LEGALLY RED

About the Author

Maurice Watkins CBE was one of the world's leading sports lawyers and sports administrators, a long-time director of Manchester United and the club solicitor. He was the Senior Partner and Head of Sport at Brabners LLP, the Chair of British Swimming – overseeing Team GB's successes in the Rio de Janeiro (2016) and Tokyo (2020) Olympics, Chair of the British Basketball Federation and a director of Lancashire County Cricket Club. Away from sport, Maurice Watkins was the Chair of Governors at his former school, The Manchester Grammar School, and Chair of the Royal Manchester Children's Hospital charity appeals board where he helped raise £68 million for the NHS. He was made Commander of the Order of the British Empire in Queen Elizabeth II's Birthday Honours 2011 for services to charity. He died on 16 August 2021 aged 79.

LEGALLY RED

MAURICE WATKINS

HODDER &
STOUGHTON

First published in Great Britain in 2024 by Hodder & Stoughton Limited
An Hachette UK company

1

Copyright © The Beneficiaries of Mr Edward Maurice Watkins 2024

The right of Maurice Watkins to be identified as the Author of the Work has been asserted by him in accordance with the Copyright, Designs and Patents Act 1988.

All rights reserved. No part of this publication may be reproduced, stored in a retrieval system, or transmitted, in any form or by any means without the prior written permission of the publisher, nor be otherwise circulated in any form of binding or cover other than that in which it is published and without a similar condition being imposed on the subsequent purchaser.

A CIP catalogue record for this title is available from the British Library

Hardback ISBN 9781399721561
Trade Paperback ISBN 9781399731249
ebook ISBN 9781399721578

Typeset in Minion Pro by Hewer Text UK Ltd, Edinburgh
Printed and bound in Great Britain by Clays Ltd, Elcograf S.p.A.

Hodder & Stoughton policy is to use papers that are natural, renewable and recyclable products and made from wood grown in sustainable forests. The logging and manufacturing processes are expected to conform to the environmental regulations of the country of origin.

Hodder & Stoughton Limited
Carmelite House
50 Victoria Embankment
London EC4Y 0DZ

www.hodder.co.uk

CONTENTS

Foreword by Sir Alex Ferguson   ix
Preface: The Phone Call   xi

1. Pride and Sorrow   1
2. The Docherty Affair   5
3. Fighting for Our Rights   16
4. Two Deaths and a Transfer   21
5. The Battle with Big Bob   28
6. The Two Gordons   33
7. The Director's Cut   43
8. The Heysel Ban   47
9. Barcelona   56
10. Getting Ferguson   64
11. The Man in the High Castle   69
12. Late-Night Shopping   78
13. Close to the Edge   84
14. Floating   91
15. The Revolution   104
16. The Deadliest Transfer   119
17. Of Sardines, Seagulls and Trawlers   135
18. Racism and Lip Reading   166
19. A Transfer with a Twist   179
20. The Boys from the Milan Tennis Club   187

21. The Bid	202
22. Stopping Murdoch	214
23. Cyril the Swan	225
24. Football Versus the European Union	231
25. A Pawn in Their Game	243
26. Gordon and Me	252
27. The Fall of the Plc	262
28. Goodbye Old Trafford, Hello World	267
Epilogue: Gandalf II	277
Endnotes	283
Acknowledgements	285
A Note from the Author's Estate	286
Photo Acknowledgements	287
Index	289

For my brother Geoffrey

Foreword
by Sir Alex Ferguson

It is my pleasure to write the foreword for my late former colleague and director of Manchester United Football Club, Maurice Watkins CBE.

It is nigh impossible to cut through his life – it would need another book! This is not a football story of tactics or how United won or lost a game. It is a story of Maurice's legal ability, and his role in all the intricate details in his long career at the club, with an amazing insight into how to quietly get the job done.

My earliest experience of Maurice was when he was one of four directors – along with Martin Edwards, Bobby Charlton and Mike Edelson – that drove to Scotland at the start of November 1986 to try to persuade me to leave Aberdeen to become manager of United.

I accepted the challenge. At my first away game, when I glanced along the passage to see him reading the programme, I whispered to Bobby Charlton, 'What's that all about?' to which Bobby replied, 'Don't worry, Alex, Maurice doesn't miss anything!'

He had an insatiable energy, which was illustrated with his involvement in other sports. The list goes on and on. To my recollection he became interim chairman of the Rugby League after leaving the Old Trafford board in 2012. He was also chairman of the Greyhound Board of Great Britain; a director of Lancashire County Cricket Club; chairman of British Swimming; and chairman of the British Basketball Federation!

His involvement in football also continued – he served as chairman of Barnsley FC from 2013 to 2017. Then there was his work for charity, particularly the millions he helped to raise for the NHS Royal Manchester Children's Hospital.

His energy levels must have been exhausted dealing with all the situations that come up at a club the size of Manchester United. But his calm demeanour and his wisdom helped to steer the ship through all manner of situations.

For instance, he navigated the club expertly through the tricky waters of Eric Cantona's trial for assault in 1995. He was always there with sound advice.

As well as his legal expertise – which saw him named International Sports and Entertainment Lawyer of the Year in 2014 at a ceremony in New York – Maurice was really supportive to me during my time as manager of United.

He was also great company, and a true gentleman.

I missed Maurice when he left the club after twenty-eight years as a director. He was an important sounding board for me and a good confidant. I'm sure you'll enjoy his story.

Alex Ferguson

Preface

The Phone Call

My mobile phone rang.

'Maurice, it's Alex. I need to speak to you, it's urgent.'

It was said in a tone that brooked no misunderstanding.

For Sir Alex Ferguson to call was not unusual. I had been dealing with Alex for almost twenty years. As Manchester United's solicitor, I had first met him in 1984 when he was manager of Aberdeen and United wanted to buy Gordon Strachan. At that time there was no thought of him becoming the 'boss' at Old Trafford. He did so in 1986 when we on the board decided Ron Atkinson could not lead the club back to the path of success that had eluded us since Sir Matt Busby had retired. I was involved in luring Alex from Aberdeen to Old Trafford and from that moment, I developed a dual role with him. On the one hand, as the club's solicitor, he and I would speak frequently whenever there was a problem with a player. On the other, the structure of the club and my role as a director meant I also had another, very personal relationship with Alex Ferguson in that I dealt with decisions regarding his contract.

However, when Alex rang that day, I knew this could not be a call about his contract as he had announced he was retiring at the end of the 2001/02 season. Yet the urgency of his voice immediately commanded my attention.

'Maurice, I have changed my mind. I do not want to retire as manager of Manchester United.'

In his autobiography, Alex said I laughed when he told me. I do not recall laughing, but to say I was surprised would be an understatement. It was now more than six months since he had told me and my fellow board members that he wanted to go, and we had been working on the assumption that we would have to replace him in the summer.

The prospect of Alex Ferguson's retirement from Old Trafford had first surfaced in a letter from his accountant, Alan Baines, on 17 December 1997. Baines wrote to me saying: 'The 1998/99 football season will, in all probability, be the final year of the most successful managerial career in world football history.'

Although Alan Baines's description of Alex was to be proved accurate, in 1997 it was hyperbole. He had not yet won the Champions League and it was a letter I was somewhat surprised to receive, for in June 1996 we had signed a new four-year contract that was meant to take Alex into the new century.

When I rang Baines to ask if this meant Ferguson was intending to retire early and not fulfil his contractual obligations to Manchester United, he quickly said he had made a mistake and that I should ignore his comment.

What I suspect is that Alan Baines and Alex had been talking about retirement as far back as 1997 and Baines had somehow misunderstood Alex's intentions.

Six months later, in the summer of 1998, the question of Alex Ferguson staying at Manchester United resurfaced once more. In his first full season as their manager, Arsène Wenger had taken Arsenal to the title and Martin Edwards, who was chairman of the Manchester United club board at that time, had responded with a not so friendly letter to Alex suggesting that he had 'taken his eye off the ball'. It was a phrase that left him deeply wounded and he would not let it lie.

On 2 July Alan Baines wrote to Sir Roland Smith, chairman of the Manchester United plc board, as follows:

THE PHONE CALL

I met Alex yesterday at Old Trafford and we discussed the fact that ideally, he would like his personal position resolved before the Manchester United tour starts on 25th July. I think what is instrumental in Alex wanting to be placed in a position of greater security is the fact that Brian Kidd was given a new four-year contract by Martin Edwards without any consultation with Alex Ferguson. You may think this is normal footballing practice but, of course, in the world you and I move outside football it would not be sensible man management to impose an assistant on a manager without taking his opinion into account.

By this time there were serious divisions opening up between Alex Ferguson and Brian Kidd, who had become Alex's assistant in 1991. The alliance coincided with a dramatic upsurge in Manchester United's fortunes that would see them win the Double three years later.

There were some in the game who thought Brian had been the catalyst for the revolution at Old Trafford. He had been offered the manager's job at Manchester City and Everton and that December he would – against Alex's advice – accept an offer to take over at Blackburn. They would be relegated five months later.

However, by the summer of 2000 it was clear Alex was once more thinking of leaving. He, Roland Smith and I had met in London in July. Roland wrote a note of the meeting which is worth quoting.

The purpose of the meeting was to begin dialogue with Sir Alex Ferguson so as to understand some of his intentions with regard to his own future. It was the wish of the Manchester United Plc Board that Sir Alex Ferguson should never feel isolated on his planning of his future career. The stance which Maurice and I took during the discussion was to leave the initiative with Sir Alex and thereby enable him to make any suggestions or proposals regarding his future.

What became clear in the first few minutes was that Sir Alex had no wish to see himself continuing in the role of manager of Manchester United after the completion of his present contract which ends in 2002.

He believes the pressures of being the manager of Manchester United had always been considerable but are becoming greater with the continued success of the present team and the more international basis for our footballing activities. He has no wish to have the pressures beyond his 60th birthday.

He says that he is looking forward to his pensionable years when he can enjoy some travel, spend some more time with his family and do some of the things he has always wanted to enjoy but because of the pressure of being the manager of Manchester United he has never had the time to relax and enjoy life.

Maurice suggested that when the season begins again, he will become more keen to continue in management – but he was adamant that the next two years were the last he would have in management as manager of Manchester United. He talked about possible successors without suggesting anyone in particular.

Sir Alex intends to develop a number of advisory or consultancy roles – maybe with commercial enterprises – once he finishes his contract as manager. So far, he has received no approaches to work for Government in any capacity – nor is he expecting anything from Government when he finishes at Old Trafford. Finally, Sir Alex Ferguson made it clear that he wanted to work on several e-commerce and internet opportunities with Goldman Sachs and his two sons.

Sir Alex was clearly unsure about some of his intentions – but in my view Sir Alex Ferguson is firm and clear about one aspect of his future – he does not wish to go beyond the age of 60 in football management. Nor does he want to continue as Manchester United manager after his present contract comes to an end. All that is absolutely clear. Maurice may take a different view.

I did take a different view. I knew Alex better than Roland, largely because I saw so much more of him and I was convinced that when the date approached, he would once again draw back.

In that sense he was like Margaret Thatcher or Tony Blair, who could not envisage a life beyond Downing Street. However, I was surprised that in all subsequent meetings I had with him, Alex seemed set on leaving. His determination appeared absolute.

Now, suddenly and out of the blue, here he was telling me that, after all this, he wanted to stay. His timing was impeccable because Peter Kenyon, the club's chief executive, and I were due to travel to London to ask the FA for permission to approach the England manager, Sven-Göran Eriksson, to become manager of Manchester United. Had Alex Ferguson delayed his phone call by by a couple of days, our deal with Eriksson might well have been done and the FA informed he was leaving England for Manchester United.

I asked if he had discussed this with his wife, Cathy. Cathy has always played a huge part in Alex's life; the Tottenham chairman, Irving Scholar, felt it was her refusal to move from Aberdeen to London that had scuppered his attempt to lure him to White Hart Lane in 1984. She was now the chief instigator behind his U-turn.

Alex added he had also been encouraged by two of his sons, Mark and Jason, and he made it clear to me that his family were very strongly of the view that he really was too young to retire.

His world was football and he wanted to continue in it. Specifically, he wanted the centre of his world to remain at Old Trafford.

He added that in recent months he had found life a little easier. He had cut back on his media work and felt the coaching positions were satisfactory. The Carrington training centre had opened eighteen months before and was a state-of-the art facility. The academy would move into new purpose-built accommodation in the summer. Manchester United had won three straight Premier League titles. Logically, there was no reason to leave.

There was one other factor in helping him change his mind. Since Alex had announced his retirement, the club had been talking of entering into a consultancy agreement with him. He made it clear that the proposals suggested for his retirement would not do at all. It was also clear that he still harboured old resentments. He had not forgotten Martin Edwards's comment that he had 'taken his eye off the ball' in 1998. Another remark by the chairman also festered.

In the wake of United's victory over Bayern Munich in the Champions League final, Martin had been asked about Alex's future once he retired. He had replied: 'We do not want a Matt Busby situation.' Once he had stepped down as manager in 1969 after nearly a quarter of a century at Manchester United, Busby had kept an office at Old Trafford, played golf with the senior players at his local course, Davyhulme, and negotiated contracts and transfers.

His two immediate successors, Wilf McGuinness and Frank O'Farrell, found the atmosphere suffocating and Manchester United were relegated in 1974, six years after becoming champions of Europe.

Ferguson thought it outrageous he would be tempted into the same kind of back-seat driving. He never forgot what he felt was an insult.

Now that he had decided to stay, I asked Alex how much longer he intended to carry on? He replied immediately: 'Two more years.'

He then asked: 'Why Eriksson?'

Alex Ferguson was fishing. He knew Manchester United were well advanced in their search for a successor. We had mulled over likely choices including David O'Leary, Martin O'Neill and Fabio Capello without me giving anything away. Our first choice had been Arsène Wenger but after a meeting with Martin Edwards and Peter Kenyon at the Arsenal manager's house in north London, he had turned us down.

Martin felt it was because of a loyalty to David Dein, the Arsenal vice-chairman who had been instrumental in his appointment.

It was in this context that Sven-Göran Eriksson's name was mentioned. Like a good forward, Alex was probing my defences. I was not a bad defender whether at full- or centre-back, and now I did not allow him to get goalside of me. According to him, I had replied: 'You may be right, you may be wrong.'

The deal was almost done. Our move to make Eriksson the next manager of Manchester United had begun, appropriately enough, at a casino. On 3 December 2001, not long before the fateful phone call, I had gone to Crockfords in Mayfair to meet Pini Zahavi, the one-time Israeli journalist who had turned himself into the world's first 'super-agent'.

Zahavi wanted to know how our search for a manager was going. When he told me Eriksson would be interested in the job, I was taken aback. His power and prestige as England manager were then at their height.

When the effortlessly charming Swede succeeded Kevin Keegan in January 2001, the consensus was that England would fail to qualify for the World Cup in Japan and South Korea. Instead, under Eriksson, they had first annihilated Germany, 5–1, in Munich's Olympic Stadium. In October, at Old Trafford, David Beckham's stoppage-time free-kick had sent England to the World Cup as group winners. England were notorious for the aggressiveness of their media but Eriksson was now untouchable.

However, as Zahavi explained, Eriksson understood that honeymoons do not last. In seven months' time, England would be involved in the 2002 World Cup, which he did not expect to win. Such was the level of expectation surrounding England's prospects, Eriksson imagined anything less than total victory would be seen as failure. He knew how many of his predecessors had been forced from office and wanted to take his leave with his audience demanding more.

Just over a week later, we had another meeting at Crockfords and this time Eriksson was present. We did not directly discuss a move to Old Trafford. The meeting was to get to know the man who might become Manchester United's next manager. I had met him before but not in such circumstances. I must say I liked him.

Ten days later, on 21 December, Manchester United's plc board met at Old Trafford. Peter Kenyon talked through a list of successors to Alex Ferguson. We discussed salary, bonuses and length of contract. It was unanimously agreed that Sven-Göran Eriksson was our preferred choice and that Peter and I should meet him to finalise the matter.

Straight after United's dramatic 3–2 win at Fulham on 30 December, which left the club fifth in the Premier League table, we left Craven Cottage to drive through London streets, still strewn with festive lights, to Pini Zahavi's flat in Marylebone. Sitting in his living room was Sven-Göran Eriksson.

The meeting went well. Eriksson was very interested in becoming our next manager. If he wanted to return to club management, what could be better than Manchester United? Unsurprisingly, he wanted a binding agreement. His main concern was how to handle the negotiations without damaging England's prospects for the World Cup.

On the surface, the FA knew nothing about these talks, although Adam Crozier, the FA's young chief executive, had his suspicions. Even before our first meeting with Eriksson, he had warned me about poaching him.

This had been in November. Adam and I had been trying to broker a peace deal between the players' union, the Professional Footballers' Association, and the Premier League over the share the PFA received from the league's television deals. The PFA, arguing that players warranted compensation for surrendering their image rights for the broadcasts, had called a strike ballot of its 2,315 members. Only 22 voted against. The walkout was due to begin on the weekend of 1 December.

THE PHONE CALL

On 23 November, a deal was thrashed out at the Hilton Hotel at Manchester Airport with the Premier League agreeing to pay the PFA £52.3 million over the three remaining years of its broadcasting contract.

Soon after the press conference Adam and I boarded a flight to London. As we flew over the Midlands, he turned to me and said, 'I know you are looking for a successor to Alex. Keep your hands off my manager.' With that Adam laughed. I joined in the laughter although I was aware of the irony. Soon after Adam had taken over at the FA, in 2000, he had tried to poach Alex Ferguson to become England manager in the wake of Kevin Keegan's resignation. Adam was always proud of the fact that Alex had a soft spot for him. Both grew up in sight of the Clyde, although Crozier's upbringing on the Isle of Bute was very different from Ferguson's on the Glasgow docks.

The Scottish connection made no impact. Crozier's offer was turned down flat. It was not just national pride that made Alex say no. He had not enjoyed his time managing Scotland in the World Cup in Mexico and he had only taken the job after seeing Jock Stein, a man he truly loved, collapse from a fatal heart attack by the side of the pitch in Cardiff. Stein was 62 and that played a part in Ferguson's apparent determination not to remain in football beyond the age of 60.

The fact that Sir Alex Ferguson wanted to stay as Manchester United manager did not mean his wish would be granted.

As soon as I got off the phone with Alex, I phoned Peter Kenyon, Roland Smith and David Gill, who in July had been promoted from the club's finance director to its group chief operating officer, overseeing Manchester United's marketing and sponsorship activities.

Initially, there was a feeling Alex had left it too late and we should tell him that. However, by the evening our views had softened as we recognised it would be difficult to tell Alex he could not change his mind. The main area of discussion was whether we should offer him a two- or a three-year contract.

However much Alex had told us it was Cathy and the boys who had made him change his mind, we wondered what role Manchester United's Irish connection had played.

John Magnier owned and ran the Coolmore Stud in County Tipperary, Ireland. It was one of the most successful horseracing studs in the world and an Irish law exempting bloodstock profits from tax had made Magnier around £500 million.

His partner, JP McManus, began in construction, went into bookmaking and would own horses that would win the Cheltenham Gold Cup and the Grand National. In 2004, he would begin work on a stately home in his native County Limerick that would reportedly cost up to £170 million. According to the *Irish Independent*, the wine cellar was the size of a one-bedroomed apartment.

Together, they were known in the media as the Coolmore Mafia. They were close to Alex and had invested heavily in Manchester United. It would be in their best interests if he were to stay as manager. Now Alex had made clear his intention to remain at the helm, we wondered if Coolmore would make a formal bid to take over the club.

I had a chance to discuss this with Alex when we flew to London on 9 January to meet Peter Kenyon and Roland Smith at the Royal Lancaster Hotel. The Royal Lancaster had deep football roots and was one of my favourite hotels. The Football Writers' Association had used it for their annual dinners before the FA Cup final and it was close to the FA's old headquarters at Lancaster Gate.

As we settled down in the 2:30pm shuttle to Heathrow, Alex opened up about his U-turn. The pressure had come from his family over Christmas, with Cathy and his sons questioning him very hard on whether he really wanted to retire.

He was also motivated by the fact the club was not doing well in the Premier League, which said a lot about him. Another manager,

THE PHONE CALL

knowing he would be leaving in May, would not have been able to summon the energy to lift the team, but Alex was determined to turn things around.

When I raised the Irish question, he told me that Magnier and McManus both played things close to their chest, but he was surprised that, having bought the shares, they had not gone any further.

When I suggested that one of the reasons why they had not pursued a takeover was because they were uncertain about Manchester United's future, Alex replied Magnier had mentioned he thought he was retiring too early but nothing more than that had been said.

By the time the plane touched down, we had also talked in detail about the length of any contract, his workload, support staff, the academy and future retirement plans.

At the Royal Lancaster, Alex confessed that his decision to retire had been conditioned by events over the previous few years. Martin Edwards's 'You have taken your eye off the ball' letter was an issue. We agreed it had been a mistake to publicise so far in advance the fact Alex was leaving at the end of the season.

We talked about a possible three-year deal and Alex wondered if he could have a little bit more free time. There was a discussion about bringing in a new number two to give him more support. Steve McClaren, who had taken over from Brian Kidd, had been appointed Middlesbrough manager in 2001 and since he had expected to retire at the end of the 2001/02 season, Alex had not replaced him.

We agreed to meet as quickly as possible with Alex's advisors to discuss draft terms so that we had draft heads of agreement available for the next plc board meeting. Alex suggested he would use his son, Jason, as his advisor; however, Roland, Peter and I felt that as a member of the Ferguson family, it was simply too close a relationship.

Alex appointed an Aberdeen lawyer, Les Dalgarno, to negotiate for him. He had known Dalgarno since his move from Glasgow to take charge of Aberdeen in 1977.

There was, however, an elephant in the room. Sven-Göran Eriksson. Five days later, I phoned Pini Zahavi in Israel to talk about Eriksson, and the following day Peter Kenyon and I flew to London to meet the England manager. First, however, we would talk to Les Dalgarno and Jason Ferguson at the Royal Lancaster. A mile away, at the Leonard Hotel on Marble Arch, we saw Eriksson, hoping that Ferguson had not put a tail on us.

If we were running two horses, then Team Ferguson was also sparring with us. This became clear when Peter and I flew to Aberdeen on 24 January for a further meeting with Les Dalgarno and Jason Ferguson. In all our negotiations, Dalgarno played the role of good cop. The Ferguson boys, Jason and Mark, were the bad cops. They could be obdurate and gave the impression they felt Manchester United had never given their father his due.

Jason made it clear that his father wanted to continue in management. In a perfect world, it would be at Manchester United. If not, it would be elsewhere. There were risks to both sides. Ferguson might not be successful outside Old Trafford. We might be accused of letting the greatest manager in the club's history slip away.

I could see what Team Ferguson were trying to do, but even at this stage it was by no means certain that we would decide to keep Alex and we were not yet prepared to burn our boats with Eriksson.

On 27 and 28 January we had several meetings in London with Alex and his advisors. Alex brought his son, Mark, to one and Jason to another. At the same time, Peter and I also had a fairly lengthy meeting with Eriksson and Zahavi on 28 January that lasted an hour and a half. The need to keep the England manager in play became even more urgent when the following day Dalgarno rang to say that Alex had told him he wanted to discuss matters with his sons before making a final decision. This, in Dalgarno's view, would be a difficult process.

With the Fergusons playing hardball, we had no alternative but to keep Eriksson in play. We returned to the Leonard Hotel on 1 February

THE PHONE CALL

to meet Zahavi. The basic contractual terms were looked at again and he confirmed they were acceptable. It was agreed that Eriksson would meet Adam Crozier on Monday, 4 February to inform the FA that he intended to join Manchester United after the World Cup.

Whether Alex got to hear of this or not, things then changed very quickly. The next day, after Manchester United had beaten Sunderland 4–1, we had a meeting in Alex's room at Old Trafford and we agreed we would finalise a deal at the Manchester Airport Hilton. Dalgarno came with Jason and this time the good-cop, bad-cop routine had been discarded. They said that provided Alex was paid a bonus at the end of his contract which was not linked to success or winning trophies, he would agree a deal.

We had no problem with that. Now it was a question of bidding goodbye to Sven-Göran Eriksson before he walked into Crozier's office and told him he would be quitting.

Peter and I went straight from Manchester Airport to Heathrow and met Zahavi at Les Ambassadeurs. Our involvement with Eriksson had begun at one Mayfair casino and it would end at another. We told him terms had been agreed with Sir Alex Ferguson.

We owed Eriksson a face-to-face explanation and the next day, hours before he was due to meet Crozier, we saw him at the Leonard Hotel.

Peter and I approached the meeting with some foreboding. But it went better than we expected. We told Eriksson that Alex was staying on and that we could not take our discussions any further.

Eriksson showed no emotion. He may well have been forewarned by Zahavi. Perhaps, mixed in was the relief of knowing that he had now been spared a difficult conversation with his employer.

The meeting was not a short one. Peter Kenyon and I did not want to give the impression we were just there to have our say and then depart. We felt relieved at the way Eriksson had taken the news. Relations between the England manager and Manchester United would remain cordial.

However, when Eriksson published his autobiography in November 2013, a few months after Sir Alex Ferguson had finally retired as manager of Manchester United, he presented a version of events that differed from our recollection. He claimed he had signed a contract to succeed Ferguson, who he suggested had vetoed his appointment. Neither was true as far as I was concerned. Sven had not even been sent a draft contract.

Back in early 2002, for more than a month we had discussed the most high-profile management position in English club football in three cities without a word appearing in the press. Then on 5 February the story broke.

We issued a statement to the Stock Exchange confirming that we were in discussions with Sir Alex Ferguson for him to remain as manager of Manchester United. At the end of the month, we issued a further statement confirming that he had signed a new three-year contract that would take him to the end of June 2005.

Alex Ferguson would describe his decision to retire in 2002 as the greatest mistake of his managerial career. By the time he finally departed, in 2013, he had won another Champions League trophy and six more league titles. His place as the greatest manager in the history of the English game was now beyond dispute.

1

Pride and Sorrow

The Manchester I was born into was pitted and scarred by war. The Blitz had come to the city at Christmas 1940. The Cathedral, the Royal Exchange and the Free Trade Hall were all hit.

On 11 March 1941, Old Trafford, which had been pressed into service as an ammunition depot, was so badly damaged that Manchester United were unable to use it until four years after the war's end. By the time I came into the world in my grandparents' front room in Milwain Road, Levenshulme, on 30 November 1941, the Luftwaffe had turned its attention to the Soviet Union; after the war's end we moved, first to Blackley, in the leafy northern suburbs, and then closer to the centre in Chorlton.

When we made the second move, my mother had already taken two jobs to afford the fees to send me to Oldham Hulme prep school. However, as a 7-year-old I had to take three buses to get there. It would not be tolerated now.

The effort was all worthwhile because not only did I pass the Eleven Plus, I secured a Foundation Scholarship to The Manchester Grammar School (MGS). I had come in the top 50 of 2,000 applicants.

Manchester Grammar was the city's oldest and most famous school. It had been founded in 1515 by Hugh Oldham – a friend of Henry VII's mother Margaret Beaufort – who had made his money in corn mills. Its task was to prepare boys for Oxford and Cambridge and from there into the Church or the legal profession. It was to play a huge part in my life.

In 1998, I became chairman of the bursary fund, which at the time of writing, delivers 200 bursaries for those who would otherwise not be able to afford the fees. Ten years later, I was chairman of MGS's board of governors, where my proudest task was helping to oversee the creation of the New Islington Free School, a primary in Ancoats, one of Manchester's most deprived suburbs.

Within the school there are twenty-three languages spoken in twenty-seven ethnic groups. Its first Ofsted report, delivered when the teaching was being delivered in Portakabins, rated the New Islington Free School as 'outstanding'. Ancoats, coincidentally, is where Hugh Oldham, Manchester Grammar School's founder, is supposed to have been born.

The postwar Labour government had made MGS into a direct-grant grammar school, which meant no fees were payable if you passed the Eleven Plus. In 1976 another Labour government abolished the direct grant and MGS became a fee-paying independent school.

When I joined the school, in 1953, it was the time of the great High Master, Eric James. He stood out against the prevailing demands for universal comprehensive education, arguing that grammar schools could propel working-class boys into careers that would otherwise have been beyond them.

All that mattered to Eric James was academic performance. Boys whose families had connections to the school were given no special treatment when it came to gaining admission. During his tenure, MGS was sending up to forty-five boys a year to Oxford and Cambridge. In 1959 he entered the House of Lords as Baron James of Rusholme.

I played first-team cricket for the school and in 1960 I made an appearance in *Wisden* as Manchester Grammar's leading wicket taker. When we played the MCC, I bowled to Cyril Washbrook, who would rival Mike Atherton as the greatest opening batsman Lancashire ever produced, although by that time he was 44.

I also became a troop leader in one of the school's five scout troops. Not everyone can say they had Jesus Christ and Gandhi in their patrol but both Robert Powell and Ben Kingsley were members of my troop: Robert would play the lead in *Jesus of Nazareth* in 1977 while Ben would take the title role in Richard Attenborough's 1982 epic *Gandhi*. Powell studied law at Manchester University, and there was a significant legal influence in my family; my father and my uncle Walter were both solicitors' clerks. It seemed the right career to embark on – in May 2016 I would be given a certificate from the Law Society to mark fifty years on the Roll of Solicitors. I studied law not at Manchester but at University College, London, graduating as first a Bachelor and then a Master of Laws.

I returned to Manchester in 1964 to work at Skelton and Co, based in the city's main thoroughfare, Deansgate. After qualifying, I had spells at Pilkington Brothers, the glass manufacturers based in St Helens, and the Co-operative Insurance Society. From there I joined James Chapman and Co.

When I came home, in 1964, Manchester United had been reborn in the shape of the Trinity whose statues now stand guard outside Old Trafford. It was the time of Best, Law and Charlton, but because I played for MGS Old Boys in the Lancashire Amateur League, I rarely made it to Old Trafford on a Saturday afternoon.

There would soon come a time when football and even the law would seem frivolous. Not a day goes by when I do not think of the summer of 1966 with a sense of absolute sadness.

My brother, Geoffrey, was five years younger than me. He had gone to school at Burnage Grammar and, like me, had been offered a place at University College London to read law. Geoffrey, however, did not enjoy the course and was contemplating a move to Manchester University to study a different subject. During the summer holidays he died in a swimming accident in south-west France. He was 19.

His death proved a devastating loss to our family which was keenly felt by my parents. After enrolling as a mature student, my mother had become a qualified teacher and had spent time in Paris on courses at the Sorbonne. The stuffing was completely knocked out of her; but she did some wonderful work back in Manchester in junior schools based in some of the city's most deprived areas. She even designed an innovative early-learning book that helped children develop their reading skills through the use of codes.

I thought I might stay with James Chapman and Co for two or three years. I would spend the next thirty-eight years there. There was a reason for that. Ever since the Munich air disaster, James Chapman and Co had acted as solicitors for Manchester United.

2

The Docherty Affair

Manchester United came into my life one winter night in 1976. At James Chapman, the club was the province of two of the most senior partners, Bill Royle and Arthur McKenna. Both had been presidents of the Manchester Law Society and had reputations that extended beyond the North West.

However, a late-night phone call informed me that Bill Royle had died at a meeting of the Law Society. He had been due to go to a board meeting at Old Trafford the following day. The firm had tried to contact other solicitors, but none was available and I would have to step in. The papers would be sent to my home so I could prepare.

The club was proposing a rights issue, a way of raising money by offering more shares to existing shareholders in proportion to their holding. That morning I was shown into the boardroom at Old Trafford. I had never met any of them, though I knew of the chairman, Louis Edwards, and the club secretary, Les Olive. The others, including the bankers from Kleinwort Benson, were total strangers.

Louis Edwards had been chairman of Manchester United since 1965. His business was in meat processing, and he owned 74 per cent of the club. He was close to Matt Busby who in February 1958 had offered him a seat on the team plane to watch the European Cup quarter-final with Red Star Belgrade. Because he was not yet a director, Louis declined. His place was taken by another of Busby's friends, Willie Satinoff, who was killed when the plane crashed at Munich.

The day after the disaster, Louis was voted on to the board while Les Olive became club secretary replacing Walter Crickmer, who had also lost his life in the Munich Disaster.

I explained why Royle was not there and Louis, who knew Bill well, expressed his sadness at the news. However, it soon became clear this was a very preliminary meeting. The rights issue, which was opposed by Busby – who, perhaps because he did not have the money of the other directors, would have preferred United to have raised the money through a bank loan – did not go through until September 1978. It would raise £1 million. Three-quarters of this came from the Edwards family.

When I attended the meeting, Manchester United were managed by Tommy Docherty, who appeared finally to have thrown off the shadow of Busby. Best, Law and Charlton had left the club and, although Manchester United had been relegated in 1974, an exciting, rebuilt side had won promotion after one season. The 1976 FA Cup final may have been lost to Southampton, who were a division below, but Docherty had taken United to third, just four points behind the champions, Liverpool.

Louis Edwards got on very well with Docherty. Both were men who enjoyed the finer things in life – the chairman was known as 'Champagne Louis'. They would enjoy meals and go horse-racing together. Docherty, a Glaswegian brought up amid the grim poverty of the Gorbals, had an impish sense of humour, laden with one-liners, which Louis relished.

The high-water mark of Tommy Docherty's reign came on 21 May 1977. Liverpool had already retained their league title and were on course for the treble that Alex Ferguson would complete twenty-two years later. They would play Manchester United for the FA Cup.

Manchester United beat them 2–1 and Docherty posed with the lid of the FA Cup on his head. The next morning he was spotted in Hyde Park with some of his players, still in his Cup final suit, clutching a bottle of champagne.

Four days later, in Rome, Liverpool overcame Borussia Mönchengladbach to win the European Cup.

There was a year remaining on Docherty's contract, but Les Olive had already called me to draft a new one that would take their manager to the summer of 1981. Derby, who two years before had been league champions, were starting to look for a replacement for their current manager, Colin Murphy. Tommy's salary at Old Trafford was £18,000 – worth about £85,000 now. Derby were offering him an additional £10,000. Docherty had informed Matt Busby and through him the rest of the board. They needed to act.

However, soon after, there was another call from Les. They now wanted to dismiss Tommy Docherty. He had fallen in love.

Although he never liked the term, for the past three years Tommy Docherty had been having an affair with Mary, the wife of Manchester United's physiotherapist, Laurie Brown.

Matt Busby had been informed of the relationship by Paddy Crerand, one of the men who had won the 1968 European Cup but who had enjoyed an unhappy spell with Docherty as his assistant manager. Busby appears to have kept this news to himself, although, according to Docherty's autobiography, when he told Sir Matt of the relationship after the story had broken, he denied knowledge of it, saying: 'You bloody fool, Tom, why didn't you let me know all about this? [...] If I had known about matters earlier, I could have spoken to people, important people.'[1]

Just before the story made the front pages of the newspapers, Docherty phoned Martin Edwards, who told him that as far as he was concerned, it was a private matter. Martin was then 31. The older members of Manchester United's board would prove less understanding.

Les Olive told me that the club was concerned about what Tommy had done. The question they had to consider was whether the terms of Docherty's contract allowed Manchester United to sack him because of his behaviour. Laurie Brown, who had punched Docherty as he sat in his car outside Brown's house, indicated he had no wish to stay on at Manchester United.

A couple of days later, on 29 June, I went to Old Trafford to meet Les and Denzil Haroun, who was Louis Edwards's uncle and a director of the club. Olive and Haroun were concerned that Docherty's affair would have an unsettling effect on morale, discipline and performance at Old Trafford. They also felt it could influence the parents of young players who were considering joining Manchester United's youth teams. Parents might not want their sons to join a club where the manager's private life was 'notorious'.

It was certainly chaotic. After Docherty's wife, Agnes, had thrown him out of his house in Mottram, Tommy was living with Mary in an annexe of the Browns's home. Laurie and the children were in the main house.

However, Docherty still had the support of the Edwards family. He had gone to their magnificent house in Alderley Edge and both Louis and Martin had given him their backing. As they owned nearly three-quarters of Manchester United, their support was critical. But this began to waver when Laurie Brown paid them a visit. He threatened to reveal other affairs within the club which would do nothing for Manchester United's reputation. He said that Tommy had been visiting Mary during the day while Laurie was working and that Docherty would ask him to spend longer at the training ground so the manager could spend more time with the physio's wife.

Louis called a board meeting at his home on 4 July. Tommy had also been invited to Alderley Edge, but was in a separate room. The entire board, including Sir Matt Busby, was in the living room. I felt like an academy player about to make his first-team debut. The only person I knew even reasonably well was Les Olive. I had never met Matt Busby or two of the other directors, Alan Gibson, the vice-chairman, and Bill Young, who was a farmer.

The key figure was Matt Busby. The Edwards family were still inclined to stick with Docherty. Matt, however, was adamant that he had to go.

Seen through Busby's eyes, the affair was not the only issue. He had heard that Docherty had sold Cup final tickets on the black market and had also asked money from fans who wanted a picture of him with the FA Cup. I told him those allegations needed to be substantiated.

However, Busby's views prevailed and Louis Edwards was won over. Despite his fondness for Docherty, Louis now accepted he had to remove his manager. When a vote was taken, it was unanimous.

However, we could not simply call Tommy in from the next room and tell him: 'Because of your affair with Mary Brown, you are now sacked.' I told the board they had to be mindful of saying anything that could land the club in legal trouble. And so it was decided that I would draft a brief statement which Louis would read to Tommy. I drew out my legal pad and wrote something along the lines of: 'It is the unanimous decision of the board that you are in breach of the terms of your contract and your engagement is terminated forthwith.'

As I left, Tommy followed me in. I glanced back and can still picture the scene of Matt Busby and Tommy Docherty in that room. Many things they knew, or felt they knew, about each other were not said. Docherty would later claim that Busby kept a mistress in London and would visit her every time Manchester United played in the capital. Docherty did not confront him with what appeared to be an act of gross hypocrisy because he knew he would need another job in football and Busby's views still carried great weight across the game.

Before I left the meeting, I told the board that if Docherty raised the issue of compensation he should be informed that this was a matter for his solicitor. For all the bond Louis felt with Tommy, this was a line he stuck to.

Docherty had one final question for the board. Could they let Derby County know he was no longer manager of Manchester United. The Rams appointed him in September. Docherty and Mary Brown married, had two daughters and lived together happily in rural Derbyshire until Tommy's death on New Year's Eve, 2020.

I drafted a formal statement to the press, which Les Olive read out, adding the rider that all applications to become manager of Manchester United should be sent to him at Old Trafford. I thought this rather unnecessary.

Manchester United did not have to look too hard. Matt Busby had tried to appoint Dave Sexton six years earlier. Sexton, then at Chelsea (where he had succeeded Docherty in 1967), had refused. But he had steered Queens Park Rangers to second place in 1976 – the highest finish in their history – and he would not be turning down Sir Matt Busby twice.

We expected to hear from Tommy Docherty's solicitor and we did in the form of a claim for unfair dismissal. He also began an action against Louis Edwards for libel and slander accompanied by an injunction restraining any further defamatory comment.

We decided to retain the services of George Carman. He would become the most famous barrister in the country but then he was a 47-year-old QC on the northern circuit – he had been born in Blackpool. His big break would come in 1979 when he successfully defended the former Liberal leader, Jeremy Thorpe, who had been charged with attempting to murder Norman Scott, a male model.

However, in September, when Docherty was appointed as manager of Derby, the High Court action was withdrawn with both sides agreeing to pay their own costs.

While all this was going on, Tommy walked into the offices of James Chapman and Co and I asked him where he was heading next? He pulled out a list of solicitors' names, each one of which had a different job attached to it. Docherty was clearly a man with plenty of legal problems on his plate.

The most sensational was to be the libel proceedings he instigated against Willie Morgan, a Scottish winger who had been brought to

Manchester United by Matt Busby in 1968 but sold by Docherty seven years later.

Morgan had appeared on a Friday night football chat show called *Kick Off*. When the presenter, Gerald Sinstadt, asked him to name the best manager he had played for, Morgan replied: 'I have played for the best and the worst. The best was Sir Matt Busby, the worst was Tommy Docherty. Docherty was the worst manager there has ever been.'

Docherty had not seen the programme but was persuaded that he had a case against both Morgan and Granada Television, who had broadcast the interview. It went all the way to the High Court and was heard in November 1978.

Morgan, who was told he would probably have to sell his house if he lost the case, had prepared 29 separate allegations including statements from Paddy Crerand, Denis Law and Lou Macari about Docherty's style of management.

Docherty had hired an expensive barrister in the shape of Richard Du Cann, who was chairman of the Criminal Bar Association. His brother, Edward, had been chairman of the Conservative Party.

Morgan was represented by John Wilpshire, who had told the player that every time Docherty lied when giving evidence to Du Cann he should tug on his gown. Morgan recalled that when Docherty spoke, his evidence laced with anecdotes and gags, he tugged Wilpshire's gown constantly. When Docherty related the story of Denis Law's transfer to Manchester City, it was almost pulled off.

When Wilpshire stood up to begin cross-examination, he demolished Docherty's evidence line by line. When he came to the Law transfer, he put it devastatingly: 'You told a pack of lies to the jury about this, didn't you?'

Docherty shrugged his shoulders and said: 'Yes. It turned out this way. Yes.'

The case collapsed. Docherty was charged with perjury, although the case against him would be dismissed. Manchester United, however, were not yet done with Tommy Docherty. We needed him as a witness.

Ted MacDougall was a Scottish striker who exploded into celebrity in November 1971 when, playing for Bournemouth against Margate, he had scored nine goals in an FA Cup tie. Bournemouth, managed by the ebullient figure of John Bond, had just been promoted to the Third Division. They would fail to gain a second successive promotion by three points. MacDougall was hot property.

In September 1972, Manchester United's manager, Frank O'Farrell, brought him to Old Trafford for £175,000. United had agreed to pay Bournemouth a further £25,000 if MacDougall scored twenty goals in competitive football for the club. Such performance-related clauses are now very common in football but in 1972 they were rare. O'Farrell lasted three more months before his dismissal. Despite the fact MacDougall scored the first goal of Tommy Docherty's reign, in a 1–1 draw with Leeds, he was not rated by the new manager. Docherty thought him 'not fit to wear a United shirt'.

In February MacDougall was sold to West Ham. He had played eighteen matches for Manchester United and scored five goals. Bournemouth, however, claimed the extra £25,000 because they argued the transfer implied that MacDougall would be given 'a reasonable opportunity' to score those twenty goals. This, the Cherries claimed, Manchester United had not done. To say we were surprised by this would be an understatement. United informed Bournemouth there was no question of them being given any extra money.

Bournemouth complained to the Football League, but the League's management committee rejected the claim, saying there was no evidence to substantiate a claim that the transfer to West Ham was made to avoid a further payment to Bournemouth.

It says something for the slow pace of litigation in this country that by the summer of 1978 the matter was still ongoing, and so Bournemouth had filed a case in court.

I had instructed Patrick Russell, perhaps the leading barrister on the northern circuit, to act for Manchester United. Russell, who would become a Lord Justice of Appeal and president of Lancashire County Cricket Club, told us we had no case to answer.

However, our case was complicated by the fact we had to go to Docherty – a man we had sacked, in circumstances that were both acrimonious and controversial – and ask him to act as a witness for us. I met Tommy at his offices at the Baseball Ground, where he was now manager. When he was at Old Trafford, he had given the club a statement about MacDougall's transfer. Now he added that MacDougall had played seven games for him and the goal against Leeds had been his only return.

After the debacle of the Willie Morgan trial, however, we were very concerned about how Tommy might perform in court. His relationship with Louis Edwards had fallen apart. Paddy Crerand would be another of our witnesses and the two men were barely on speaking terms.

The trial was held at Winchester Crown Court before Mr Justice Talbot. Our fears about Tommy Docherty were not realised. He was untroubled in the witness box and by the end of the trial his relationship with Louis Edwards was something close to what it had been.

In the bar, Les Olive asked Louis Edwards if he would like a drink. He was told 'a small one'. I thought the chairman meant half a pint of the local bitter. What he actually wanted was half a bottle of champagne.

There seemed no reason to doubt the verdict would not be in our favour, but Mr Justice Talbot said he would reserve judgment until 10 November. I was due to fly to Southampton on the morning to hear the judgment but, although it was a beautiful morning in Manchester, all south coast airports were fog-bound.

Manchester United had to have someone in court to hear the verdict so I quickly assembled a team of local lawyers. When they phoned back from Winchester, I could not believe what I was hearing. Manchester United had lost.

Contrary to what Patrick Russell had advised me, Mr Justice Talbot found there had been an implication in the contract that MacDougall would be given a reasonable opportunity to score the number of goals that would trigger the additional payment. Mr Justice Talbot did, however, discount the award by 20 per cent to cover 'the uncertainties in a footballer's life' such as disastrous injury.

We could not let the judgment stand. Patrick Russell advised that Talbot's judgment was wrong in law. There was nothing in the contract that implied Manchester United should be required to retain MacDougall's services 'for a reasonable period' so he could have the opportunity to score twenty goals. Talbot had accepted the club had acted in good faith.

Given the sums of money involved, an appeal was fully justified and had a reasonable prospect of success. We went to the Court of Appeal and since Patrick Russell and our junior counsel Keith Goddard were no longer available, a new team had to be assembled. I went for George Carman and Raymond Machell, a young barrister who excelled in personal injury and clinical negligence cases; he would become a QC in 1988.

The appeal was heard on 24 May 1980 before a stellar bench composed of the Master of the Rolls, Lord Denning, and Lord Justice Donaldson and Lord Justice Brightman. Denning was famous for his inquiry into the Profumo Affair, while Donaldson had been the presiding judge in the trials that had wrongly convicted four people of the Guildford pub bombings in 1974. Two years earlier, John Brightman had ruled that Bobby Moore and Geoff Hurst should not have to pay tax on bonuses they were paid after England had won the World Cup.

The stage was set for Carman who was flush with his Old Bailey success of overseeing Jeremy Thorpe's acquittal for conspiracy to murder. He did not disappoint.

THE DOCHERTY AFFAIR

The case was Manchester United's to lose but lose it we did – 2–1. Denning and Donaldson supported Bournemouth while Lord Justice Brightman was the only one to score for United.

In one of those curious twists of legal judgment, both Denning and Donaldson said that in finding for Bournemouth they were making no criticism of Tommy Docherty in coming to the conclusion that MacDougall did not fit into his ideas for Manchester United.

It is never good to lose a case, particularly one so high profile and in the Court of Appeal. The usual practice after defeat in court was to cross the Strand and go for a coffee or something stronger. Then you would hear phrases like: 'We did everything we could, but the law is a lottery.' It is not what the client wants to hear, but it is the best that lawyers think we can do.

Carman, however, simply would not accept the judgment and wanted leave to appeal to the House of Lords. On returning to Manchester, I wrote a long report for the board. The chief argument was financial. It would cost us a further £12,000 plus interest to seek leave to appeal to the House of Lords. This would be to save £60,000 in the value of the claim, interest and costs.

The High Court judgment had come in for plenty of criticism, especially from the influential *New Law Journal*. However, I told the board that although we had a good case, litigation is to a degree speculative and it would be difficult to predict the outcome in the House of Lords. The board decided enough was enough.

Some good did come of it. I was determined Manchester United should never again face another MacDougall case. This was all the more necessary since, by 1980, transfers were no longer settled by a single payment. There would be a down payment and then a number of potential payments relating to how the player and the club performed. I redrafted all our contracts so that in future no selling club could take United to court claiming there had been 'an implied agreement'.

3

Fighting for Our Rights

Football clubs seeking money is not a new story, but in the 1970s there were not many sources of finance.

The clubs themselves did not earn much and those running them earned virtually nothing at all. In 1977, the total dividend paid by Manchester United was £323. It paid the same the following season, by which time the purchase of Joe Jordan and Gordon McQueen from Leeds had turned a half-million-pound profit into a loss of £290,000.

The most straightforward way to raise money was by a rights issue. This enabled existing shareholders to buy more shares in the company. Since buying the shares was not compulsory it meant shareholders with money could increase their stake in the company at the expense of those who had less access to ready cash.

Louis Edwards had long wanted a rights issue. It had been the reason for my first contact with the board of Manchester United and nearly two years later, in July 1978, the United board met to consider a memorandum from the investment bank, Kleinwort Benson. The aim was to raise £1 million, which was to be spent on players. Kleinwort Benson recommended a rights issue over a loan 'because of the volatility of the transfer market and the risk involved in purchasing players who may become injured or lose their form'. A loan of £1 million would also cost the club £100,000 in interest payments.

For every share held by a current shareholder, they could buy 208 new ordinary shares at £1 each. They could also buy preference shares, which unlike ordinary shares gave you a fixed, guaranteed dividend and greater protection if the company became insolvent. They did not, however, give you voting rights. For every one preference share held by a current shareholder, they could buy 21 new preference shares at £1 each.

The Edwards family already owned 74 per cent of Manchester United and announced that they would underwrite the share issue and purchase any shares an existing shareholder did not wish to buy.

This guaranteed that Manchester United would raise the full million, but it also ensured that the power of the Edwards family within Old Trafford would continue to grow. This was something that seemed to alarm the FA.

Manchester United were required to seek the FA's approval for the rights issue. Although it was given, the FA wrote to the club wondering 'whether the proposal is in the best interests of the club and of football in general'.

The letter expressed concern that the rights of minority shareholders would be eroded by the rights issue, which would give the family 'overriding power to control any future policy or sale of shares'. The FA added:

> It is really for the present minority shareholders to consider whether the reasons given in the board's statement . . . are satisfactory and to determine whether the proposal represents a desirable policy or whether it involves possible danger for the future welfare of the club. It is hoped they will express their opinions at the Extraordinary General Meeting.

The FA's letter was a clear declaration of support for Sir Matt Busby, who opposed the rights issue partly because he did not see the need to raise money and partly because he thought it could be better done via a bank loan. It was also true that Busby did not possess the financial resources of the Edwards family and that a rights issue would dilute his power at Manchester United.

It would be interesting to speculate whether Busby had a word with the FA before their Emergency Committee met to discuss United's proposal. It could not stop Louis Edwards but it could signal its distaste for what he was doing.

However, when the board met on 21 November to discuss the proposal, Busby did not oppose it. He said he had 'considered the matter very deeply and decided that for the sake of unity within the club [he] would be prepared to go along with it'.

There was a problem at the heart of the rights issue. The Edwards family had committed themselves to paying £739,000 for the 73.9 per cent of shares they already owned. If none of the other shareholders took up their options, they would be liable for the full one million. However, their core meat-processing business, Louis Edwards and Sons, had been unable to pay a dividend for several years and appeared to be in financial trouble.

Martin Edwards, who alone would have to borrow £400,000 to finance his part in the rights issue, tried to reassure the fans: 'We have the money,' he said. 'It comes from our own pockets. We have had to work that out, basically, through bank borrowing. We have had to use collateral from our investments and from shares elsewhere.'

Martin also revealed that the family was in talks to sell Louis Edwards and Sons. In February 1979, James Gulliver, the former chairman of Fine Fare, bought the business for £100,000, renaming it Argyll Foods. Within ten years, the company would swallow up 130 Safeway supermarkets and be worth £1.7 billion. Gulliver also paid Louis £250,000 for 100,000 shares in Manchester United.

The way appeared clear for a successful injection of funds into Old Trafford. Then, up popped John Fletcher, the 61-year-old managing director of Trumanns Steel. Eighteen days before the extraordinary general meeting that was to approve the rights issue, he wrote to all shareholders and copied the letter to every section of the media.

Fletcher was a supporter, rather than a shareholder, of Manchester United but he argued that the price of £1 a share was a long way below the true market value and, although existing shareholders might eventually make a profit, the deal was not in the best interests of the club.

He proposed that if the club were floated on the Stock Exchange it would bring in '£2 million and probably more'. He wanted the EGM, scheduled for 18 December, postponed. He claimed to have £2 million to fund his campaign. When asked why he was prepared to put so much money into a campaign, Fletcher stated:

> I can tell you quite simply there are three things that mean a great deal to me in my life. The first is my family, the second is Manchester United football club and the third is my cycling club, Manchester Wheelers.
>
> United have given me great memories like winning the European Cup and beating Sheffield Wednesday after the Munich Disaster. I believe in repaying debts and I owe United a debt for all the pleasure they have given me.

Fletcher's proposal to float Manchester United was revolutionary but ahead of its time. In December 1978, the country was being gripped by freezing weather and waves of crippling industrial action that was to become known as the Winter of Discontent. There was no appetite to float a football club, however big, on the Stock Exchange.

Fletcher attempted to seek an injunction to halt the EGM. On 14 December each of Manchester United's directors came separately to my offices in Chepstow Street and dropped his writ on my desk. The hearing was the next day. We would have to move very fast.

We briefed a counsel experienced in company law and secured secretarial facilities at the offices of our London agents, Herbert Smith.

Martin Edwards, Les Olive and I shot down to London by train and booked a hotel in Russell Square, which was convenient for the law courts. We were joined by John Nelson of Kleinwort Benson, who had just finished a stint as chairman of Lloyds of London, and we finished preparing our case at three in the morning.

At seven in the morning, while we were scrambling about on the floor, putting documents together, we were joined by Kleinwort's deputy chairman, Andrew Caldecott. It was Kleinwort's first involvement in football and they were amazed that someone, who had no financial interest in the company, would try to stop a normal commercial arrangement, particularly one sponsored by them.

Once we got into court, we did not have too much difficulty in persuading Mr Justice Goulding that the rights issue should go ahead. It was approved at the EGM by a vote of 37–3 in favour.

Fletcher accepted defeat gracefully and paid Manchester United's costs. His company Trumanns Steel is, however, better remembered at Manchester City rather than Old Trafford. The advertising hoarding that proclaimed 'Trumanns for Steel' was a prominent feature at Maine Road and a banner with 'Trumanns for Steel' was draped from the stands when City moved to what was to become the Etihad Stadium in 2003, by which time most Premier League clubs had accepted John Fletcher's wisdom of becoming public limited companies.

Nonetheless, the rights issue, which diluted Matt Busby's power at the expense of Louis Edwards and his family, did little to heal a growing rift between the two men. There had long been a tacit agreement between Matt and Louis that their sons, Sandy and Martin, would join them on the board. Martin had joined in 1970. Sandy had not been asked and as it became clear he never would, what remained of the friendship continued to rot.

4

Two Deaths and a Transfer

In February 1980, the geography of Manchester United changed abruptly when Louis Edwards was found dead on his bathroom floor. He had suffered a massive heart attack at the age of 65.

Martin immediately took over as chairman of the club. Although Louis had been in poor health and weighed eighteen stone when he died, Martin was convinced that an investigation, broadcast by Granada Television's *World in Action* programme, had contributed to his death.

The documentary, produced by the 25-year-old Paul Greengrass, who would become a Hollywood director (the Jason Bourne films among his works), alleged that Louis had put pressure on small shareholders to sell to him before the rights issue.

Greengrass believed that Louis had been persuaded by Roland Smith, the professor of business studies at Manchester University, that owning top-flight football clubs would one day become a lucrative business and he should aim to control as many shares as he could, despite their historically low return.

The 'victims' included the daughter of Walter Crickmer, the Manchester United secretary who had lost his life in the Munich air disaster.

Greengrass also alleged Louis had offered young footballers, including Peter Lorimer, illegal financial inducements to join Manchester United. Lorimer, who had been offered £5,000 (the equivalent of £72,500 today), joined Leeds but others had come to United.

Most damaging were allegations that Louis Edwards's meat-processing company had employed bribery to win contracts with council catering departments.

Louis did not sue Granada for libel but spent the next four weeks preparing a detailed and vigorous defence of his position, which he was still compiling when he died. Although his relationship with Sir Matt Busby had been a distant one, Busby agreed to give the valediction at the Church of the Holy Name in Manchester.

Busby turned it into an attack on Granada Television, calling *World in Action* 'a programme in which Louis, a person of admirable qualities, was vilified so viciously, whose good character was attacked with such concentrated venom'.

The rift between the two men was healed in death.

Far more painful for me was the death that was to come thirteen months later. My son, Christopher, died on 2 March 1981 from cystic fibrosis. He was 10 years old and his fight against the disease that clogs the lungs and the pancreas had been an inspiration to everyone around him.

We knew from the moment he was diagnosed that Christopher's life would be a short one, as treatments at the time were only of limited value – but it still came as a huge shock when we realised that his time was up.

He had made a second home of the Duchess of York hospital in Burnage, which was across the road from my parents who would call in with breakfast for him. I often used to sit with him at night, working on my files.

It was a Saturday afternoon when I called in to see him after playing for Old Mancunians in the Lancashire Amateur League. On my way to the ward, I was intercepted by a doctor who told me that, because of the increasing damage to his lungs, Christopher was now very near the end.

We had tried to give him as normal a life as we could. Much to the obvious displeasure of the hospital medical staff, he went to a local junior school and we took him on foreign holidays. Foreign trips could be a little nerve-wracking as it was sometimes necessary to leave at a moment's notice if Christopher's condition deteriorated and he needed treatment back home. He took it in his stride, although we had to fly back from Agadir and Minorca in our beachwear.

I spent the summer of 1981 coming to terms with Christopher's loss on the beaches of Devon. It had been an exhausting few months, made worse by Manchester United's disastrous tour of the Far East.

Now it would be known as selling the brand. A tour of the Far East to raise Manchester United's profile and build up the commercial contracts that would underpin the finances of the biggest football club in the world. In June 1981, Manchester United had embarked for the Far East without a manager and without enough footballers to field a team.

Ron Atkinson had been appointed to succeed Dave Sexton but he would not take over until 9 June, by which time the party would already have played their first game of the tour. The tour was managed by Jack Crompton, one of Manchester United's great goalkeepers, who had won the FA Cup in 1948 and the league title four years later. He was now United's reserve-team coach.

We had signed a contract with Keytours, who specialised in arranging matches overseas. They agreed to pay us $100,000 plus all travel and accommodation costs.

However, there was also a side deal. The biggest sports agency in the world was IMG, the International Management Group. They were an American company and the core of their business was golf, tennis and Formula One – their clients included Jack Nicklaus, Björn Borg and Jackie Stewart.

We had an agreement with IMG, who had never worked on a football tour before, to provide Manchester United players for various sponsored events. However, there were not that many United players to choose from. We agreed to field our optimum team. However, the tour coincided with a crucial round of qualifiers for the World Cup in Spain. England, needing to beat Hungary in Budapest, had called up four United players: Gary Bailey, Steve Coppell, Ray Wilkins and Mike Duxbury. The game, at the Nep Stadium on 6 June, was won 3–1 but, since United's first match was a day later, none would be available for any part of the tour.

Mickey Thomas would be playing for Wales against the Soviet Union on 30 May while Sammy McIlroy and Jimmy Nicholl would be in Sweden for Northern Ireland's qualifier on 3 June. Mickey would join the tour party in Manchester while the Northern Irish pair would meet up with us at Heathrow. However, the coach that would take the tour party to Manchester Airport had only ten players. An eleventh player was found in Garry Worrall, a young winger on his way back from a youth tournament in Switzerland who was met by his parents at Manchester Airport with a change of clothes. Mickey Thomas also made it to the airport.

Jack Crompton had been expecting to meet McIlroy and Nicholl at Heathrow and was taken aback to find them at Manchester. They were, however, only there to tell Crompton they would not be travelling at all because they were exhausted. A furious row ensued, and the two men were persuaded to join the flight to Heathrow, only for McIlroy to get off the plane while it was on the tarmac.

While waiting at Heathrow for the flight to Kuala Lumpur, Nicholl and Thomas also walked out of the airport and out of the tour. Manchester United arrived in Malaysia with eleven players, who managed a goalless draw.[2]

The second game, scheduled for Singapore six days later, was switched to Borneo, which allowed United's England players, minus Ray Wilkins, to join up. The players were appalled by the state of the hotel and only agreed to stay if they were given bonus payments.

Fixtures in Beijing and Hong Kong had already been cancelled so the party returned to Kuala Lumpur for a third and final match. Crompton was relieved when the flight took off to return the party to England. His relief would only extend so far. On his arrival back in Manchester, Martin Edwards, who had taken over from his father as chairman, sacked him as United's reserve-team coach.

We fined McIlroy, Nicholl and Thomas and were met with a furious reaction from IMG. They were used to perfectly organised sports PR, fronted by the likes of Arnold Palmer and Gary Player. We had presented them with a near shambles. They told us they would be withholding a significant amount of our tour fee.

There were two sides to IMG's complaints. They were unhappy at reports of players 'cavorting in the hotel swimming pool' and dancing and drinking into the small hours the night before a match.

They also accused us of being in breach of contract. We had agreed that our training sessions would be filmed with the players wearing shirts with the logo of the Malaysian subsidiary of Ovaltine. However, Jack Crompton had been so frightened of the players picking up any injury – which would have meant he could not field a team – that there had been no training sessions. He had allowed the sponsors to take photographs of the tour party wearing orange shirts with the sponsors logo. However, the mutinous atmosphere that dogged the tour meant the players had been in no mood to fulfil scheduled appearances with the media or with fans.

I became engaged in some lengthy correspondence and phone calls between Manchester and New York. Mainly because we had squeezed in the unscheduled second match in Borneo, they finally agreed to pay us in full. IMG would, however, continue to see tennis and golf as a safer sporting option.

Once Ron Atkinson had installed himself at Old Trafford, he became determined to buy Frank Stapleton to spearhead United's attack.

Stapleton had just turned 25 and had played in three FA Cup finals for Arsenal and been the club's top scorer for the past three seasons. Although Stapleton was out of contract in the summer, clubs were still able to retain the player's registration and demand a fee. The Bosman ruling was fourteen years in the future.

The board at Highbury was naturally keen to keep him in London and had offered Stapleton generous personal terms on a new contract. If Atkinson was to get his way, they wanted £2 million for the player, which would have been a record transfer for an English club. Our offer was £750,000. The matter seemed set to be decided by the Football League appeals committee.

The committee had just changed its rules, which allowed the buying club to withdraw from the transfer if the fee they were set was more than the club could afford. Before this, the transfer had to go through at the price the committee set.

I had taken the paperwork on the Stapleton transfer with me to Devon and while reading it, I became very uncomfortable and spent many hours in a telephone box by the beach, ringing Martin, the club's accountants and their tax advisors, Price Waterhouse.

In my experience, in almost all acquisitions of players, proposals are put forward to encourage the deal by making it appear cheaper than it was. For example, if we could not meet the player's wage demands, we could offer them a car or we could sort out a house for them and would settle the outstanding rent or mortgage. All this had implications for the Inland Revenue.

In the end the practicalities of dealing with the paperwork became impossible from a public telephone box and I returned to Old Trafford to meet Martin. My concerns were that the scheme to fund the Stapleton transfer breached FA and Football League rules, would create problems with the Inland Revenue and breach the 1967 Companies Act.

Martin backed me and the negotiations were simplified when Stapleton's solicitor, Michael Kennedy – who went on to represent a legion of Irish footballers – told us the package Arsenal were offering his client. All we presumably had to do was match it.

The appeals committee met at the Midland Hotel in Manchester on 20 August and set the fee at £900,000. This was very acceptable to us but less than half of the money Arsenal had wanted. The Arsenal chairman, Denis Hill-Wood, was displeased with the result and suggested the directors' traditional pre-match meal in Highbury's oak-panelled boardroom might be put off. 'We have always asked the United directors to come early and have lunch with us,' he told the press. 'I don't think we will be doing that again.'

When we played Arsenal at Highbury, a month after Stapleton had signed a five-year contract, we were given lunch, which was rather more entertaining than the football, which finished in a goalless draw.

5

The Battle with Big Bob

Robert Maxwell was a man who never forgot a slight and if you wanted to find the reason for his sudden desire to take over Manchester United, you would have to go back to a League Cup game with Oxford United.

Maxwell's core business, Pergamon Press, was based in Oxford and he had bought the city's main football club. In December 1983, his first big moment in the footballing limelight came when Oxford, then in the Third Division, knocked Manchester United out of the League Cup.

Ron Atkinson, who had captained Oxford, could not hide his anguish: 'I feel worse than I have ever done in football,' he said in the wake of the 2–1 defeat.

The road to that feeling had been long and laborious. This was the third time the clubs had met in the space of three weeks. The first game, at the Manor Ground, had been drawn 1–1. The replay at Old Trafford ended with the same scoreline and now it had been settled on a Monday night in Oxford.

It was then customary for clubs to share the gate receipts. The secretary of the away team would be handed the attendance and the takings shortly after half-time. The first replay at Old Trafford had attracted a crowd of 27,459. Oxford were given half the takings.

When Les Olive was handed the figures, we struggled to believe them. The official attendance at the Manor Ground had been 13,912. The club told the BBC, which was televising the game, that they had taken record receipts. People had clambered on the roof of a stand to watch the game. Martin Edwards told Les to question the information.

We were told that some of the home allocation had been sold to Oxford's supporters' club at higher than their face value. They were not prepared to share that money with Manchester United.

Robert Maxwell told the *Manchester Evening News* (20 December 1983):

> The chairman of Manchester United, instead of coming to the dressing room to congratulate us, tried to get extra cash out of us that he is not entitled to.
>
> United will receive their share of the gate receipts on the face value of the tickets sold. We raised extra money by selling a number of tickets at higher prices. We are not prepared to put that money into the pot. It belongs to our supporters' club.

I am convinced that it was this row, this feeling that he was being accused of dishonesty, that triggered Maxwell's decision to try to take control of Manchester United. He did it in a fit of pique.

Robert Maxwell had an 'in' at the club in the shape of Professor Roland Smith, who was not only close to the Edwards family but acted as Maxwell's financial advisor. He put the bid to Martin but at this stage no price was forthcoming.

On 2 February 1984 there was a full-scale meeting involving Martin, his brother Roger, and Roland Smith. During the meeting, calls came in from Maxwell's people asking for information about the club. Provided they agreed not to disclose it, we agreed.

It would be limited, and it did not mean we were ready to sell the club to Maxwell, but we needed to find out what exactly he had in mind. In a sense we were in a game where we wanted to find out what Maxwell's real motives were. We did not, however, wish to make it public.

There was no chance of United being able to hold that line. The following day we were digesting the front page of the *Daily Mirror*, a paper Maxwell would buy five months later. The headline proclaimed: '£10m To Take Over United!'

Not only had our request for discretion been hurled back in our faces, it was the first time we knew the price Maxwell was willing to pay.

Martin did not seem to oppose the bid, believing that Maxwell's finances could give Manchester United the resources to take on Liverpool, who were on their way to their fifth title in six years.

Speaking to the *Manchester Evening News*' United correspondent, David Meek, as reported on 10 February 1984, Edwards said:

> What really interests me is that if we can get a man like Robert Maxwell to Old Trafford, then we shall have someone with real financial clout at the club, someone perhaps who will want so badly to make Manchester United the number one club that he will lend his tremendous resources to help get a player like Diego Maradona.

Maxwell told Martin he would be appointing Coopers and Lybrand to investigate Manchester United's assets and report back. On 9 February, I met their representatives, who were particularly interested in the properties the club owned, and was contacted by Sam Silkin, who had been attorney general in the previous Labour government and was now working for Maxwell.

Four days later, Martin and I agreed to meet Maxwell at his London offices in Worship Street. We were promised 'a quiet lunch' with Maxwell and Roland Smith.

After watching United demolish Luton Town 5–0 at Kenilworth Road the previous evening, we stayed overnight at the Royal Lancaster, where we were joined by Roger Edwards. After breakfast, we went to the Savoy to meet James Gulliver of Argyll Foods, who after buying Louis Edwards and Sons had been offered a seat on the United board. Then we joined John Nelson of Kleinwort Benson, who had advised us on the rights issue.

We pointed out that when the *Daily Mirror* had publicised the £10 million price Maxwell had put on Manchester United it was not clear whether this was for the whole club or the 70 per cent of the shareholding Martin and Roger owned. We agreed we should sell the club for not less than £15 million (£43.5 million in today's terms).

John Nelson advised on what would happen when we arrived at Maxwell House, as his offices were grandly titled: 'The first thing he will do is invite you on to the roof to show off the view.'

We were met by Maxwell and Roland Smith and were duly invited up onto the roof. There, it became apparent very quickly that Maxwell had no clear strategy. It seemed he was looking to acquire only a minority stake in Manchester United. Roland suggested to Martin that he might like to sell Maxwell a limited number of his shares. I did not think much of this idea as it would have diluted Martin's influence at Old Trafford and left him with no satisfactory exit strategy. I told him not to pursue this idea on any account.

We then went to lunch. Far from being the promised quiet affair, the dining room at Maxwell House was jammed with the owner's senior employees and advisors.

News then came through that Yuri Andropov, the leader of the Soviet Union, had died. Maxwell knew his likely successor, Konstantin Chernenko, and he was forever asking his aides whether the media needed a comment from him. Every now and then Maxwell would bark loudly to his subordinates: 'Get me the Kremlin.'

It is unlikely the Communist Party of the Soviet Union needed advice from Robert Maxwell as to who should lead the world's second superpower. Like showing off the view from the top of his offices, it was a tactic to demonstrate his power to his visitors.

Watching Robert Maxwell eat was a mesmerising and revolting experience. I could not take my eyes off what was in his mouth or cascading down his chin. While all this was going on, it became clear we were not actually discussing a deal. The whole thing had been a publicity stunt.

After two hours we agreed we would issue a joint press statement that would bring an end to the takeover talk. I told Maxwell: 'Give me a chance to get back to the office and I'll draft something.' I need not have bothered. We were driving back to Manchester when we heard Maxwell's statement over the radio:

> Robert Maxwell has withdrawn from negotiation about the possible acquisition of a majority stake in Manchester United ... Mr Maxwell made it clear he could see no justification for the price of £15 million which was being asked, although he recognised why this figure was put forward and he accepted that Manchester United is unique in that it is difficult to put a precise figure on a team with this reputation.

Martin was relieved but he was also anxious about the whereabouts of his wallet. We had been so exhausted by the meeting that as soon as we left we decided we needed a drink. When Martin reached into his jacket pocket to pay for one, there was nothing there. It was somewhere back in Maxwell House, a place to which we had no desire to return.

Many years later, I was in Israel, advising one of its biggest clubs, Maccabi Haifa, and was driven past Maxwell's grave on the Mount of Olives.

I wondered what would have happened had he in fact taken over Manchester United. When he died in November 1991, Oxford United were forced to return every car and mobile phone the club owned and put every saleable player onto the transfer market.

Manchester United were a vastly bigger institution but in 1991, when it was floated on the Stock Exchange, it was valued at £47 million. Maxwell's debts were almost ten times that. We would have been swept away in the avalanche.

6

The Two Gordons

It is 250 miles from Manchester to Edinburgh. Martin Edwards and I could have driven.

We could have taken the train to Waverley Station. Instead, we decided to fly to meet Gordon Strachan.

There were no scheduled flights between the two airports, but a private plane was available. It was much smaller than we imagined, a propeller-driven, three-seater aircraft. We were given a flask of coffee when we clambered on board, but the conditions were so bumpy we couldn't pour anything into a cup.

As the little plane bucked and weaved, I tried to make conversation with the pilot. 'Which airlines did you fly for before you set up this company?'

'Oh nobody,' he replied. 'I only do this for a hobby. I work in a garage in Worsley during the day.'

I slumped back into my seat, glad that Martin, who was a nervous traveller at the best of times, had not heard the pilot because of the noise of the engine.

We landed safely enough and went to meet Gordon Strachan and his accountant, a man called, rather confusingly, Alan Gordon.

It was 3 May 1984 and Manchester United's season that had begun at Wembley with victory over Liverpool in the Charity Shield was spluttering to its conclusion. A 4–1 win over Coventry on 21 April had put United second, three points behind Liverpool, but Bryan Robson would tear his hamstring, Juventus would knock us out of the Cup Winners' Cup at the semi-final stage and we would not win another match.

Signing Strachan would provide some compensation. He was 27 and had driven the Aberdeen midfield that had won the previous season's Cup Winners' Cup. Aberdeen were on course to win the Scottish Premier League and had just been denied a place in a second successive Cup Winners' Cup final by Porto.

Strachan had also performed well for Scotland during the 1982 World Cup in Spain. Alex Ferguson had contacted Ron Atkinson and offered him Strachan, who was out of contract in the summer, for £500,000. He gave Ron the phone number of the player and that of his accountant. It seemed an excellent piece of business.

We knew why. Ferguson and Strachan disliked each other. Ferguson could not stand the player's quips from the back of the dressing room and the feeling that he was somehow apart from the rest of the team.

Strachan found the routine of the Scottish season, where you might end up playing Celtic or Rangers ten times, stifling. When he told Ferguson he was 'bored', his manager told him to 'unbore' himself. When he dropped Strachan towards the end of the season, Strachan criticised him in his column for the *Daily Express*. Ferguson ordered him to stop the column.

Aberdeen were also keen for Strachan to be sold to an English club. If, as an out-of-contract footballer, he went abroad, the fee would be determined by the European multiplier system, which set the fee judged on the player's age and his current salary, multiplied by eight. Based on that, the most Aberdeen could expect was £200,000.

Compared to the turbulence that surrounded Strachan in Aberdeen and the turbulence that had buffeted us all the way to Edinburgh, the meeting with Strachan and Alan Gordon was very smooth, helped by the fact that the player had brought his family with him.

Terms were quickly agreed and after another meeting the following morning Martin spoke to Aberdeen to finalise the transfer fee.

Strachan's playing contract with Manchester United would be signed on 18 May. We flew back to Manchester happy, partly because this time we were being flown by a professional pilot.

No sooner had we landed than we went straight to the Excelsior Hotel, which stood right outside Terminal One, to finalise another transfer – that of Ray Wilkins to AC Milan. They were prepared to pay £1.4 million – a British record – for one of the game's most cultured midfielders, and their representatives, led by the Milan president, Giuseppe Farina, were waiting for us.

We would be sorry to see Wilkins leave. He was a lovely, intelligent man. My abiding memory of him is seeing him at Stringfellows after the 1983 FA Cup final against Brighton. It was the final defined by the phrase 'and Smith must score' uttered by the BBC radio commentator, Peter Jones. Smith did not score and Manchester United escaped with a 2–2 draw. Wilkins, who had found the net at Wembley, was in a euphoric mood that night, convinced that Brighton had blown their chance and that United would win the replay – which we did, 4–0.

At Manchester Airport, we were joined by Gianni Rivera, one of the greatest midfielders ever to play for Milan and Italy. He was now the club's vice-president. Also in the room was the agent Dennis Roach, who those days seemed to be involved in every transfer.

It was a Saturday and we had to wait for Wilkins, who was playing in a 1–1 draw with Everton at Goodison Park. When Ray eventually arrived, he surveyed the room, pointed at Dennis Roach and asked: 'What's he doing here?'

'I assume he's your agent,' I replied.

'The only agent I have is my solicitor, Michael Kennedy.'

At this point we all turned to Roach and asked him to leave. He made no fuss. He had tried it on, and he knew this particular game was up. He went with a smile.

Wilkins then had his own discussions with the Milan delegation and agreed a deal around midnight. By now Martin and I had our minds on other matters because in the intervening period we had taken a phone call from Gordon Strachan.

We were ushered into another room to listen to a very agitated footballer. He told Martin he could not join Manchester United because he had already signed an agreement to play for Cologne.

Martin was so nonplussed by this and so aware we were needed back in the other room to talk to the Milan delegation that he didn't say anything to Gordon other than 'okay'.

As soon as the meeting with Farina was over, I phoned Alan Gordon, who said he had informed Alex Ferguson of what had happened with Cologne. Ferguson's reaction was stunned silence. He said he was so shocked he could not lose his temper. I then spoke to Gordon.

A fortnight before the semi-final with Porto, Strachan had met Karl-Heinz Thielen, who as a player had won two Bundesliga titles with Cologne and was now a vice-president of the club. He was also an agent.

Speaking to Gordon and his wife, Lesley, Thielen had given him a draft contract which he had taken home and was still unsigned. There had been a second meeting just before the semi-final in which Thielen had made it clear that if Gordon was unhappy with the contract, he should say so and Cologne would tear it up.

He cited the example of Tony Woodcock, who had signed for Cologne in 1979, immediately after helping Nottingham Forest win the European Cup. During the negotiations, Woodcock's wife expressed doubts about the move and Thielen had reassured her that if they did not want to go through with the transfer, the club would not object. Woodcock was reassured by a phone call with Kevin Keegan, who was playing in the Bundesliga with Hamburg. Some 8,000 fans turned up to his first training session and Woodcock spent five happy years at Cologne over two spells.

Strachan then signed a contract. Aberdeen had no knowledge of any of this and had not given permission for Strachan to talk to the Germans. When I asked Strachan why he had done it, he said he had not been playing well – Ferguson thought his display against Porto had been poor and he would eventually drop him. He said he felt he needed to protect himself and was still banking on Thielen's assurance that the contract could be torn up if he were unhappy with it.

When I asked him why he had not mentioned this at our meeting in Edinburgh, Gordon became evasive. However, he did say that after the meeting on 3 May he had told Cologne that his preference was now to join Manchester United. Strachan clearly expected Thielen to say that, given his assurances, that would be fine. Instead, Thielen had told him that now the contract had been signed it was out of his hands and the next decision would have to come from the Cologne board.

When Strachan's Aberdeen teammate Mark McGhee – who was negotiating his own move to West Germany to join Hamburg – told him the matter was being reported to UEFA, he really began to panic.

He phoned Cologne and told them that next season he would be playing his football not at Pittodrie, nor at Old Trafford, but at the Müngersdorfer Stadium. That should have settled it. He then told me that what he really wanted was to join Manchester United and he would like us to tell Cologne.

It was clear that Strachan was in such a confused state of mind that he should have no direct further contact with Cologne. If anyone was going to talk to them, it should be his accountant, Alan Gordon.

I asked him to ring Thielen, hoping it would sort matters out. It did not. Thielen told Gordon that he trusted Strachan and was sure he would come to the Bundesliga. He then put the phone down.

We needed a face-to-face meeting to try to resolve the issue. On 9 May, Martin and I met Alex Ferguson, Gordon and Lesley Strachan, and Alan Gordon in the boardroom at Old Trafford. It was the first time I had met Alex and he impressed me with the calm, thoughtful manner he considered the options.

The discussions lasted nearly four hours. We considered what action Cologne might take and the UEFA rules on approaches being made to a player under contract, because they were different from those that operated within the domestic game.

I drafted the player contract. Naturally, the agreement would be subject to a medical, a clause we were more than usually interested in because Arsenal had withdrawn their interest in Strachan when they heard he had a problem with his pelvic area.

The contract would also give us the right to withdraw and cancel the agreement before 30 June if Cologne instigated proceedings against Manchester United. We could also cancel the agreement, if it was shown to our satisfaction that the agreement between Strachan and Cologne was legally binding.

If Cologne instigated proceedings against Strachan personally, Martin agreed he should have the right to withdraw from the contract, unless Manchester United indemnified him against any costs or claim resulting from legal action.

Legally I could not advise that the situation was totally watertight from United's position, but I said it was sufficient for the club to take the risk in order to acquire such an important player.

Fifteen days later, Cologne made their move in the form of an exclusive in Scotland's biggest paper, the *Daily Record*. The headline was: 'Cologne To Sue Strachan'.

The paper revealed that the German club considered Strachan to be in breach of contract and that the West German FA had already registered him as a player. They had a copy of a contract with Strachan's signature upon it. If Strachan refused to honour the contract, Cologne would sue him.

Martin Edwards was quoted saying it was Manchester United's understanding that if Strachan was not happy with the terms of the contract Cologne had offered, he would be released from it. Aberdeen had not given Cologne permission to speak to Strachan and that permission would be required to make the contract legally binding.

By now Martin was in Australia. I sent him a fax: 'There is a serious threat of action by Cologne and it is one we should take seriously now, particularly bearing in mind the cover we have in our agreement with Gordon that expires on 30th June 1984. I have kept in close contact with Alex Ferguson and Aberdeen and his feeling is that Cologne are upset and that they are looking to save face.'

The matter had still not been resolved by the time Martin returned and we flew to Cologne on 20 June. We told Cologne that Strachan and his family wished to play for United and that he had already found accommodation in the Manchester area. The Germans' attitude was that once Gordon came to Cologne he would not want to play anywhere else. Having seen their magnificent training facilities, we could see the substance in their argument. The rebuilt Müngersdorfer was only nine years old.

We then flew to Zurich for a UEFA tribunal. Aberdeen, Cologne and the Scottish FA were also represented. They need not have bothered. The tribunal decided they needed to hear evidence from Strachan and Ferguson before they could make a ruling. They convened another meeting, in Rome, on 23 July. There, UEFA decided they were not competent to come to a decision and referred the matter to the world governing body, FIFA.

Three days later, following a representation from the West German FA, FIFA informed the Scottish FA that Gordon Strachan could not play for any club until his future was resolved by the FIFA Executive Committee. This was a serious stalemate and, if it were not resolved quickly, Strachan would not be eligible to play for Cologne or Manchester United in the UEFA Cup.

Back in Manchester, I phoned the Aberdeen vice-chairman, Chris Anderson, and Bernard Schäfer, who was on the board at Cologne. We agreed to meet at the Paris InterContinental on 7 August. Cologne's season was due to begin in six days' time. Manchester United had more breathing space. Our first match, at home to Watford, was not until 25 August.

Bernard and Chris fought their case with dignity and charm. The discussions went on deep into the night. By the time I wrote an agreement by hand on the Hotel InterContinental's headed notepaper, it was morning on 8 August.

All three of us signed an agreement that allowed Strachan's transfer from Aberdeen to Manchester United. In return, Cologne received an agreement that United would play a friendly at the Müngersdorfer. For whatever reason, that match never took place. The transfer of Gordon Strachan was one when a lot of people said a lot of things that did not happen.

It was not long, however, before we realised the other transfer of the summer, the one that had sent Ray Wilkins to AC Milan, was not working out quite as anticipated.

There had already been delays in payment of the transfer fee instalments and in receiving the letters of credit from Milan. Then, on 24 September, *The Times* reported that Wilkins and Mark Hateley, who had also signed for Milan for £1.5 million from Portsmouth in the summer, were both ready to walk out of the club. Wilkins had persuaded Hateley to join him at the San Siro during England's summer tour of South America. The deal was negotiated by Dennis Roach.

When Ray and his family arrived in Milan, they were put up in the luxury of the Principe di Savoia Hotel, along with Hateley, his wife and two daughters. However, the apartments they were shown were far too small for a family of four and, instead of the promised Mercedes, they were driving Fiat rental cars.

Neither man had been paid and when they were moved out of the Principe di Savoia and found themselves each crammed into a single hotel room, their patience snapped. Their mood was not improved when they discovered the German striker, Karl-Heinz Rummenigge, who had been signed by Inter Milan, was living in a beautiful lakeside home with a Mercedes on the drive.

The Times reported that they had bought their airline tickets back to London but had been persuaded not to drive to Malpensa Airport by Milan officials. The president, Giuseppe Farina, gave them the promised Mercedes and eventually they were presented with beautiful apartments in the town of Legnano, halfway between San Siro and the club's state-of-the-art training base at Milanello. Hateley celebrated by scoring the winner in the derby with Inter.

However, getting Manchester's United's transfer fee paid proved a much more drawn-out process. Despite the fame of their name, Milan were not a club flush with funds. A match-fixing scandal had seen them relegated in 1980, and although they were now back in Serie A, they were facing bankruptcy with debts of £2.5 million.

Eighteen months after the Wilkins transfer, we had whittled down the amount that was owed to us to £275,000. Then we heard that Farina had fled Italy for South Africa amid allegations of misappropriation of club funds.[3] Neither Wilkins nor Hateley had been paid for months. I wrote to the Italian FA asking for help in securing the remainder of the transfer fee and in January 1986 Martin Edwards and I flew to Milan. When we arrived at Malpensa we were greeted by an urbane, English-speaking Italian.

When Martin asked him who was taking over from Farina, our smooth guide looked at his watch and said: 'In ten minutes it will be Signor so-and-so.' It signified that the new man, Rosario Lo Verde, was regarded as rather insignificant in the great scheme of things. The club was being stalked by the media magnate, Silvio Berlusconi.

We spent two days with the 71-year-old Lo Verde and Milan's English lawyer, Ronnie Teeman, while Berlusconi implemented his takeover. Lo Verde agreed he would speak to Berlusconi over the next few days and get a date when the debt would be paid.

Berlusconi formally took over AC Milan in February 1986. The debt to Manchester United was paid in April with interest that for part of the time had run to 15 per cent. In July, Berlusconi was unveiled as the club's new president, arriving in Milan in a helicopter with loudspeakers blaring out Wagner's *Ride of the Valkyries*.

Berlusconi had the same sense of showmanship as Robert Maxwell but there was far, far more substance to him. By 1988, AC Milan were champions of Italy. The following year, they were champions of Europe. And, as everyone knows, that did not mark the end of Silvio Berlusconi's ambitions.

7

The Director's Cut

A few months after Robert Maxwell's retreat from Old Trafford, I joined the board of Manchester United. Martin Edwards wanted to refresh the board and thought my legal experience might be helpful.

When Louis Edwards died in February 1980, there had been some on the board who thought Sir Matt Busby would make a more convincing chairman of Manchester United than Martin. He had faced down that revolt and made Matt president of the club. It was a strictly honorary position that marked the end of Busby's real power at Old Trafford, although he and Martin enjoyed a good working relationship.

Alan Gibson, who had been vice-chairman, and Bill Young were also pushed upstairs to become vice-presidents. In their place came me, Michael Edelson and Bobby Charlton.

Michael was a good friend of Martin's and joined the board earlier than me, in December 1982. His family ran a well-known firm of furriers that had encountered increasing opposition from the animal-rights lobby. Edelson closed the business abruptly when one of his stores was firebombed. He went into developing shell companies and became known as 'The Shellmeister', boasting an impressive list of contacts.

Charlton was appointed because he possessed a football knowledge that was superior to anyone else on the board. Eleven years after his retirement, he was still England's most famous footballer and his value to Manchester United as an ambassador across the world was incalculable. He was the first United player to join the board since Harry Stafford, who had been captain of Newton Heath and was instrumental in its transformation into Manchester United in 1902. Stafford lasted two years before he was forced to resign for making illegal payments to players.

The other members of the board were James Gulliver, Roger Edwards and Martin's uncle, Denzil Haroun, who was Martin's uncle by marriage and whose business was in the clothing trade. Denzil seemed more taken by reserve- and youth-team football than he did by the senior side.

The business of Manchester United was always my primary concern rather than the results on the pitch and in that I differed from Bobby Charlton.

Soon after I became a director, we trooped back into the boardroom after United had drawn. I remarked that my club, Old Mancunians, were usually happy with a draw. Bobby shot me a look of utter astonishment. The only thing that counted for him was that Manchester United won.

He was still very competitive. When he agreed to play for my law firm, James Chapman and Co, against a team of our clients at Manchester United's training ground, the Cliff, he went to everyone telling them just to enjoy the match. A few minutes after kick-off he was snapping at his teammates to watch their passes, demanding that they look for space and shouting at us to make sure we won.

Les Olive, the club secretary, was the guardian of tickets for the directors' box and they were treated like precious stones. A few weeks after I joined the board, I asked Les during a meeting if I could have a couple of extra tickets for the next game.

The room went very quiet. I did not realise that such a request was never made. All eyes turned to Les, who to my very great relief, kindly acceded. Interestingly, other directors had taken note and from then on reasonable requests from board members generally went through.

When I joined the board, I already owned 1,800 shares. Shortly afterwards, Roger Edwards, the club's second-largest shareholder, said he wanted to sell a block of shares to fund a business venture.

Martin was reluctant to up his stake in the club but Oscar Goldstein, a partner with Price Waterhouse and one of Manchester United's tax advisors, suggested we buy them between us. It was a very substantial outlay for me and, although I did not believe I would lose money on the deal, I did not think I would ever make much if I sold them. It would, however, increase my influence on the board.

I took out a loan with my bank, Williams and Glyn, and in July 1984 I became the proud owner of 50,000 shares in Manchester United. There would be an early return on the transaction. Having not paid a dividend for a number of years, the club made a profit of £280,300 and declared it would pay a dividend of 15 pence per ordinary share. I had made £7,500. Buying Roger Edwards's shares was to prove a very good investment.

There were, however, side-issues to being a director and shareholder. When Manchester United floated on the Stock Exchange in 1991 and became the subject of takeover bids by Michael Knighton, BSkyB (British Sky Broadcasting) and, later, the Glazer family, the press, and especially the local press, delighted in telling their readers just how much the major shareholders stood to make.

This speculation generated a certain amount of envy among my legal partners at James Chapman and Co. There was always the suspicion that I might want to lay down my pen and take up some other, more lucrative, kind of work.

Manchester United had qualified for the UEFA Cup and had drawn the Hungarian club, Raba Gyor. The first leg was won comfortably enough, 3–0, at Old Trafford. As a director, I went with the team to Gyor, an elegant city by the Danube.

The night before the game, Martin Edwards and I were walking along the banks of the river when we saw a policeman trying to stop a young woman plunging off a bridge. As she seemed about to slip, we grabbed her arms and between us we wrestled her to safety. The policeman took her away and we never even discovered her name.

Manchester United would return to Hungary five months later, in March 1985, to play Videoton, a club based in Szekesfehervar, which was once the capital of the old kingdom. Rather more prosaically, the club was named after the local factory that produced televisions and radios.

Nobody who watched or listened to Manchester United being knocked out of the competition on penalties could have predicted this would be the club's last game in European football for five years.

8

The Heysel Ban

The mood when Manchester United set off on a post-season tour of the Caribbean was buoyant. For the second time in three years Ron Atkinson's side had won the FA Cup, beating the league champions, Everton, in the final.

It was the first season with Gordon Strachan and Jesper Olsen in midfield and had we not been badly beaten at Watford just before the FA Cup final, we would have finished second. There was a sense of momentum building at Old Trafford.

The tour, which had been organised by the football agent Dennis Roach, consisted of three matches against Southampton played on three islands. The highlight was checking into the Port of Spain Hilton, in Trinidad. The hotel is built into the side of a mountain, so reception is on the top floor and the rooms are below. Everything else was not nearly so spectacular.

The tone was set by the parachute display that was supposed to open our first match. The parachutists were supposed to land in formation in the centre circle. As we watched them drift in the wind, it became clear none of them would make the stadium. They ended up scattered amid the streets of Port of Spain.

The tour finished in Jamaica, where we had been promised a few days' holiday in Montego Bay. One look at the bus that was going to take us there was enough to ascertain that its best days were behind it. Two of our players, John Gidman and Arthur Albiston, point-blank refused to board it and hired a taxi.

Martin and I sat at the front by the driver on the grounds that if there was a head-on crash our lives were worth less than those of our players. There was, naturally, no air-conditioning and it was almost a relief when the bus broke down so we could at least get out while we waited for the repair truck. The accommodation, which had been provided by the Jamaican FA, matched the bus. The hotel had hot and cold running water, but much of it was running down the walls. Martin rather testily pointed out that the swimming pool was smaller than the one in his home in Alderley Edge.

With a full-scale rebellion on our hands, Martin, Dennis Roach and I marched down to the local tourism office and rebooked the tour party into the Royal Caribbean Hotel while Martin, Dennis, Ron Atkinson and I stayed in the Half Moon Club, a series of villas that led on to the evocatively named Sunset Beach.

We were in heaven, but 5,000 miles away an event was taking place that would propel football into its own version of hell.

On 29 May, Martin and I settled down in the Half Moon Club, an elegant, lemon-painted mansion, to watch the European Cup final between Juventus and the holders, Liverpool.

An hour before kick-off the football became irrelevant as Liverpool fans charged the Juventus fans, breaching a fence that separated them from a 'neutral' area. A concrete retaining wall gave way and 39 fans, mainly Italians, were killed. Another 600 were injured. Despite the carnage, UEFA ordered the final to go ahead. Juventus won, 1–0. A world away by the beaches of the Caribbean, Martin and I agreed the consequences for English football would be severe.

Even before Heysel, hooliganism had gripped the English game. The FA Cup quarter-final between Luton and Millwall had seen Kenilworth Road smashed up by hooligans who had travelled from London, armed with knives and billiard balls – which they hurled at the directors' box – with the express purpose of demolishing the ground. It was the lead item on ITN *News at Ten*.

Although her husband, Denis, had been a qualified rugby referee, Margaret Thatcher had no interest in football. In March 1985 all that had changed. David Evans, the chairman of Luton, who was the Conservative prospective parliamentary candidate for Welwyn, was summoned to meet the prime minister. Evans recommended a ban on away supporters and the introduction of membership cards.

Ironically, given what was to happen in Brussels two months later, the lead was taken by the Liverpool chairman, John Smith. In a meeting with Mrs Thatcher seven days after the rioting at Kenilworth Road, Smith called for decisive action against four problem clubs which he claimed had a strong National Front presence. These were Chelsea, Millwall, West Ham and Leeds.

Mrs Thatcher's principal private secretary, Robin Butler, itemised the steps Smith wanted to take.

> When a club's supporters had misbehaved, they should be banned from travelling to away matches in organised coaches or trains... The use of closed-circuit television should be extended as a priority to those problem clubs... When there had been trouble at a ground, there should be a ban on alcohol for the rest of the season.

Butler's document also recorded: 'Unless fines were large, they were ineffective: a more effective penalty would be a requirement to be present at attendance centres on Saturday afternoons.' Smith thought there was 'much to be said' for 'the police parading the ground with police dogs, as a warning' and recommended a 'specific offence to encroach on the ground'.

Butler's memorandum concluded: 'Mr Smith said that he was not in favour of identity cards because he thought that large numbers of supporters would fail to present them and would cause trouble outside the grounds when they were refused admittance.'

Smith also wanted to tackle trouble at international matches through 'an offence of behaving in a way likely to bring the nation into disrepute'.

The behaviour of Liverpool fans in Brussels had brought the nation firmly into disrepute. As we prepared to fly back from Jamaica, we were told the FA had unilaterally withdrawn English clubs from all European competitions for the 1985/86 season: Manchester United would not be playing in the Cup Winners' Cup, which would be won by a brilliant Dynamo Kyiv side.

On 2 June, UEFA banned all English clubs for 'an indeterminate period of time'. On 6 June, the ban was made worldwide by FIFA.

At Old Trafford, we recognised that some steps had to be taken to curb hooliganism. Something had to be done. People had died at a football match, and we had left our own stain in Europe. In September 1977, Manchester United supporters, some armed with bottles and knives, had attacked Saint-Etienne's home fans in a Cup Winners' Cup tie. United appealed successfully against their expulsion from the competition but were forced to play the return leg a minimum 200 miles from Old Trafford. That turned out to be Plymouth.

However, I thought that in withdrawing all English clubs from European football for the 1985/86 season, the FA had acted hastily. The decision was taken by a so-called emergency committee composed of just two people: the chairman, Bert Millichip, and the vice-chairman, Arthur McMullen, who had been secretary of the Bedfordshire FA.

The FA also seemed to have missed the wider implications of banning their clubs from Europe but allowing England to continue to play internationals. In 1980, the referee had been forced to suspend England's European Championship match against Belgium because of the sheer amount of tear-gas pouring on to the pitch as Italian police struggled to control our fans in Turin.

The Football League called a meeting at the Great Western Hotel near Paddington with all the clubs affected by the European ban – Everton (league champions), Manchester United (FA Cup winners),

Norwich (League Cup winners) plus Liverpool, Southampton and Tottenham who had qualified for the UEFA Cup because of their league position. They would announce a Super Cup competition between the six teams with a two-legged final. It would attract very little interest and be won by Liverpool.

To me this seemed an ideal opportunity to discuss the legality of the UEFA ban. Before I travelled to London for the meeting on 19 June, I discussed the situation with Gordon Taylor, the secretary of the Professional Footballers' Association, and their solicitors, George Davies and Co. The PFA were concerned about the impact of the ban on their players and were prepared to be associated with any proposed action. Once I arrived at the Great Western, I told the clubs that the PFA would support our action. Alan Woodford, the chairman of Southampton, was a solicitor and he suggested we recruit Robert Alexander QC.

Alexander was a good choice. Working for Kerry Packer, he had successfully overturned the ban on six English players who had signed for World Series Cricket from representing their counties. Geoff Boycott, whom Alexander had cross-examined at the High Court, thought him 'alert and wily'.

Liverpool, however, told us they would not be joining in any legal action. They had already imposed their own one-year voluntary ban and the following day they would receive notification of the sanctions determined by a special meeting of UEFA. They also thought that, given what had happened at Heysel, their presence could only hinder the other clubs.

I needed to know if the Football League would back us. The League secretary, Graham Kelly, said he would discuss it with his president, Jack Dunnett, and come back to us. I told Kelly that time was very much of the essence. Nominations to enter the three UEFA competitions had to be in by 30 June. We had eleven days. I needed a decision immediately.

I rang him that evening and Kelly said Dunnett's view was that the Football League could not lead any legal challenge. He said that even if the League wanted to join us, it could only be done after backing from the League Management Committee. They were not due to meet until 28 June. That was too late.

The next day I had an emergency consultation with Robert Alexander, who in 1977 had used restraint of trade legislation to overturn the Test and County Cricket Board's ban on the Packer players. We would use the same tactic now.

Alexander was unable to represent us as he was about to start an action for the British government in the European Court in Strasbourg. He did have time for a consultation and our discussions centred on whether we could go to law in Switzerland, where UEFA and FIFA were based, and how quickly we could do it. The draw was due to take place on 4 July. He said it was essential the clubs made interlocutory (provisional) orders against the FA, UEFA and FIFA.

He suggested we employ Christopher Clarke QC as lead counsel. Fifteen years later, he would be the lead counsel in the Saville Inquiry into the Bloody Sunday shootings. Gerald Barling would be junior counsel because of his knowledge of European Community law. The team was completed by my partner, David Marsden, and Peter Leaver, a barrister who had been a director at Tottenham and who would become chief executive of the Premier League.

On 21 June, the representatives of four clubs – Everton, Manchester United, Tottenham and Southampton – plus the PFA met and decided to launch legal action in the Chancery Division of the High Court. Norwich did not attend.

Our case against the FA was that they had breached the implied terms of their contract by failing to submit the names of its clubs who had qualified for European competitions. They had also breached the rules of natural justice in punishing clubs who had no connection whatsoever to the events at Heysel. They had also breached restraint of trade legislation and the terms of the Treaty of Rome.

Against UEFA and FIFA, it would be restraint of trade, breach of natural justice and infringement of the Treaty of Rome.

THE HEYSEL BAN

The clubs wanted the High Court to order the FA to enter the clubs into the appropriate European club competitions they had qualified for. They wanted UEFA to accept the nominations and enter the clubs into the draw for their competitions and for FIFA to raise its ban against English clubs to enable them to compete in these competitions and to participate in the matches against non-English clubs. Proceedings were issued on 25 June.

Christopher Clarke's advice was reassuring. He felt we had a good case against the FA and a reasonable one against UEFA and FIFA. These organisations had infringed European Community law and failed to hear the arguments of the clubs. The bans were far too wide and unjustified. The PFA agreed to join the action and agreed to be responsible for an equal share of the costs.

We were aware our legal action might be misunderstood by the public. We issued a press release making it clear that we 'utterly condemn the action of those who caused the appalling tragedy in Brussels'. However, we pointed out that we were trying to protect clubs who were being punished for events they had no part in. It was:

> an attempt to mitigate the extremely serious consequences for football clubs and professional footballers in England that would undoubtedly flow from the cumulative effect of the action of the FA, UEFA and FIFA.
>
> Those actions were taken without any consultation with either the clubs or the PFA and without giving the clubs or the PFA the opportunity to make representations.

Copies of the writ were served on UEFA and FIFA by me and the Everton club secretary, Jim Greenwood. We also engaged lawyers in Zurich to be ready for any proceedings in the Swiss courts.

Driving back to Manchester after serving the papers, I was astonished to hear on the radio that Tottenham were withdrawing from the action. They had just agreed the press release and had pledged to support the action and pay their share of the costs.

When I contacted White Hart Lane for an explanation, I was told their chairman, Irving Scholar, had decided that since the government supported a ban on English clubs, they should withdraw.

The hearing took place at the High Court on 28 June. Although UEFA did not accept English courts had any jurisdiction over them, they attended the hearing and were represented by counsel.

The case was heard by Mr Justice Vinelott, who often took his spaniel with him to court. John Vinelott considered that UEFA and FIFA were outside the jurisdiction of the English courts and ruled the application should be stood down to a later date.

During the Second World War, Vinelott had served in destroyers, and that ruling torpedoed our action. Nominations for the draw had to be submitted in two days' time. We had run out of time and further litigation was now pointless.

Ted Croker, the secretary of the FA, did not even attend the hearing. He had a prior appointment playing golf. He remarked he was surprised the clubs had even appealed against the ban. 'I thought most people, in and out of football, had agreed the time had come for a year out of Europe,' he said. 'Let us hope it is no more than a year. It is the only way to try to bring some sense to those idiots who follow us around Europe.'

Croker would have been shocked by UEFA's ruling. It was not one year, it was five – and by the time the ban was lifted, Croker would have left the FA. English clubs and players who had no involvement in the tragedy of Heysel were massively affected by the ban.

The clubs believed Croker had sacrificed them in order to keep the England national team playing World Cup and European Championship fixtures. Almost immediately after the Heysel disaster, England were due to fly to Mexico to play three matches in preparation for the following summer's World Cup. The first of those was against

Italy and, although there was speculation that the match might be called off, the FA was keen for it to proceed.

With an eye to the 1986 World Cup in Mexico, Croker was at great pains, when commenting on FIFA's decision not to ban England, to say that 'there had not been significant problems with the supporters of the English national side outside Europe . . .'

In the past fifteen years there had been only one major tournament staged outside Europe and English fans had caused no trouble at the 1978 World Cup in Argentina because England had failed to qualify for it. In October 1977, there had been serious violence when England travelled to play Luxembourg. During the 1984 European Championship in France there had been no repeat of the depressing scenes in Italy four years earlier because once more England had failed to qualify. When they did make it to the 1988 Championship in West Germany, there were more than 400 arrests.

The fact is the FA, as the supreme football body in this country, instead of taking some responsibility, was washing its hands of the whole thing as if it was not its concern. This was well summed up when Croker told Margaret Thatcher that the behaviour of the fans was a reflection of society and the responsibility of the government. Croker's remark did not go down well. When he stepped down from the FA in 1989, he was not awarded a knighthood, an honour that someone in his position might have expected.

The following year when English clubs, except Liverpool who served an extra season's ban, returned to Europe, they had no co-efficient points, which determined their seeding and how many clubs would be allowed into the UEFA Cup. It would take four years before the Football League returned to the level it had been prior to Heysel.

As they had been in 1985, Manchester United were FA Cup winners and entered the 1990/91 season's Cup Winners' Cup, which they won, beating Barcelona in driving rain in Rotterdam. The story had come full circle.

9

Barcelona

When the door to European football slammed shut, it made many players yearn for abroad.

You did not have to travel far to reach abroad. Scottish clubs were still allowed to play in Europe. Aberdeen under Alex Ferguson had beaten Bayern Munich and Real Madrid to win the Cup Winners' Cup in 1983. The following year, Dundee United reached the semi-finals of the European Cup and would make the final of the UEFA Cup in 1987. And under Graeme Souness, Glasgow Rangers would have the money and access to European football that the likes of Terry Butcher would find attractive.

Serie A had cash and glamour while Barcelona under Terry Venables would become a refuge for the likes of Steve Archibald and Gary Lineker. It also attracted the attention of a fierce young centre-forward from north Wales.

When the Heysel ban was imposed in 1985, Mark Hughes was 21 and had scored twenty-five goals in a season that had climaxed with Manchester United winning the FA Cup. The goalscoring continued into the following season, one in which United managed to win their opening ten games – a start which would not be enough to see them win the league.

The passion of his play and the fact he had joined Manchester United at 17 meant Hughes was a huge favourite at Old Trafford but his contract expired in the summer of 1986.

We were still pre-Bosman and, as Arsenal had done with Frank Stapleton, we could still charge a fee for Hughes's registration. However, if he moved abroad, the transfer would be subject to something many selling clubs feared – the European multiplier system. If clubs from differing associations could not agree a fee, it would be set by a formula multiplying the player's wages by the length of his remaining contract.

In 1985, Bryan Robson was Manchester United's highest-paid player, earning £93,000 a year (worth £247,000 now). Hughes was on £200 a week.

We knew Barcelona were interested and in the words of Ron Atkinson, 'we did not have a leg to stand on.' If Venables wanted Mark Hughes, then applying the European multiplier system he could have one of the hottest properties in British football for £200,000. We needed to renegotiate his contract and we needed to do it quickly.

Strictly speaking, the football authorities did not then recognise agents and only did so after the bungs scandal of the early 1990s in which a number of prominent managers were the subject of allegations, which in the case of George Graham led to his sacking. Back then, they posed as people who helped organise tours and other major events. Players usually employed a solicitor or an accountant to negotiate their contract, but increasingly they were using agents who were experienced in the entertainment industry such as Eric Hall.

Dennis Roach was in the furniture business when a chance encounter with Johan Cruyff on holiday in Portugal changed his life. In the summer of 1973, Cruyff had been offered the chance to go from Ajax to Barcelona. Roach, who had no knowledge of the football business, somehow persuaded Cruyff he could negotiate a better contract and travelled with Cruyff to Catalonia to do the deal.

Six years later, his company Pro International negotiated the first £1 million transfer in British football when Trevor Francis left Birmingham to join Brian Clough's Nottingham Forest.

Roach was now not only Terry Venables's agent, he acted for Mark Hughes. It would not be hard to guess how a deal might come about. We agreed with Roach that Hughes would get a new contract that ran until June 1990, which gave him a bit more money than £200 a week. There would, however, be suitable release clauses in the contract which would give Barcelona an opportunity to make their move, provided they could agree personal terms with the player.

The first buy-out clause could be exercised at the end of the 1985/86 season or the 1986/87 season. It was £1.8 million. The second could be invoked at the end of any of the remaining three seasons and was priced at £2.3 million. On 2 December 1985, Roach and I flew to Barcelona.

Terry Venables had agreed to meet us at the airport. When we arrived at El Prat, we were whisked through immigration and customs, which to us demonstrated the standing the club had in Catalonia. Terry escorted us to his car, which turned out to be a small Seat. Dennis Roach was a big man and we had to cram ourselves in. The man at the wheel was the manager of the champions of Spain. Ron Atkinson drove a top-of-the range Mercedes coupe which the club provided. Terry explained that he had to buy his own car – nothing was provided in his contract. When he first arrived at the Nou Camp, Joan Gaspart, the club's vice-president, had told him that the fans at Barcelona would either build a statue to him or set fire to his car. The choice of a cheap Seat was perhaps understandable.

The next day I would meet Gaspart, the power behind the throne at the Nou Camp. He had been appointed vice-president in 1978 and would hold the position for another twenty-two years. His business was hotels. In 1930, his grandfather had founded the Husa group – which was now Spain's third-largest hotel chain – and by the age of 25 Joan was managing the elegant Oriente on Las Ramblas.

By no means would this be the most difficult transfer Joan Gaspart had ever had to conduct. In 1982 he had travelled to Buenos Aires to negotiate the transfer of Diego Maradona from Boca Juniors. Such were the fears that the Boca fans would try to prevent the move by physically attacking him, that Gaspart was taken back to the airport in a light tank. It was the time of the junta.

We quickly agreed that Barcelona would pay £1.8 million for Mark Hughes and the fee would be paid on 1 August 1986. We would finalise everything at another meeting three days later in Paris.

Ron had told me to ask whether Barcelona would be prepared to sell Steve Archibald, whose goals had won Aberdeen the Scottish title in 1980 and Barcelona La Liga five years later. He would be 30 in September, but Ron thought he would be a useful addition to his attack. Gaspart wanted £680,000 for Archibald while Ron was not prepared to go beyond £250,000. Gaspart turned us down but did add he would give Manchester United first refusal if they decided to sell him. When Archibald did return to British football, it was to Blackburn Rovers.

I then flew back to Manchester and met Roach at the Four Seasons Hotel near the airport. Hughes would sign a five-year contract on 12 December, knowing full well it would last less than eight months. By the time I met Gaspart in Zurich twenty-eight days later, he confirmed Hughes had already signed a playing contract with Barcelona.

As I flew back from Switzerland, I wondered how long we could keep this deal under wraps. The answer was ten days.

On 19 January the back page of the *Sunday People* read: 'Sell Out Scandal'. The paper revealed Barcelona's option on Hughes and claimed it 'smells of stupidity by Manchester United's board and management. Worst of all, it treats the supporters like mugs. They dream of United's first championship for 19 seasons while the club connives in selling their top scorer.'

The timing could not have been worse. Manchester United's electrifying start had started to lose momentum and the *People*'s back page appeared the day after a 3–2 home defeat to Nottingham Forest had cut the lead over the chasing pack, led by Everton, Liverpool and Chelsea, to just two points. Nerves were starting to fray.

Martin Edwards responded with an interview with David Meek in the *Manchester Evening News*. He said he was incensed by the *People*'s suggestion that Manchester United were 'more interested in money than keeping Mark Hughes at Old Trafford'. He claimed that the deal had to be done because Hughes would be out of contract in June and the most Manchester United could hope to get for him was around £350,000 – and that was only if he joined another English club.

Martin added:

> We would have been irresponsible if we had not done something to safeguard ourselves financially . . . Mark Hughes did not want a new contract unless we gave him an option to leave us at the end of each year. Barcelona had already approached us and said that they were interested at £2 million pounds.

By 16 March Manchester United's season had all but unravelled. A 1–0 defeat at Queens Park Rangers was the third in five matches – and amid all that, we had been knocked out of the FA Cup by West Ham. Ron Atkinson's side had slid to third, seven points behind the leaders, Everton, albeit with a game in hand.

Since the deal with Barcelona had been concluded, Mark Hughes's form had disintegrated and he had not played at Loftus Road. He would, however, be involved in the aftermath of the defeat.

That morning's *News of the World* contained an article by Hughes under the headline: 'Black Mark: Why I Don't Deserve Shabby Treatment'. Even allowing for the fact it had been ghost-written, the content was jaw-dropping. It is worth quoting Hughes's words at length.

> I am entitled to ask my club Manchester United this angry question today: What the hell is going on?

It's not long since I put my name to a new five-year contract with United. And, for me at any rate, that meant security as a United player.

Now look what's happening. They're acting as though I was already out of the door. Just like a player of the past. I've gone from first to fourth choice striker almost overnight and my boss, Ron Atkinson, gives me the boot without even having the courtesy to tell me first.

United have signed an agreement with Barcelona for my £2 million transfer. But nobody asked me. I haven't even talked to anyone about a move from Old Trafford. The Chairman Martin Edwards told me he genuinely wanted me to stay. And I believed him . . .

I was amazed that Dennis Roach, who had travelled with me to Barcelona to negotiate the deal and who presumably had kept Hughes informed at every stage of the proceedings, should have allowed his client to talk to the *News of the World* – much less to put his name to an article that was so disingenuous.

I phoned him immediately and on the Tuesday he and Hughes came to Old Trafford to discuss the matter with Atkinson, Edwards and me. We decided calling a press conference would be too risky because we would not be able to control the line of questioning. Instead, we issued the following statement signed by Hughes and the club.

Mark Hughes has signed a contract with Barcelona FC to play for them next season, conditional only on a medical. Mark has apologised to the club for his recent newspaper article and wishes to put on record his appreciation of the treatment he has always received at Manchester United.

Both club and player now hope that all speculation will stop and Mark will be allowed to get on with playing football for the remainder of the season and contributing his part in United's attempt to win the League Championship.

Manchester United finished fourth, twelve points behind the champions, Liverpool. Mark Hughes left for Barcelona in the summer. The transfer had been the principal reason his form had fallen apart as the season reached its climax – not because he could not wait to drink in the adulation of the Nou Camp but because he did not really want to leave. Hughes was a boy from Ruabon in north Wales who was faced with moving to one of the centres of world football to play in a country whose language he did not understand and which he suspected he never would. In a Manchester United podcast in 2021, Mark revealed that, deep down, he wanted to stop the transfer but could never summon up the courage to do so.[4] The nearest he came was in that article in the *News of the World*.

His fears were well grounded. Mark Hughes's physical game was not suited to La Liga, where he continually fell foul of referees. Barcelona did not employ a player liaison officer to help new signings integrate and Hughes became isolated and unhappy. A loan move to Bayern Munich was more successful, but by 1988 he was back at Old Trafford.

In the summer of 1986, I was at a meeting of First Division clubs at Highbury when I was told I was wanted on the telephone. It was Joan Gaspart. He wondered if I could recommend a top-ranking coach.

He did not make it clear whether he was asking on behalf of Barcelona or another Spanish club. Terry Venables had just taken Barcelona to the European Cup final, a match which proved traumatic for the Catalans. It was staged in Seville and played against a limited Steaua Bucharest side. It should have been a coronation but instead a miserable game (0–0 after 120 minutes) was lost even more miserably on penalties (2–0).

In hindsight the European Cup final marked a turning point in Venables's time at the Nou Camp, but at the time a man who had won

La Liga and taken Barcelona to their first European Cup final in a quarter of a century did not seem in immediate danger. I decided Gaspart had to be asking for someone else.

   I told him to go for Alex Ferguson, who had just led Aberdeen to another Scottish League title and was fresh from overseeing Scotland's World Cup campaign in Mexico. Ferguson, I told Gaspart, would make someone an excellent manager.

10

Getting Ferguson

As November nights go, it was bleak. The day before Bonfire Night we had been thrashed 4–1 at Southampton in the League Cup. In the league, Manchester United were fourth from bottom and were only out of the relegation zone on goal difference from Chelsea. In that season, the fourth-bottom club in the First Division would go into a play-off featuring the third, fourth and fifth-placed teams from the Second Division. Crowds at Old Trafford had dipped below 40,000.

The change in United's fortunes had been dramatic. A year earlier, having won the FA Cup, Ron Atkinson's side had won their first ten games. On 4 November 1985 we had been ten points clear of Liverpool at the top of the league. All the talk at Old Trafford had been of a first championship in nineteen years. Now parallels were being drawn with the relegation season of 1973/74.

The slide had begun on 18 January with a 3–2 defeat to Nottingham Forest at Old Trafford. Liverpool had won the league and, for good measure, the FA Cup to become only the third English team in the twentieth century to win the coveted Double (Tottenham in 1960/61 then Arsenal ten years later). The sickly pattern had continued into the new season.

Martin Edwards had been at the Dell but was back at Old Trafford for a meeting with me that had been arranged long before the rout at Southampton. Inevitably, we discussed Ron's future. As we talked,

Bobby Charlton popped his head round the door and joined the conversation. Soon after, Mike Edelson, who had been at the match and flown back with Martin, also telephoned to speak to Martin. When he realised that the three of us were together talking over the match, he said he would come and join us. The four members of the Manchester United board were together in one room.

There had long been suggestions we would be looking to Alex Ferguson to take over. During the World Cup, where he was working as a commentator for ITV, Atkinson was approached by Lawrie McMenemy, who was then in charge of Sunderland. He apparently told Ron that Ferguson had already been sounded out about taking over at Old Trafford.

Ferguson was managing Scotland at the Mexico World Cup, and just before they faced Uruguay, Bobby Charlton told him that should he ever want to manage in England, he should give him a call. In his autobiography, *Managing My Life*, Ferguson remarked: 'I don't think that could be considered an offer.' [5]

I agree, but what I can say is that when the four of us met that morning at Old Trafford, I was the one who said we should get Alex Ferguson. I had got to know him during the Strachan affair and was confident in his abilities. There was talk of Terry Venables, but it was soon clear we all wanted Ferguson.

We knew we had to move quickly. Martin did not want a repeat of the process the last time he had changed manager. In 1981, he had sacked Dave Sexton and been rejected by McMenemy, Bobby Robson and Ron Saunders before Atkinson agreed to take charge. We could not ring Alex directly at Aberdeen as it would immediately raise suspicion and prompt accusations that we were 'poaching' their manager. So, Mike Edelson, with his best Scottish accent, rang Alex claiming to be Gordon Strachan's accountant, Alan Gordon.

Ferguson's first words were: 'How are you doing, you ugly bugger,' before he realised he was not speaking to Alan Gordon. Edelson asked

Alex to hold on and the phone was passed to Martin, who gave Alex his number and asked him to ring him back so he could be certain it was not a crank call.

Alex rang back almost immediately, and Martin asked if he would be interested in the Manchester United job. A year earlier, Alex had fulsomely praised Ron Atkinson in his book about his time at Aberdeen, *A Light in the North*, saying, 'It wouldn't surprise me if Ron's Manchester United side become one of the greatest sides in the club's illustrious history.'[6] Now it was a very different story. He said he was interested, and it was clear that, whatever he may have felt about Atkinson, he was being given the opportunity to manage Manchester United and he was not going to spurn it.

We did not want to waste any time and it was agreed we would meet in Scotland. Martin asked Alex to suggest a place and he rang back to say the motorway service station in Hamilton, Lanarkshire, at 7pm.

While we told nobody about the journey to Scotland, Ferguson informed three people. One was Archie Knox, who had been his assistant at Aberdeen when they won the Cup Winners' Cup, and was now back at Pittodrie after a spell managing Dundee. Alex wanted him as his number two in Manchester.

He phoned Jim Rodger, a journalist at the *Daily Record*. Rodger had been a miner in the Lanarkshire pits with Jock Stein before they both changed profession: one into newspapers, the other into football. Rodger had been close to Bill Shankly, and Ferguson regarded him as a mentor.

The third and most important conversation was with his wife, Cathy. Two years earlier, he had been offered the chance to manage Tottenham but had rejected the move, partly because the Spurs chairman, Irving Scholar, was not prepared to give him a five-year contract but also because Cathy did not want to move to London.

At Old Trafford, the four of us agreed we would drive to the Tickled Trout Hotel, which lies off the M6 near Preston, leave our cars, and

Mike would take us to Hamilton in his Jaguar XJ6. We arrived early and, because car phones were not then common, we looked for Alex's number plate in the darkness. We somehow found each other, and Martin got into Alex's car for the drive to Ferguson's sister-in-law Bridget's house in Bishopbriggs on the outskirts of Glasgow. A very nice supper had been laid on for us.

Alex made it quite clear he would be interested in joining Manchester United, though the potential salary disappointed him. With bonuses it would be less than what he was earning at Aberdeen.

It was pretty late when we left Bishopbriggs and across the border in Cumbria we stopped off at a fish-and-chip shop, where Bobby Charlton had been recognised. However, although the owner told him how honoured he was to have a World Cup winner in his shop, the questions went no deeper.

As we drove back, we agreed a plan of campaign. Martin and I would meet Ron Atkinson and his assistant, Mick Brown, separately after training and, once they had been dismissed, we would fly to Aberdeen to meet their chairman, Dick Donald.

Ron and Mick had their suspicions when they discovered their boots had not been laid out for training but there was no animosity shown. Ron had offered to resign in the summer, after the 1985/86 season that had promised so much had fizzled out. His words to Martin were: 'Perhaps I should get out of town for everybody's sake.' The chairman was stunned by the remark.

I had always liked Ron Atkinson. He was somebody who if you asked him to do something would always oblige. He even played football for James Chapman & Co when we played clients, usually insurance companies, at the indoor centre at the Cliff. He was very competitive and did not like losing.

In one game, against the Eagle Star Insurance Company, we had a 50-minute second half instead of 30 minutes. Ron made it clear to the referee that he could not blow for time until we were ahead.

Martin and I arrived on a British Airways flight at Aberdeen just before four o'clock, when it was already nearly dark. Dick Donald, a man whom Ferguson thought of as a father-figure, recognised what an opportunity this was for Alex. His son, Ian, who was also at the meeting, had represented Manchester United as a youngster.

We agreed to pay Aberdeen £60,000 in compensation and stage a friendly at Pittodrie in March. Aberdeen would be guaranteed £30,000 from the gate. Anything over that would be split between the two clubs.

We then met up with Alex to discuss his contract and later in the evening with Archie Knox. The meetings were very much exploratory, but we were looking at a three-and-a-half-year deal for Alex, from 7 November 1986 to 30 June 1990. After another meeting between me, Martin Edwards and Alex, I sent Martin a copy of the draft service agreements for both Alex and Archie. In the letter I wrote: 'Mr Ferguson's salary has been left blank.'

The arrival of Alex Ferguson did not quickly improve Manchester United's fortunes. His first match was lost at Oxford, and a goalless draw against Norwich left us languishing in the relegation zone. We were eliminated from the FA Cup at home to Coventry a few months later. By the end of the season, however, the team had found enough rhythm to finish eleventh.

11

The Man in the High Castle

It was a phone call out of the blue skies of a July morning in 1989. The voice on the other end belonged to Martin Edwards.

'I'm at Manchester Airport and I wonder if I can come round and talk. I've just sold the club.'

I was stunned. Martin had never even suggested he was ready to sell Manchester United. As I waited for him to arrive, I wondered who he could have sold the club to and why he had not even mentioned it to any of the other directors?

As he sipped tea in my living room, Martin told me he had just flown back from Scotland. He had been to Killochan Castle in Ayrshire, built a few years before the death of Mary, Queen of Scots, and now owned by a man called Michael Knighton. They had been introduced through Barry Chaytow, who was the chairman of Bolton Wanderers and a friend of Michael Edelson.

There, he had agreed to give Knighton an option over his shares which valued his holding at £10 million. It would wipe out Martin's personal debt which then stood at nearly £1 million. Knighton had also promised money to make the Stretford End an all-seater stand. It was the summer after the Hillsborough disaster.

The draft of the Taylor report into the deaths of 96 Liverpool fans at Hillsborough on 15 April 1989 was due to be published the following month and we already knew it would demand all-seater stadiums. The North Bank at Highbury, the Kop at Anfield and the

Stretford End would have to be completely remodelled. When the full report appeared the following year, it set a deadline of the start of the 1994/95 season for stadiums in the top two divisions to become all-seater.

The Stretford End was then Old Trafford's biggest stand and could hold 20,000. Rebuilding it would cost another £10 million. From what Martin told me, Knighton seemed an attractive prospect and we agreed to meet at Old Trafford three days later.

Martin needed a lawyer to represent him in the sale and as I was on the board of Manchester United it could not be me. I had known Peter Cole since our days as law students at University College, London. He was now a senior corporate partner at Alexander Tatham's in Manchester and had a feel for this kind of transaction. He agreed to look after Martin's interests.

Proceedings were delayed by Manchester United's participation in the Mitsubishi World Soccer Tournament which saw us play Everton and Japan in Kobe and Tokyo, respectively. When we returned to Manchester, Martin signed a formal agreement with Knighton's company, MK Trafford Holdings Ltd, for the sale of all his ordinary and preference shares in Manchester United. The board was formally notified of Martin's transaction the following day, 18 August.

He told them Knighton was offering £20 a share and wanted all directors to remain on the board subject to them retaining at least 25 per cent of their shareholding. The deal was conditional on an accountancy report, and everything was scheduled to be finalised by 30 November.

The one dissenting voice came from Amer Al Midani, who had joined the board four years earlier. Midani was a Lebanese property developer who had owned the Warrington Vikings basketball club. Martin had always thought Manchester United should become a multi-sport club in the manner of Barcelona, and in 1985 he had invited Midani to join the board and move Warrington Vikings to Trafford, where they were renamed Manchester United.

Midani had previously expressed an interest in buying Martin out, and now he wondered why he had not been given the opportunity to do so and why Knighton had been handed a clear run at the club. Knighton then joined the meeting and outlined his proposals to redevelop Old Trafford and rebuild the team.

Martin was aware that news of the sale of Manchester United would not go down well with the fanbase and felt it was imperative to call a press conference.

Michael Knighton was an unknown to the football media and the press conference presented him with a wonderful opportunity to talk about himself, something he did with a flourish. He had a good back story. He said he had been destined for a career as a professional footballer and was a ground-staff boy at Coventry City when he suffered a serious thigh injury that had thwarted his dreams. He said he wanted Manchester United restored to its position as 'the greatest club in Europe'.

He added: 'This will be achieved through the marriage of sound business management, a genuine love of football and a deep understanding of the needs of the players and supporters alike.'

The following day (19 August), Manchester United opened their season against Arsenal. I was not at Old Trafford because I had taken my family to Malta for the week. That evening I was rung at my hotel by Michael Edelson. His first words were: 'You will never believe what happened at the match.'

I did find it hard to believe what Edelson was describing. Before kick-off, Knighton, in full United kit, had run on to the pitch, juggled with the ball on his head (with some skill, apparently) and then lashed it into an empty net.

The fans loved it, especially since it was followed up by a resounding 4–1 win over the champions. However, many others did not. Michael

Knighton soon realised that his showmanship would expose him to intense media scrutiny which he was not equipped to withstand.

One newspaper pointed out that five years before his dramatic appearance at Old Trafford, Knighton had been a prep-school teacher and been supported by his wife's parents who had sent them food parcels.

His company, MK Trafford Holdings, was registered in the Isle of Man and controlled by a trust of which he owned 60 per cent. The other 40 per cent was owned by Robert Thornton, the former head of Debenhams. Knighton had bought Killochan Castle with a £565,000 mortgage from the Midland Bank.

Not long after the dramatic victory over Arsenal, Michael invited us to Killochan. The other members of the board employed excuses of varying degrees of seriousness not to go. I went to Scotland, accompanied by my wife and baby son, Timothy. I was curious and wanted to preserve some measure of friendliness with our potential new owner.

We ate at a long, baronial table with Knighton's advisors and contacts from institutions in Glasgow and Edinburgh. It appeared they had been invited at the last minute to cover for the missing Manchester United board members. After everyone had gone, we joined Michael and his wife, Rosemary, for coffee and liqueurs. Also in the room was the entertainer, Rod Hull, thankfully minus Emu. He was wearing slippers. He was staying in one of the castle lodges and was clearly a regular visitor to Killochan.

There was a fair amount of laughter in the room, but it was not driven by Rod who, although at the height of his fame, seemed withdrawn and did not put on a performance. Off stage, Rod Hull could be melancholy, believing that the puppet that had propelled him to fame had completely boxed in his career. Producers wanted him but only if he brought Emu. He was a fan of Manchester United, and tragically fell to his death in March 1999 when trying to adjust his TV aerial on the

Even after all the glory with United, taking the most wickets in a season for The Manchester Grammar School's 1st XI remains one of my proudest achievements.

At The Manchester Grammar School presenting pupil Matthew Slim with the Maurice Watkins Award, given every year to the footballer who displays the highest levels of sportsmanship.

With my brother Geoffrey (left), who died aged 19 in a swimming accident in France, in the summer of 1966.

Holding Christopher, my beloved firstborn who passed away at 10 years old from cystic fibrosis.

With Bobby Charlton, Martin Edwards and Michael Edelson, the old guard of Old Trafford.

Martin Edwards (bottom left), David Gill (top left), Alex Ferguson (bottom centre), Peter Kenyon (bottom right). The team behind the team.

Alex on his way to his first match in charge, away at Oxford United in 1986. Manchester United lost 2–0.

Unveiling Gary Pallister at a press conference on 29 August 1989, having signed him for a record £2.3 million fee from Middlesborough. How times have changed!

Lee Martin's match-winning goal against Crystal Palace in the 1990 FA Cup final replay at Wembley, 17 May 1990.

Mark Hughes raises the European Cup Winners' Cup for Manchester United after scoring both goals to beat Barcelona 2–1 in the final in Rotterdam, 15 May 1991.

A bit late in the day to sign him, but a pleasure to have hosted Pelé in the Directors' Box at Old Trafford in the '90s.

Above: Club secretary Ken Merritt (far left), Bobby Charlton (second left), Mike Edelson (third left, Sir Matt Busby (centre), me (third right), and Martin Edwards (far right) with the European Cup Winners' Cup.

Left: Winning the first ever Premier League title, in 1993. Twelve more have since followed.

It was a privilege meeting Nelson Mandela on Manchester United's tour of South Africa in 1993.

Andrei Kanchelskis completes his hat-trick against Manchester City in a 5–0 hammering, 10 November 1994.

Eric Cantona's infamous kung-fu kick on an abusive fan, moments after he had been sent off against Crystal Palace, 25 January 1995.

Almost as famous as Eric Cantona's kick is his cryptic statement at a press conference following his successful appeal at Croydon Crown Court: 'When the seagulls follow the trawler, it's because they think sardines will be thrown into the sea. Thank you very much.'

roof of his house in an effort to get a better picture of United's Champions League quarter-final with Inter Milan.

Michael Knighton was very good company. He lived in a striking venue and I was particularly impressed with the bathroom in one of the turrets. Whether that made him a fit and proper person to buy Manchester United was another matter.

The first indications that things were not quite as they seemed came in mid-September when it was announced that Knighton had removed Robert Thornton from MK Trafford Holdings. Thornton had lobbied for Knighton to be replaced by Stanley Cohen, whose family owned Betterware, a company that sold household products door to door. Cohen, a veteran businessman, had been a significant backer of the takeover. As the major shareholder, Knighton had won the battle and bought Thornton out.[7]

On 20 September, MK Holdings' offer went unconditional, which meant Michael had to make a general offer for the whole of the issued share capital in Manchester United. He could, if he wished, buy all our shares and become the sole owner of the club. The offer had to be in by 11 October. Knighton went public, announcing to the press:

> I have done it. I've put together a £20 million package in three-and-a-half days and shall go unconditional in my offer to shareholders later today.
>
> I have been vilified. This was my own deal from day one and it remains so. It was upsetting to say the least to lose two business partners [Thornton and Cohen] three months down the line with them.
>
> There is no bitterness and I am simply reverting to how I started out. I have no backers. I have used purely my own business resources and financial contacts. I have pledged my personal funds and assets. I don't think my personal commitment can be questioned.

That evening Michael and I flew to Portsmouth to watch Manchester United win the first leg of their League Cup tie, 3–2.

In 1989, Manchester United did not run a press office. I was the club's spokesman as well as its lawyer. I felt we needed the help of a heavyweight City firm. The obvious choice was Kleinwort Benson who had worked with Manchester United before. I spoke to John Nelson, who had helped us with the abortive Maxwell takeover, and Kleinwort's director, Simon Robertson, who would later become chairman of Rolls-Royce.

Simon came back to me with the news that Kleinwort had decided they did not want to represent the club. Both John and Simon had been in favour, but they were overruled. I was surprised because Kleinwort had had good experiences working with Manchester United. I can only assume they did not like the publicity Knighton was generating.

Robertson recommended a smaller finance company, Henry Ansbacher and Co. On 28 September, I met their managing director, Mark Phythian-Adams, and four days later they were appointed as the club's financial advisors.

At Old Trafford an increasing tension gripped the board. It was fuelled partly by the uncertainty surrounding the takeover and partly because some directors thought they might be better placed than Knighton to bid for control of Manchester United. Some thought they should enter into a partnership with him. The board was also irritated by Knighton's continual press briefings.

In order for Knighton to buy his shares, Martin had provided his advisors with confidential documents and information about Manchester United which were never intended to be made public. Based on this, Knighton's accountants had prepared a report on the club and its finances. This was also not for the public domain. We soon discovered, however, that his information was being supplied to people who were not involved in the deal. We also learned that Knighton was trying to sell a controlling interest in MK Trafford and we were concerned he had not told the board the name of the company's financial advisors, which he was required to do by law.

Knighton may have had grand plans for what he wanted to do with Manchester United, but it seemed he did not have the money to complete the purchase. Confidential information had been passed to at least two people. One was Eddy Shah, who had sold his *Today* national newspaper and was looking for new investments. The other was Owen Oyston, the chairman of Blackpool FC, who had sold his estate agency business for £37 million and owned magazines and radio stations across the north of England.

A number of directors met at Old Trafford on 4 October and were joined by Martin Edwards. We agreed time was running against us and that Martin had to move quickly. Board members met late at night in their cars in leafy Cheshire lanes to compare notes as we tried to discover what had been leaked and to whom.

The following day, we arranged a confidential hearing at the High Court before Sir Igor Judge, who granted an injunction preventing Knighton releasing any further confidential information.

However, even at this late stage, we still felt there was a deal to be done with Knighton. In a spirit of compromise, we altered the scope of the injunction to allow his professional advisors sight of documents which would otherwise be confidential. The High Court adjourned the matter for further consideration until 12 October.

By then the only question that mattered was whether Knighton had the money to buy Manchester United. The matter would be settled in the Midland Hotel, the venue in Manchester where Mr Rolls first met Mr Royce. It was soon clear that a similarly happy merger was not going to happen.

All around the hotel there were little groups of people discussing the various deals now swirling around Manchester United. As I toured the hotel, I wondered what hotchpotch mix of investment and ownership might result from these conversations. What was happening surely could not be in the best interests of the club or its supporters. Something had to be done, so I spoke to Martin, who by now wanted nothing more than the whole Knighton experience to disappear. I suggested we meet urgently with Knighton and ask him to cancel the deal. Even if he did get the funding together, his position was becoming more untenable by the hour.

It would be a humiliation for him and we would need something to sweeten the deal. I told Martin we could not offer Knighton any money to withdraw but we could offer him a place on the board. This would play to his ego, which as we saw from the way he had announced himself to the crowd at Old Trafford, was considerable.

The meeting was at a venue considerably less grand than the Midland. It was the Novotel near Trafford Park. Michael had realised that the deal which had started so promisingly was no longer obtainable. Even if he did succeed in raising the money, there was no guarantee the investors would be remotely right for Manchester United. He wanted an honourable exit and when I offered him a seat on the board, he immediately accepted.

On 11 October we announced that the deal between Martin Edwards and Michael Knighton had been cancelled and that Knighton was now a director of the club. The press statement was carefully worded to make it appear that this was a friendly separation. The press release did not state that Knighton did not have the money to buy Manchester United and said the board accepted that he had acted in 'the best interests of the club'. We were grateful for 'the bold action which he [Knighton] has taken to bring an end to the uncertainty surrounding Manchester United'.

In the years to come, I was always asked to propose Knighton for re-election to the board of Manchester United. Was this my punishment for first suggesting he become a member? I always took the view that it was worth it because the alternative was unthinkable. Knighton always had to be re-elected by a vote using Martin's majority shareholding. He would not have been re-elected on a show of hands.

Michael Knighton was ahead of his time. Unlike Robert Maxwell, he had the vision but not the money. He thought Manchester United should exploit its commercial advantages with television deals, overhaul its merchandising operation and build a hotel near Old Trafford. Knighton predicted that in fifteen years' time the club would be worth £150 million. Events proved his prediction to be unusually conservative; in 2004, according to *Forbes* magazine, Manchester United was the most valuable football club in the world, worth £655.5 million.

By then Michael Knighton was no longer in football. He left the Manchester United board in May 1992, after the club had been floated on the Stock Exchange, and became chairman of Carlisle United, where he would step down ten years later. There would be a promotion in 1995 and a successful trip to Wembley for the Football League Trophy a couple of years later but not, as he had promised, the Premier League. Killochan was sold to a relative of the Kaiser – Wilhelm II, not Franz Beckenbauer.

Knighton made himself manager of Carlisle in the 1997/98 season. 'You need a JCB to move all the bullshit that's been written about coaching,' he said. Anyone, he believed, could manage a football club. It was a theory disproved by his record of nineteen wins in sixty-eight matches. It was a theory that Alex Ferguson – who may not have survived had Michael Knighton taken control of Manchester United – would surely have disagreed with.

12

Late-Night Shopping

One Sunday evening, at the height of the Knighton takeover, I got a call from my next-door neighbour, Ernie Craig, to say that Alex Ferguson was on his way round. It may sound strange, but I lived at number 25 and Ernie was at 25A, so he often had to deal with people who came knocking for me, including the manager of Manchester United.

We were going shopping for a centre-half, which meant driving to Middlesbrough to meet Gary Pallister. Alex had inherited two Irish centre-backs from Ron Atkinson. The first, Paul McGrath, was a world-class defender, whose time at Old Trafford had been undermined by alcoholism and injury. The other was Kevin Moran, who in 1985 had become the first footballer to be sent off in an FA Cup final. Ferguson would describe Moran as 'a punch-drunk boxer' because he was involved in so many clashes of heads.

Pallister was 24. He had been instrumental in Middlesbrough's rise from bankruptcy which had seen them win successive promotions to the top flight. Alex thought he could deliver the steady, consistent performances he wanted week-in and week-out from his team.

The long drive gave us the chance to discuss how we were going to manage the negotiations. First, we would meet with Gary's agent, Jon Smith. If we could agree personal terms, we would meet Middlesbrough. Once we had agreed terms with Pallister, they would not be able to hold on to him.

Jon Smith was a young, confident man who was well on his way to becoming England's most successful sports agent. He would manage the off-field affairs of the England football and cricket teams. His most famous client was Diego Maradona.

We met in the car park of a hotel, just off the A1, called the Cleveland Tontine. (A tontine is a legal device, much loved by crime writers, where the inheritance goes to the last named beneficiary who is still alive.) The discussions were held in Alex's Mercedes with the rain splattering against the windows as Smith tried to wring out much more money than I knew Manchester United could agree to. We had a well laid-out salary structure that included a basic wage, a signing-on fee and bonuses for appearances, wins and trophies. We were not going to break it for Gary Pallister.

I knew exactly how high we were prepared to go and while I never lost my temper, I refused to be swayed by the various arguments put forward by Smith for us to pay more. At the end of it he told Alex, 'I think I've done a reasonable job for the lad but there is a little part of me that wishes I could have found a turnkey to go a little higher.'

It was flattering to read in Smith's book *The Deal* that I was 'a ferocious but gregarious negotiator' and that, 'we ticked all Man United's boxes and pushed them as far as they would go but I pride myself on finding loopholes in the system and I couldn't do it this time.' [8]

Now it was well past midnight, but we still had to do the deal with Middlesbrough. Their manager, Bruce Rioch, was waiting for us in the car park. He and Alex knew each other well. Although Rioch had been born in Aldershot, his father was from Aberdeenshire and served in the Scots Guards.

We drove to Ayresome Park to meet the chairman, Colin Henderson, who had been the commercial manager of the ICI chemical plant in Wilton on Teesside. Henderson was a formidable figure, who in 1986 had led the consortium, backed by ICI, that had rescued Middlesbrough FC from oblivion.

Henderson said the club wanted £2.3 million for Pallister. It was the highest fee Manchester United had ever paid and the highest any English club had paid for a defender. It was several hundred thousand pounds more than we had budgeted for. But just as Jon Smith had been unable to find a turnkey at the Cleveland Tontine, I was not able to find a way through Henderson and Rioch in the boardroom at Ayresome Park. At two in the morning, I did what lawyers do when they need a change of tactic. I asked for a timeout so I could have a private chat with Alex in another room.

'How important is this player to you?'

'Very. We must secure him.' He looked at me in a very determined way.

We went back to the boardroom and agreed the fee on Colin Henderson's terms. It was the small hours of the morning so I could not phone Martin Edwards to seek his agreement. The only small breakthrough I achieved was to ask for more time to spread out the instalments. Dawn was breaking by the time we reached home.

I rang Martin a few hours later. 'Do you want the good news or the bad news?'

'The good.'

'We have secured Gary Pallister.'

'And the bad.'

'It is a record fee. £2.3 million.'

'Bloody hell!'

Although Michael Knighton was on the point of taking over the club, I had not kept him informed. I did not see at this stage why he needed to know. However, the imminence of the takeover and the knowledge that it would inject money into the club may have persuaded Martin to take a more relaxed view of the transfer.

The deal proved its value. With Steve Bruce, Pallister formed one of the great defensive partnerships in Manchester United's history.

The first impressions, however, were not good. Pallister existed on a diet of Coca-Cola, Crunchies, Rolos and Mars bars. But, as Ferguson recalled:

> [He had] a rich talent [...] his physique and his football both matured rapidly and, unusually blessed with balance and pace, he became a centre-half I wouldn't have swapped for any in the game. As a combination, he and Bruce gave us a sense of assurance and authority in defence that spread confidence through the whole team.[9]

Gary Pallister was unveiled at a press conference on 29 August. We had hoped to have Paul Ince alongside him, but that transfer had gone horribly wrong.

It was no secret that Paul Ince was coming to Manchester United.

At West Ham, he had formed a very close relationship with the manager, John Lyall, who regarded him as a surrogate son. However, Lyall's sacking had made him want to leave Upton Park and, before we had even spoken to him, he had been pictured in a Manchester United shirt. We quickly agreed terms with West Ham and three days before our trip to Middlesbrough, on 25 August 1989, we met Paul and his lawyer, Henri Brandman. We haggled for three hours before we could come to a deal, but then Ince announced he wanted to discuss the terms with his agent, Ambrose Mendy, whose core interest was boxing – he managed Ince's cousin, Nigel Benn.

The morning that we were due to see Pallister, Ince went for his medical and told the Manchester United physio, Jim McGregor, that he was in considerable pain. The problem was his groin. McGregor's advice was that Ince needed three months' rest.

We were now faced with the prospect of paying £1 million for a midfielder who would not be ready for action until the start of December. Alex and I met the club doctor, Francis McHugh, and an orthopaedic specialist, Jonathan Noble, and we agreed it was impossible to go through with the transfer.

We issued a press release, informing the media of a problem with Paul's pelvic area and concluded: 'In the interests of all parties, the matter will have to remain on ice pending further tests.'

Paul Ince was distraught and gave an interview to *The Sun*, in which he said: 'I hope and pray that I will be sitting around a table with Mr Ferguson one day in the future so I can finally sign the piece of paper that makes me a United player.'

Mendy and Brandman arranged their own medical report from two Harley Street consultants, concentrating on three specific areas – the pelvis, the left side of Ince's groin and his right foot. The reports were in within a couple of days.

They were positive enough for us to meet up on 12 September with Paul's representatives and those of West Ham for two days of talks. Ince's personal terms did not change, but we had to arrange a 'pay-per-play' deal with West Ham to protect Manchester United from the risk of Ince breaking down completely. The down payment on the transfer was also reduced. However, after a couple of years, when it became clear the injury risk we feared was unlikely to materialise, we bought out our original obligations to West Ham and put Ince on a more routine contract.

One thing I did take from the Ince transfer was knowing to stay calm when there seemed to be a serious hitch.

In April 2000, I was working on the Ruud van Nistelrooy transfer from PSV Eindhoven. The striker had not played for six weeks because of a knee injury sustained when he attempted a bicycle kick, but we had agreed a fee of £18.5 million that would break the British transfer record.

On 25 April David Gill, the club's newly appointed financial director, and I were due to give a press conference at Old Trafford announcing the transfer alongside Ruud. However, the club's medical staff were increasingly concerned about the state of Van Nistelrooy's knee and told us that on the evidence before them they could not sanction the transfer.

After journalists had been kept waiting for an hour and a half, David and I had to tell them that Ruud had returned to Holland for further treatment. He was upset by this and two days later the deal collapsed when PSV declined to carry out keyhole surgery on the knee because Van Nistelrooy feared it would jeopardise his chances of playing in Euro 2000, which was being co-hosted by the Netherlands. A couple of days later, his cruciate ligaments gave way in training.

David Gill was very downhearted at the way his first major transfer had gone. However, I reminded him of how the deal to bring Paul Ince to United had seemed beyond us. Ince had spent six years at Old Trafford and won two league titles. All was not necessarily lost.

On 23 April 2001, almost exactly a year after the aborted press conference and after some intensive rehabilitation, we once more announced Ruud van Nistelrooy as a Manchester United player. Like Ince, he would win the Premier League.

13

Close to the Edge

'It's not "Notts Forest", it's "Nottingham Forest".'

The words were delivered in the unmistakable drawl of Brian Clough. A few minutes later, when I had made the same mistake, he uttered the exact same phrase. They were the only words he ever spoke to me.

We were in the boardroom at Villa Park in July 1989 at a tribunal to set the fee for Neil Webb, who had come to the end of his contract with Nottingham Forest. Webb was a goalscoring midfielder, blessed with the gift of making a precise pass. It had been a difficult process to persuade him to come to Old Trafford and now we had to fix a fee. Alex Ferguson and I represented Manchester United. Forest had Clough and his chairman, Maurice Roworth.

Correcting my description of his club was virtually the only intervention Clough made, apart from asking if we would like 'a stiffener' before we started. We declined the offer of a drink and Clough left almost everything to his chairman.

There was a yawning gulf between the valuations United and Forest put on the player. Nottingham Forest wanted £2.2 million. Manchester United were prepared to pay £900,000. The tribunal set the fee at £1.5 million.

Neil Webb did not fulfil his promise at Old Trafford, mainly because a month after his debut for the club – which he marked with a goal against Arsenal – he tore his Achilles tendon playing for England in a

World Cup qualifier against Sweden. He made a recovery but never regained his former pace and was sold back to Nottingham Forest for £800,000 in November 1992.

He did, however, provide one of the most important passes in the history of Manchester United. It was his lovely, measured through ball to Lee Martin that gave United a 1–0 victory in the 1990 FA Cup final replay against Crystal Palace. Had Manchester United lost, I do not believe Alex Ferguson would have survived and the greatest era in the club's history would have been lost.

The match that is commonly supposed to have determined Ferguson's fate was the third-round tie at Nottingham Forest on 7 January. United were 15th in the First Division, two points off a relegation place, and, after the heavy spending in the summer, the media thought elimination from the FA Cup at the first hurdle would prove terminal for Alex.

However, the doubts expressed by the press and by some of the fans were not shared by the board. We knew how hard he worked behind the scenes and the progress he had made with players at all levels of the club.

Interestingly, when we arrived at the City Ground and glanced at Brian Clough's programme notes it seemed as if the Nottingham Forest manager feared for his future.

> Somebody put round a rumour last weekend that I was packing in after my 1,000th game at Nottingham Forest. I'm not naming names, but my mole tells me that the person responsible is Scottish . . . is now a coach and is still one of the biggest stirrers in the game . . . I'm told that the reason for him putting around this malicious gossip is that he fancies my job. But I've got news for him – and anyone else who thinks I've 'shot it' – I'm going nowhere yet.

I do not know who is the Scot that Clough mentioned. I am sure it was not Alex.

Manchester United won, 1–0, thanks to a goal from Mark Robins. The team progressed to the final via Hereford, Newcastle, Sheffield United and a hard-fought semi-final which went to a replay, against Oldham.

The final, against a Crystal Palace side managed by Steve Coppell, was also replayed after the first match had been drawn 3–3. For the replay, Alex dropped his goalkeeper, Jim Leighton, who had been with him at Aberdeen and in the World Cup in Mexico. It was an astonishing gamble, but it paid off with a 1–0 win that gave Manchester United their first trophy in five years, and threw their manager a lifeline.

Had we lost, I think it likely Alex Ferguson would have been dismissed. Martin Edwards is of the same opinion. He wrote in his autobiography that 'I could not keep defending him.'[10] I am not sure just taking us to the final would have saved Alex's job. The board may well have said: 'Thank you and goodbye.'

As it was, the board meeting that was convened the day after the cup was won recorded their congratulations to their manager, ending with the phrase: 'They hope it will be the first of many such trophies.' Never has a hope been so amply fulfilled.

When Alex took his leave of Manchester United, twenty-three years later, he had added another twenty-seven major trophies. I don't include the Charity or Community Shields because neither did Alex.

Brian Clough and Alex Ferguson, two of the great managers in British football, did not get on. Perhaps because of the club's greater financial resources, Clough disliked anyone who was manager of Manchester United.

When Ron Atkinson was manager of West Bromwich Albion, he and Clough were on very friendly terms. As soon as he departed for Old Trafford in 1981, Brian barely exchanged a word with him. Then, when Ron returned to the Midlands after his sacking by United, Clough invited him to the City Ground for drinks.

Alex also had a fractious relationship with Kenny Dalglish. The two Glaswegians are closer now than they were when they opposed each other on football's front line, when there was a sharp edge to their encounters. 'You'll get more sense out of my baby than him,' Dalglish is said to have once quipped, carrying his daughter Lauren in his arms as he passed Ferguson giving a press conference beside the pitch at Anfield.

By January 1992, Dalglish had left Liverpool and was spearheading the extraordinary transformation of Blackburn Rovers from a northern backwater to the champions of England. Financed by the money provided by Jack Walker's steel business, they could outbid any club in the country, and while others paid in instalments, Blackburn paid cash up front.

Alan Shearer was then 21, the hottest young striker in English football, who at the age of 17 had scored a hat-trick for Southampton against Arsenal. He was a month away from making his full England debut in which he would score against France.

That January, the *Daily Star* announced Shearer would join Manchester United for £4 million at the end of the season. They claimed Shearer had already agreed personal terms and that Southampton and United had settled the fee.

This was utterly untrue. Alan Shearer consulted solicitors who sought a retraction and an apology. Later that month we were due to play Southampton in the FA Cup and we wondered if we could use that opportunity to persuade Shearer to join us in a libel action against the *Daily Star*. However, by the time the tie was played, we had decided that it would be too expensive for the benefits it would bring.

Nevertheless, by the summer it was clear that Alan Shearer would be leaving Southampton. Blackburn had won promotion to the Premier League and made Southampton an offer of £3.6 million. After

Alex had been rebuffed by Sheffield Wednesday when he asked whether their striker, David Hirst, was available, we turned our attention to trying to prise Shearer from Blackburn's grasp.

It was not a smooth operation. When Alex phoned the striker, it resulted in a painful, stilted conversation, while Dalglish had better luck in a face-to-face meeting at the Haydock Park Hotel which adjoins the racecourse. He was helped by the fact that his assistant, Ray Harford, had managed Shearer at England under-21 level and that Kenny's wife, Marina, who was also at Haydock Park, hit it off with Alan's wife, Lainya.

Meanwhile, I was meeting Shearer's agent, Mel Stein, in London and making any number of phone calls to Manchester and Southampton from a phone box in Baker Street. It made for uncomfortable working and was to no avail. On the evening of 23 July, Stein informed me that Shearer would sign for Blackburn.

I notified Alex Ferguson, who subsequently informed me that there may be a problem with the transfer negotiations as David Speedie – who was the player exchange part of the contract between Blackburn and Southampton – did not fancy a move to the South Coast. It proved a forlorn hope, however, because Speedie ultimately agreed to his £400,000 transfer.

Afterwards, Alex told me our failure might have been for the best because he had not liked Shearer's attitude and wondered how committed he would have been to Manchester United.

This did not prevent him, four years later, from making a concerted effort to bring Alan Shearer to Old Trafford. Then, there was a face-to-face meeting with the player, who asked if he could wear the number nine shirt and if he could take Manchester United's penalties. The first demand was no problem, but we had a fabulous penalty-taker in Eric Cantona. Because we had won two Doubles in the space of three seasons, we were much more confident of attracting Shearer than we had been in the summer of 1992.

However, Jack Walker did not want to sell his prize asset to Manchester United, and Newcastle could offer him the emotional pull of a return to the North East. Shearer went for a world-record fee of £15 million.

The fact we had lost Shearer to Blackburn in 1992 gave an edge to the pursuit of Roy Keane a summer later.

Nottingham Forest had just been relegated and, after eighteen years, Brian Clough had left the City Ground. The squad he left behind was vulnerable to being picked apart and nobody was more valuable than their combative midfielder, Roy Keane.

Blackburn had been stalking him since it became clear that Clough's regime was falling apart. They knew Keane had a clause in his contract allowing him to leave Nottingham Forest if they were relegated.

They made their move early, agreeing a fee of £4 million with the new Forest manager, Frank Clark, while Keane accepted a salary of £400,000 – which was 25 per cent less than Alan Shearer was being paid. Keane's meeting with Dalglish was successful but because it took place late on a Friday afternoon, there was no office staff at Ewood Park to process the documents. Keane returned home to Cork and Dalglish told him he could complete the forms on Monday.

While he was in Ireland, he was phoned by Alex Ferguson and persuaded to come to Alex's home in Wilmslow on the Monday. There, over a game of snooker, he persuaded Keane – whose family were hardened Manchester United fans – that Old Trafford represented a better bet than Ewood Park.

Dalglish was apoplectic when he found out. There followed a furious conversation with Keane. 'Nobody does this to Kenny Dalglish,' he told the Irishman, who was about to go on holiday to Cyprus. He told the press that 'Keane gave me his word on three separate occasions that he would be joining Blackburn Rovers.'[11]

At this time, Keane did not have an agent and was represented by Brendon Batson of the Professional Footballers' Association. Martin

Edwards and I met Batson on 9 June to discuss his personal terms. Five days later, at the Etrop Grange Hotel near Manchester Airport, we met Keane and his newly appointed lawyer Michael Kennedy.

It was a decision that would help make Kennedy one of the most famous sporting lawyers in the country, even though he shunned publicity. He was born to Irish parents in Highgate, north London, and held a season ticket at Highbury. He became involved in football when the Arsenal defender David O'Leary, who had employed Kennedy to help with a house purchase, asked him to look at his contract. In time he would represent a host of Ireland internationals.

On 19 June, we agreed to meet Kennedy and Keane at the offices of James Chapman and Co. As Keane was not familiar with Manchester, we arranged for Roy to stand at the rear of the Midland Hotel, which was about 300 yards from our offices. We would monitor his arrival using binoculars. Once we spotted him, we sent a trainee solicitor to bring him over. Contracts were exchanged and the personal terms arranged, although Keane was unhappy with the salary of £250,000 which was considerably less than Blackburn had offered. Martin agreed to increase it by £100,000.

On 23 June, Martin and I travelled to Nottingham to meet Frank Clark and the Forest chairman, Fred Reacher. We agreed a transfer fee of £3.75 million. As I left the City Ground, my thoughts darted back to that afternoon in January 1990 when all the talk was of how Alex Ferguson was on the point of dismissal. Instead, it was Brian Clough who was no longer there, while Ferguson was now in charge of the league champions.

14

Floating

Like something out of a John Le Carré thriller, we had been given a code name. Henceforth Manchester United would be known as 'Batsman' in an attempt to maintain secrecy as the club prepared to float on the Stock Market.

I don't know why Ansbacher, the City merchant bank advising us on becoming a public limited company, chose the name. It may have been a nod to the Old Trafford cricket ground that stands half a mile from its footballing cousin.

Throughout football there was a desperate need to raise money. Attendances were still a club's chief source of revenue and they were in freefall throughout the 1980s. Manchester United was the biggest club in the country. At the start of the decade, Old Trafford's average attendance was 51,600. By 1989, it had fallen by nearly 30 per cent to 36,400.

There was little hope of rescue from television as the BBC and ITV ran a cartel and paid as little as they could get away with. In 1983, Manchester United's television income amounted to £25,000 – the same as Rochdale's.

In the early 1980s, Tottenham came up with the idea of raising money by listing themselves on the Stock Exchange.

Tottenham were highly successful on the pitch, winning the FA Cup in 1981 and 1982 and the UEFA Cup in 1984. However, their attempts to upgrade White Hart Lane by rebuilding the West Stand to house 72 executive boxes that would generate increased revenue had seen the club plunge into debt. The budgeted cost almost doubled to £6 million and the fallout saw the property developer Irving Scholar buy out the ex-chairman Sidney Wale. He was partnered by another property developer, Paul Bobroff. They decided the only way to get Tottenham out of debt was to float as a public limited company and raise money through people buying shares in the club.

On 6 October 1983, Tottenham Hotspur plc was born. The flotation raised £3.8 million, while Scholar and Bobroff underwrote another £1.1 million in new shares. However, while the share price initially did well, it soon drifted below its issue price of £1 and by January 1984 it was trading at a 19 per cent discount. The Stock Market was then nearing an all-time high, but Tottenham shares continued to bump along the bottom.

Nevertheless, the flotation had created a lot of interest and Martin Edwards and I discussed whether Manchester United should follow suit. Tottenham had gone straight in with the big boys of the Stock Exchange, but I pointed out there was also an Unlisted Securities Market where smaller companies could be floated.

If we were to float, we needed a merchant banker, so Martin and I met John Nelson of Kleinwort Benson in December 1983. There was another meeting in the new year which Roger Edwards also attended. Within weeks, Kleinwort Benson produced a discussion document. It pointed out that Tottenham's shares had done worse than the market average. Tottenham also had relatively few existing shareholders when they floated, so most of the cash went to the club.

This would not be the case with Manchester United. Partly because of the rights issue, there were a lot of Manchester United shares and most of those that would be sold on the Stock Exchange would come from existing shareholders. It would be they rather than the club who would become the chief beneficiaries.

As to how much the club was worth, Kleinwort Benson thought £9 million was a possibility but £10 million was unlikely to be reached.

When Robert Maxwell touted £15 million for Manchester United that year, he would be paying significantly above the market valuation. Perhaps because of this, his bid never developed into anything serious.

Martin got on well with Irving Scholar. In the summer of 1983, Manchester United and Tottenham were playing a friendly in Swaziland. Scholar and Edwards challenged each other to a match and captained their sides in club colours. Scholar, who fancied himself as a footballer, scored a hat-trick in an 8–4 win.

In May 1984, Martin and I met Scholar and the Spurs chairman, Douglas Alexiou, who was a divorce lawyer by trade, at Harry's Bar in Piccadilly. We were joined by Oscar Goldstein who worked for accountants Price Waterhouse.

We agreed that Tottenham and Manchester United had much in common. Our television revenue was exactly the same – £25,000. We had both won the FA Cup in recent seasons and, although Old Trafford's average attendance was nearly 14,000 more than White Hart Lane's, Tottenham's ticket prices were significantly higher.

Martin's chief concern was whether Manchester United would be able to afford the dividends which would have to be paid to shareholders if the club floated. One result of the meeting was that Oscar and I decided to buy some of Roger Edwards's shares.

For legal reasons, the deal with Oscar Goldstein would later run into trouble and Martin, much against his will, was forced to buy back Oscar's shares.

It was then that Nigel Burrows came into our orbit. He was a director of the Independent Financial Group, whose holding company administered the Manchester United pension fund. He claimed to have been a regular on the Stretford End and now, much more genteelly, was chairman of the Manchester United luncheon club. It is through that route that Burrows met Martin Edwards and offered to buy Goldstein's shares. Martin was only too glad to accept and during the

1987/88 season proposed Burrows join the Manchester United board. Nigel, who was just 34, described this as 'a dream come true'.

Martin at this time would not have been too particular as to whom he sold his shares to. As he told the *Daily Telegraph* journalist Mihir Bose:

> I had heavy debts. I had to pay those off. They were certainly seven figures. I had carried the debt since 1978 [the time of the rights issue].
>
> Indeed, my house was in debt to the bank. I was not prepared to carry on for the rest of my life being in debt to the bank. We had a situation where I was the majority shareholder, holding 50 per cent, but how could I liquidate my position? The choice was instead of selling to an individual we should go public. Plus, the fact that we also wanted to raise money to rebuild the Stretford End.

This was why Michael Knighton had seemed so attractive. The deal would produce money for Manchester United, rebuild the Stretford End and pay off Martin's debts in one go.

We also discussed whether some of the United directors might want to buy some of Martin's shareholding and reduce the financial pressure on Martin. It was then that Burrows said he might be in a position to invest. The problem was that his money was tied up in trusts, and investments could only be made on the say-so of the financial advisors that controlled them. They were based in Jersey and called TA Le Sueur and D de Sainte Croix. Coincidentally, I had booked a family holiday to Jersey and decided to investigate. It proved a complete waste of time. Nothing substantial came of any of the discussions I had with them in St Helier.

Amer Al Midani, who had brought the Warrington Vikings basketball team to Manchester United, also thought he might be able to buy Martin out, but these talks also went nowhere. Martin and I flew out to

Marbella, where the Midani family owned the Puente Romano Hotel, where Amer agreed to buy 8 per cent of Roger's holding.

The Midani family were very wealthy, but Amer was gripped by a chronic gambling addiction, which came to a head in August 2000. It was then that Al Midani made the last of five visits to the Rio Casino in Las Vegas. He ended it owing $1.6 million, debt he was unable to pay. It says something for the scale of his gambling, which was on roulette, that on the first of those visits, on Boxing Day 1999, Al Midani had won $3.8 million.

On this occasion, Amer's family would not bail him out and he faced bankruptcy proceedings in the County Court at Stockport. He asked me to help out with the case, but his solicitors would not release the paperwork until they had been paid. I paid those arrears myself, but we were unable to save him from being found bankrupt and Amer did not repay me the money I had lent him. In April 2012, he would die from a heart attack in a casino in North Africa.

The facts were that we had found no alternative to funding Manchester United and on 30 October 1990 the board instructed Henry Ansbacher's corporate finance department to prepare the club for flotation.

The following month Ansbacher's managing director, Glenn Cooper, wrote to Martin saying the spring of 1991 might be a suitable date as the Stock Market might have recovered by then. November 1990 was a time of extreme turbulence that would see Margaret Thatcher's downfall as prime minister.

Cooper was a vastly experienced City man who had absolutely no interest in football. When he met us at Old Trafford, he could not understand why there was so much excitement when news came through that Manchester City had lost. Nevertheless, he and Martin Edwards formed an instant bond.

The entire board had assembled to meet Glenn and ask him whether he thought a flotation was possible. There in that old, small, windowless boardroom, now a suite, we sat: me, Knighton, Martin, Al Midani, Mike Edelson, Les Olive, Bobby Charlton and Nigel Burrows.

Martin went round the room asking us whether we should float. Al Midani and Burrows were very keen. I probably was not keen, but it seemed the only alternative. Martin had to raise money to pay off his considerable debts, and finding suitable individuals to buy him out had not proved very successful. Martin then asked, 'Can we float Manchester United?'

Cooper hesitated for a long time before replying: 'Just.' Privately he was not very confident and thought it all might be 'a ghastly mistake'.

His doubts were based on how the City had taken to Tottenham's flotation. In the eight years since they had joined the Stock Exchange, they had not been paying regular dividends and a merchandising operation had gone seriously wrong. In a review by the *Independent* of Irving Scholar's book *Behind Closed Doors*,[12] it was noted that Scholar had been forced to borrow £1.1 million from Robert Maxwell to pay Barcelona for the balance that was owed by Spurs on Gary Lineker's transfer to White Hart Lane. In June 1991 Tottenham would be bought by a consortium led by Alan Sugar and Terry Venables.

Martin shared Cooper's scepticism. He was the only member of the board who had experience of running a public company – his father's meat-processing business. He said he was 'the last person to be convinced we should float'.

He told the *Daily Telegraph*'s Mihir Bose:

There was strong support in that board to float and I warned: 'If you float, this will no longer be a private company and you won't be able to do everything you want. You will have to look after shareholders interest and pay dividends. And although it will give us what we want in building the Stretford End there will be restraints about us in the future.'

An 'action committee' was established to prepare Manchester United for flotation and the first meeting was held in my offices on 9 December. Our flotation structure would copy Tottenham's. The existing board would become the football board and above it would be a plc board. We announced the flotation at the AGM on 10 January 1991. We had already informed the FA's chief executive, Graham Kelly.

Football AGMs are not like those of other companies. Shareholders do not expect financial rewards from their shareholding but want success on the field of play. A small group of committed fans come and all they really want to do is ask questions of the manager, usually about transfer policies.

This was our first AGM since winning the FA Cup, which had eased a lot of the pressure that had been building on Alex Ferguson. Manchester United were fifth in the First Division and had progressed well in the Cup Winners' Cup. It meant Ferguson and Edwards did not face the usual barrage of questions. The interesting one was whether Martin would continue to combine the roles of chairman and chief executive, while the media focused on the story that he stood to bank £7.5 million from selling some of his controlling interest.

When Cooper met the board on 29 January, he expressed the view that the plc board should have five members – three of whom should be existing directors of Manchester United. Since the club had seven directors, this resulted in a serious jockeying for power. Michael Knighton, Nigel Burrows, Michael Edelson and Bobby Charlton were all keen to be on the plc board. Glenn Cooper became a one-man selection panel.

He did not think any of the directors suitable to be a non-executive chairman of a publicly quoted company. Martin recommended Sir Roland Smith, who had been a long-standing friend of his father and had been vice-chairman of Louis C. Edwards and Sons.

Not only did he have an impressive record in the City but Sir Roland was also a devoted supporter of Manchester United. We felt we could not have the plc headed by someone who knew nothing about football or supported some other club.

My legal background saw me appointed on to the plc board. Glenn Cooper also wanted Amer Al Midani because he had a substantial stake in the club. Knighton he ruled out almost immediately. Cooper recalled:

> The only thing I remember about Knighton at board meetings was he was always taking notes. Whenever I looked over my shoulder, I could see him writing. I believe he was writing a book. Edelson lobbied me hard, out of an inexperienced belief that he was important.
>
> Charlton was the most grumpy. He threatened to resign at one point if he did not go on the plc board. He realised later that he was much better off sitting where he was on the football club board rather on the plc board. But he didn't feel that at that time.

Nigel Burrows, who owned 4 per cent of the club, also did not make it onto the plc board, which was probably just as well. In March 1992, Burrows resigned from the football club board and left for the United States. He faced a number of financial issues and his stake in the club, which was held through a trust and pledged as security for a loan at the Bank of Scotland, was reportedly sold to the BBC Pension Fund for £1.27 million.

Glenn Cooper also made it clear that the plc board required two directors from outside the club. This was important to keep the City happy. One of the problems Tottenham encountered was that their plc board were all recruited from within White Hart Lane, which led to a blinkered financial approach.

As chairman, Sir Roland Smith would be one, the other would be the financial director. In April 1991 we appointed Robin Launders, who was group finance director for Reg Vardy. He had been involved in floating the car showroom company and had a degree in mechanical engineering from the University of Manchester. He ticked a lot of boxes.

Robin Launders was a clever man, but he was impatient with people he thought less clever than himself. The staff at Manchester United did not always appreciate him, but, as Martin says, he proved an effective accountant and sometimes the most effective man is not the one you would wish to have a drink with.

One of Launders's financial innovations was setting up what was called the Transfer Fee Reserve Account. It was set at £2 million and could be increased from profits, cup runs and receipts on player sales.

The papers called it 'Fergie's Kitty' which it never quite was, since it was set up more for accounting purposes than anything else. Alex Ferguson did not appear especially interested in the flotation. Cooper could not recall any occasion in which the United manager actually sat in on a meeting. The only time Ferguson appeared interested was when the financial benefits from flotation became apparent. It was decided that all heads of department and senior managers would receive 25,000 shares. The one exception was the financial director, who would receive 100,000.

When Ferguson discovered Launders was getting four times what he had been offered, he interpreted this as a slight against him. Martin Edwards persuaded Alex that he was paid much more than Robin and, unlike the financial director, had an opportunity to earn substantial bonuses if the team were successful.

To create the plc, we bought an 'off the shelf' company which had no assets but was quoted on the Stock Exchange. We would then change its name to Manchester United plc. The company we bought was called Voteasset Public Limited which had been formed on 20 December 1990. Its name was changed on 25 January. It then bought all the issued shares in the football club; a task it had completed by 10 May.

Under the roof of Old Trafford, we had two very different companies. A plc, subject to the rules of the Stock Exchange, and a football club, a subsidiary of the plc, which was subject to the rules of the FA.

The rules of the FA restricted football clubs in many ways. It controlled the maximum dividend a club could pay. It did not allow its directors to be paid. Should the football club be liquidated, any surplus that remained would be given to the FA's Benevolent Fund. A copy of a club's audited balance sheet and profit-and-loss account had to be sent to the FA at Lancaster Gate.

The football club transferred all its fixed assets, including the stadium, all its non-footballing activities and its intellectual property rights to the plc, who then leased Old Trafford back to the club. The players, the coaching and management staff remained on the books of the football club. The non-football activities included concerts by Rod Stewart and Status Quo in June.

We were very aware that the supporters needed to be kept informed and took out adverts in the matchday programme that spoke of 'A great team on and off the pitch'. We emphasised the point that 'For the team to be successful, the business has to be successful.'

In subsequent years it was said the FA was wrong to give such approval because it triggered a culture of greed. I disagree. Football clubs had to change. The creation of the football club plc was necessary if football was to raise money and make the sort of changes that had to be made in the wake of Hillsborough. Football could not remain mothballed.

Many, including Alex Ferguson, predicted that flotation would destroy Manchester United's ability to win trophies as its first duty would be to serve the interests of the shareholders. Underpinned by the superb array of footballers Alex brought through, the flotation transformed the club.

As we prepared to become a plc, Manchester United beat Barcelona to win the Cup Winners' Cup; our first European trophy since 1968.

Within two years of flotation, United were league champions for the first time in twenty-six years. The progress would reach its zenith in 1999, the year of the treble.

When Manchester United was floated, it was valued at £42 million. Six years later, in 1997, it had overtaken Real Madrid, Barcelona and Juventus to become the richest football club in the world. In 2003, United recorded a pre-tax profit of £39.3 million. The rest of the Premier League clubs made a combined loss of £153 million.

Flotation opened the boardroom door at Old Trafford. The offer document detailed precisely who was offering the shares to the public. There were 1,671,882 from Martin Edwards, 427,071 from Amer Midani and his trusts, 175,925 from me, 84,718 from Mike Edelson and his trusts, and 238,007 from Nigel Burrow's trusts. When we floated, everybody could work out how much money we had. But the plc got vastly more money to fund much-needed activity at Old Trafford. The chief beneficiary was the Stretford End.

The Stretford End was at the very heart of Manchester United's support; a vast terrace with some seating on the top tier, it could accommodate 20,500 fans behind one goal. Under the planned redevelopment, the Stretford End would become all-seater with 10,300 seats and 40 private boxes. The entire stadium roof would then be fully cantilevered, giving spectators an unimpaired view of the pitch. Facilities behind the Stretford End would provide approximately 9,500 square feet of permanent exhibition space together with suites with restaurant and bar areas for up to 1,600 people. The flotation would raise a net £6.7 million and would provide a substantial part of the funds for the redevelopment.

The problem was that Manchester United did not own all the land necessary to carry out the development. A strip of land behind the Stretford End belonged to Trafford Park Estates, chaired by Sir Neil Westbrook, who had been a good friend of Louis Edwards. Trafford Park Estates had been set up in 1896 to lease land to industries alongside the newly opened Manchester Ship Canal.

In initial discussions, it appeared that Trafford Park Estates would be prepared to transfer the strip of land in exchange for a long licence on one of the new eight-seater boxes to be built in the new development.

However, they soon realised the strength of their negotiating position. We only came to an agreement on 9 June, the night before the Stock Market flotation. At two in the morning, Martin Edwards and Glenn Cooper were driven to London, arriving at Glenn's offices in Mitre Square with the dawn. With a mixture of relief and some joy I rang them and said, 'We are good to go, but it has cost £350,000.'

The immediate steps leading up to the flotation had not been easy. Glenn Cooper had found it difficult to get a stockbroker to handle the issue: six of them turned him down, scared by what had happened to Tottenham; it took him seven weeks before he found Smith New Court. Initially institutions were dubious but, once they had been shown round Old Trafford, they became enthusiastic. The documents they had read had identified Manchester United only as 'Batsman'. Seeing the ground, they realised this was a batsman who could, given the chance, make copious runs.

Glenn valued Manchester United at £42 million, £22 million more than Michael Knighton had been prepared to pay two years earlier. He was ready to float in early May 1991 but decided to wait until after the European Cup Winners' Cup final against Barcelona.

Just before the team flew out to Rotterdam, the assistant manager, Archie Knox, resigned to become assistant manager to Walter Smith at Glasgow Rangers. This came as a shock to Alex Ferguson. Knox had been his assistant when Aberdeen had beaten Real Madrid to win the Cup Winners' Cup in 1983.

When they moved to Manchester three years later, the two men shared a house in Timperley, a small town in Cheshire. Knox's decision to exchange Old Trafford for Ibrox, where he would earn more money, created a short-term falling out between them. I advised the club Knox would not be entitled to a win bonus because he would not be part of the club at the time of the final. We did, however, invite him to Rotterdam as a guest of the club. He declined. In teeming rain, Barcelona, managed by Johan Cruyff, were beaten 2–1.

The fact we had won a European trophy gave a sheen to the flotation. However, the return of the Maxwells ensured the share price did not remain at £3.85 for very long. Robert's son, Kevin, the chairman of Oxford United, having indicated he was a long-term investor with 5 per cent of the club, suddenly decided to dump his shares. Within a week, the share price had slumped to £2.60. Manchester United, floated at £42 million, was suddenly worth £26 million.

By July 1991, the *Manchester Evening News* was describing the flotation as 'disastrous' under the headline 'United Go One Down'. The fact was that Manchester United would win this financial match and Robert Maxwell's empire was just five months away from collapse.

15

The Revolution

The formation of the Premier League in May 1992 was not English football's first attempt at a breakaway but it was the one that succeeded.

What became known as 'The Big Five' – Manchester United, Arsenal, Liverpool, Tottenham and Everton – first threatened to form a Super League in 1985. Then, the Heysel disaster, the Bradford fire – which killed 56 spectators and injured many more, and a ban on televised football – because the Football League could not agree a deal – had pushed the game into crisis. A breakaway was averted by the Football League offering Division One clubs 50 per cent of television and sponsorship revenue and giving them one-and-a-half votes in any election.

Three years later, when the BBC and ITV deal, worth £6.2 million a season, expired, the scenario of a breakaway was revived.

Psychologically, the leading clubs felt that 'tails wagged the dogs'. These were the most important teams but they were not in control; the voting structure militated against any changes and the management committee running the league was not representative of the interests of the leading clubs. So 1988 was a crucial year given the need to conclude a new exclusive television contract with ITV for four Football League seasons 1988/89 to 1991/92. Although I was a Manchester United director, the Football League, particularly their sales and marketing manager, Lee Walker, wanted my help, because of my experience in negotiating and drafting the new heads of agreement. Lee

Walker and I met with ITV's head of sport, John Bromley, and contracts manager, Jonathan Higton, at ITV's offices in Birmingham.

One important aspect which arose from my involvement with the negotiation and drafting of the heads of agreement was that there should be no suggestion of a conflict of interest in my attending any of the meetings and assisting Lee Walker in the negotiation of the revisions of the heads of agreement submitted by ITV. Accordingly, I recommended to Walker that he make it quite clear to the management committee the reasons why I was there, what my input and knowledge was, and the shortage of time in obtaining assistance from the Football League's own lawyers.

On 18 October 1988 an Extraordinary General Meeting of the Football League Ltd was held at the Dean Park Hotel in Watford where resolutions were passed removing the Everton chairman Philip Carter as chairman and director of the Football League together with Arsenal's vice-chairman David Dein as vice-chairman and director of the Football League. Bill Fox, chairman of Blackburn, was elected president of the Football League.

Carter and Dein had defended themselves by arguing they had substantially increased television revenues and that the emergence of a new channel, British Satellite Broadcasting (BSB), who were prepared to offer significant sums for exclusive rights, could only increase the funds.

In June 1990 the 'Big Five' were approached by Greg Dyke of ITV about the next Football League contract. A meeting of the Big Five was organised and, led by David Dein, conversations spread to a discussion about creating a new league and whether ITV would be interested in purchasing its TV rights, which it was. Those who took part in the meeting/dinner were Martin Edwards, Irving Scholar (Tottenham), David Dein (Arsenal), Philip Carter (Everton) and Noel White (Liverpool).

To move these radical changes forward it was agreed that the Football Association should be approached. This led to the FA producing a *Blueprint for the Future of Football*. They concluded that all other associations, leagues and clubs should be subordinate to the FA.

Historically, there had been a constant power struggle between the FA and the Football League. The effect of that lack of unity had, in the FA's view, undermined the government of the game to the disadvantage of football as a whole, including the Football League.

The Football League, in its publication *One Game, One Team, One Voice*, presented a case for an equal share of power within the FA, but that proposition was rejected by the FA Council.

The Blueprint for the Future of Football was published in June 1991. The summary of the main recommendations were as follows:

- That the FA should establish a Premier League within its own administration.
- That the League should be named 'The Football Association Premier League'.
- That the Football Association Premier League should start in the season 1992/93.
- That Regulation 10, which required clubs to give three years' notice to quit the Football League, should be disallowed.
- That the transitional period from 22 clubs to 18 clubs should take place between the start of the seasons 1992/93 and 1996/97.*

In an early briefing paper prepared by Alex Flynn of Saatchi & Saatchi examining the issues and the need for change, the establishment of a Premier League was expressed in the following terms:

---

* *The Blueprint for the Future of Football* (Football Association, 1991) was only an aspirational document. The size of the old First Division varied. Until 1987 it was 22 clubs. It had 21 in 1987–88 and then 20 between 1988 and 1991. For the final season before the Premier League was introduced it was 22. The Premier League began in 1992 but did not reduce its numbers to 20 until the start of the 1995/96 season.

- There should be massive investment in stadia;
- English clubs have to be geared to compete at least on equal terms in Europe which means retaining their best players and raising the overall level of technical ability;
- The national side needs to be given the fullest possible support.

The existing structure, of an English Football League comprising ninety-two professional clubs divided into four divisions, was not conducive to a positive response to those challenges. There was a tremendous gap between the clubs at the top of the Football League and those at the bottom, both in terms of aspirations and problems.

Indeed, the major clubs were rather dismissive of the management of the Football League and tended to regard it as an organisation of little consequence and concerned only with the lower divisions. The voting structure of one-and-a-half votes for each of the twenty First Division clubs and one vote for each of the Second, Third and Fourth Division clubs militated against any change, and the management committee running the League was not representative of the interests of the leading clubs.

The FA summoned a meeting of its Football Association Premier League rules, regulations and player registration working party, one of four working parties established under the Blueprint and of which I was a committee member, for a meeting on 24 April 1991. The starting point of the discussion document was the authority of the Football Association to run the Premier League. Also on the agenda was the abolition of Football League Regulation 10, requiring clubs to give three years' notice if they wanted to resign their membership of the Football League.

A meeting was held on 7 May with the main participants of the new League, Everton, Arsenal, Manchester United, Tottenham Hotspur and Liverpool. It was followed the next day with a meeting of the FA and all First Division clubs to receive information about the FA Premier League.

The FA had received advice from its solicitors that it should not proceed on the assumption that Regulation 10 could be ignored. A number of clubs had received advice that, at least between the clubs, the Football League Regulation 10 should be regarded as valid.

This would provide possible grounds for action for damages by the Football League to prevent clubs leaving in breach of the notice provisions. They might even obtain an injunction to prevent the resignations. If the FA were to encourage and induce clubs to break away from the Football League in breach of that notice requirement, then the FA could be liable for damages on the basis of 'inducement of breach of contract'.

Shortly afterwards, legal proceedings were instigated by the Football League against the FA.

Rick Parry, working for Ernst & Young Chartered Accountants, was a mainspring of the discussions and it was agreed he would act as the independent chairman. Following a meeting on 25 June, the First Division chairmen were invited by Rick Parry to a meeting on 17 July at the FA Council Chamber at Lancaster Gate. At that time, Rick had been seconded to Manchester's bid team for the 1992 Olympics.

It was at this meeting, which only lasted a few hours, that the First Division chairmen signed the historic 'Founder Members' Agreement' stating their belief that a separate Premier League needed to be established and declaring to the Football Association their support of the initiative taken by the FA in proposing the setting up of a Premier League in its *Blueprint for the Future of Football.*

The founder clubs were Arsenal, Aston Villa, Chelsea, Coventry City, Crystal Palace, Everton, Leeds United, Liverpool, Luton Town, Manchester City, Manchester United, Norwich City, Notts County, Nottingham Forest, Oldham Athletic, Queens Park Rangers, Sheffield United, Sheffield Wednesday, Southampton, Tottenham Hotspur, West Ham United and Wimbledon. Because of relegation, two clubs, Luton and Notts County, would, it seemed, never play in the league they founded.*

The signing of the Founder Members' Agreement was a momentous occasion, and I was amazed how quickly terms were agreed. The terms were written up in less than half a day; this is quite extraordinary given the fact that they included the financial terms which have remained constant. Included among these clauses was the sharing equally of principal sponsorship contracts and overseas television contracts, which would certainly have been drafted differently if its future impact had been realised.

For a long time, I seemed to have the only copy of the document and kept being called upon by the football authorities to supply copies. The Big Five did not have any greater influence on the drafting of the document than the other clubs. This demonstrates further the significance of the agreement.

The following day, Rick Parry wrote to the First Division chairmen reporting on a meeting with Second Division representatives on the afternoon of 17 July, explaining that the meeting was designed 'to achieve change in as painless a way as possible'.

Parry was asked to provide a simple statement of the First Division's position, which he did in the following terms:

> At a meeting of the First Division clubs on 17th July, it was agreed that:
>
> - the clubs will resign from the Football League in order to establish the FA Premier League;
> - the FA Premier League should ultimately comprise a single division of 20 clubs;

---

* Note from editor: That is, until Luton won promotion to the Premier League in 2023.

- ideally the FA Premier League should commence in 1992/93 with those clubs which would otherwise comprise the First Division of the Football League;
- in order to commence in 1992/93, it will be necessary to remove Regulation 10 by democratic means;
- the cooperation of the Second, Third and Fourth divisions will be sought so that change can be achieved in a constructive manner. It was recognised that it will be necessary to give assurances which include the following:
- there will be three promotion and relegation places while there are 22 clubs in the FA Premier League; the intention is that this shall drop to two places when the number of clubs reduces to 20;
- the FA Premier League clubs shall continue to play in the League Cup;
- the merits of maintaining the office at Lytham St Annes to administer the FA Premier League and the Football League are recognised and the practicalities of this must be investigated;
- all possible steps will be taken to ensure that existing commercial contracts are not jeopardised;
- even at this late stage, every possible step must be taken to persuade both the Football League and the Football Association to cease legal action, which will serve no useful purpose.

The litigation between the FA and the Football League came to court on 22 July 1991. The background to the case was that the Football League had entered into a contractual relationship with the FA by virtue of the fact that in accordance with the FA rules it applied annually for the FA's sanction to run the four divisions comprising the League.

In 1988 the League had adopted Regulation 10, requiring any club to give three full seasons' notice of its intention to terminate its membership of the League or to indemnify the League if it terminated membership earlier. Regulation 10 provided that any club which was in breach of the provisions of the regulation must on demand indemnify the League against all losses suffered or incurred by the League resulting directly or indirectly from such breach, including any loss of income or profits from sponsorship or broadcast contracts.

The FA had recently amended its own rules to say that any regulation that forced clubs to give a longer notice of termination than required by the FA was itself null and void.

Mr Justice Rose, the High Court judge hearing the case, dismissed the Football League's application for judicial review, saying the FA was not susceptible to judicial review at the instigation of the League with which it was contractually bound.

The FA was a domestic body whose powers existed in private law only. He also found that the League could not enforce its Regulation 10 against the clubs because to do so would be to force the clubs to accept a contract inconsistent with their contracts with the FA.

If the FA had thought that their victory in the High Court would lead to a smooth transition for the new Premier League, they were seriously mistaken. The League appealed.

A reconvened EGM of the Football League was called for 23 September. If the three-year rule was voted out, the Football League said it would not pursue its appeal. The offending rule was voted out with 51½ votes in favour of removal, 9 against and 1½ abstentions.

With the regulation gone, there had to be a series of much more detailed negotiations to set up the Premier League and to govern its working relationship with the FA and the Football League. A meeting of the First Division clubs was held on 10 October 1991 at the FA. The meeting confirmed that while they recognised they would come under the overall jurisdiction of the FA, the First Division clubs wished to have independence with regard to the day-to-day running of the Premier League.

They wished to form a limited company and to have their own legal 'personality' but recognised that there may be taxation implications and asked Rick Parry to obtain the appropriate professional advice as a matter of urgency. They reiterated their decision in the Founder Members' Agreement – one club, one vote, and a two-thirds majority before changing any rules. They confirmed that they did not wish to see a reduction in the Premier League from twenty-two clubs, unless and until such time as it was evident that the loss of income that would result from a reduction in fixtures was replaced from other sources.

Rick Parry was appointed chief executive until the start of season 1992/93; on the payroll of the FA but to be funded by the clubs. Permanent terms of reference were to be considered at a later date. It was also agreed that a non-executive chairman should be appointed.

Working parties to consider in detail the compilation of the 'Rule Book' and players contracts, registrations and transfers were set up and I was subsequently appointed to these. I was also asked to investigate and report back on certain commercial arrangements.

On 8 December, the clubs unanimously agreed to invite Sir John Quinton, the chairman of Barclays Bank, to take up the post of Premier League chairman. It was also agreed to set up and organise the League's principal office at the Football Association.

One of the issues we had to settle was payments from the FA and Premier League to the Football League for five seasons so that Football League clubs did not suffer financially because of the formation of the Premier League.

Considerable time was also taken up with negotiations with the PFA. It received 5 per cent of the Football League's television revenue, which amounted to approximately £700,000, although the League regulations said it could get 10 per cent. We in the Premier League did not want to pay 10 per cent. The negotiations were contentious and the PFA threatened industrial action by calling a ballot of its members. Finally, after much deliberation, on 27 March 1992 the Premier League agreed to offer the PFA 5 per cent of their domestic television revenue, with a minimum guarantee of £1 million per annum. The proposal was supported by nineteen clubs with three abstentions.

The duel between ITV and BSkyB for exclusive television rights was played out at the Royal Lancaster Hotel on 18 May. BSkyB won the vote by 14 to 6. ITV's supporters included Arsenal, Manchester United, Liverpool, Everton and Aston Villa. It was the smaller clubs who led the charge for Sky.

When I got to the Royal Lancaster Hotel at the start of the meeting you could cut the atmosphere with a knife. There was intense lobbying. Notes were passed round; telephone calls were made, and people were going in and out of the rooms all to influence the voting. For my part I felt that this was going to be a long-drawn-out meeting so I left the Royal Lancaster with Martin Edwards and went off to another meeting thinking that I would have ample time to get back for the crucial vote.

I was mistaken. Tottenham had supported ITV in 1988 but now Alan Sugar, who had taken over the club from Irving Scholar, decided to back Rupert Murdoch's company. Had Irving Scholar still been running Spurs, he would have backed ITV. There was an attempt to get Sugar disqualified as an interested party since his company, Amstrad, supplied BSkyB satellite dishes, but this failed. Spurs changing sides was decisive. Had they stayed with ITV, a 13–7 vote would have denied BSkyB the necessary two-thirds majority.

Rick Parry had led the negotiations for the Premier League and reported on the offers, which kept changing, to the clubs. After the vote and the acceptance of the £304 million offer from BSkyB, Rick Parry asked all the disappointed parties to accept the result and allow him and the clubs to concentrate on creating a successful League. That did not happen.

ITV went to the High Court to try to obtain an injunction to frustrate the deal, claiming the Premier League had acted unfairly by disclosing the terms of ITV's ultimate bid to BSkyB and not giving ITV a further chance to top BSkyB's winning figure. ITV claimed that the entire procedure was irregular and arbitrary, and each bid should have been presented and analysed in the same manner. ITV's application was unsuccessful.

On 13 August the League signed an agreement for five seasons with BSkyB for the televising of Premier League football matches within the United Kingdom and the Republic of Ireland. The following month, the Premier League signed an agreement with the BBC for five seasons of recorded highlights to be broadcast in the UK and Ireland.

The distribution of domestic television income for seasons 1992/93 worked out as follows (some figures have been rounded):

	£	£
BSkyB Rights Fee	35,500,000	
BBC Rights Fee	4,500,000	40,000,000
Less Payment to PFA		2,500,000
Available for distribution		37,500,000
Equal Shares		
25 payments of £750,000		18,750,000
Merit Payments		
£37,055 per share (first place represents 22 shares)		9,375,000
Facility Fees		
BSkyB – 60 matches; 120 payments of £69,335 per club	£8,320,200	
BBC – 62 Saturday matches and six midweek matches; 136 payments of £7,755 per club	£1,054,800	

The club finishing in first place in 1993 would receive a merit payment of £815,210 and the bottom club £37,055.

The Founder Members' Agreement is without doubt the most important document in the history of the Premier League and the rock on which the league stands. Over the years problems in the Premier League have been solved by reference to the Founders' Agreement. Here is my copy (signatures have been blurred).

THE PREMIER LEAGUE

THE FOUNDER MEMBERS AGREEMENT made on 17th July 1991 by the Clubs whose names are listed at the end of this Agreement ("the Clubs")

1. The Clubs believe that a separate Premier League needs to be established and have declared to The Football Association their support of the initiative taken by The Football Association in proposing the setting up of a Premier League in its Blueprint for the Future of Football

2. The Clubs declare that basic principles for the establishment of a Premier League are:-

   * The Premier League must have constitutional independence with its own rule book

   * The Premier League must have commercial independence

   * There will be entry criteria after an agreed time period

   * There will be promotion to, and relegation from, the Premier League

   * Member clubs will meet on a regular basis and all business will be conducted on a "one-club, one-vote" basis. All decisions will require a majority of not less than two-thirds of the votes cast

   * There will be no Management Committee; policy agreed by the clubs will be implemented by a competent executive team

   * Revenue from the domestic television contract will be shared on the following basis:

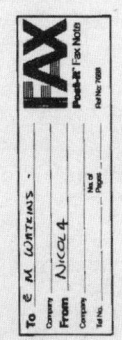

- 50% to be divided equally amongst the clubs

- 25% to be shared on merit; this will be related to positions in the league table at the end of the Season

- 25% to be allocated as facility fees which will be divided equally between the home club and the visiting club
  It is intended that each club will appear on at least one live televised match each Season

- Revenues from principal sponsorship contracts and overseas television contracts will be shared equally amongst the clubs"

3. The Clubs will continue to work together and with The Football Association and (as far as practicable) with The Football League and the Professional Footballers Association to do what is necessary to establish The Premier League so as to commence at the expiration of the Notices referred to below or sooner should this become possible

4. The Clubs will be the Founder Members of the Premier League on its commencement irrespective of their then position in The Football League unless the commencement date is brought forward to the beginning of the 1992/93 or 1993/94 Seasons when the Founder Members will consist of those Clubs which would then be the members of the First Division (i.e., less those relegated at the end of the previous Season but with those promoted) on the assumption that there is "free" promotion and relegation on the existing basis. It is recognised that any of the Clubs who have signed this Agreement and who will not be eligible in either of those two Seasons to be a Founder Member shall be entitled to fair compensation for having

supported thus far the establishment of the Premier League. The precise basis for calculating the compensation is one of the matters to be determined by the Clubs in their continuing discussions and work to establish The Premier League, but the intention is to ensure that any such club should receive a share of the income from sponsorship and sale of television rights equal to that received by those who are members of the Premier League

5. The Clubs will give on or before 15th August 1991 notice to The Football League Limited in accordance with Regulation 10 of the Football League Regulations to terminate their membership of The Football League after expiration of 3 full Seasons from the date of the notice and will authorise Mr Rick Parry to deliver to The Football League the Notices which he is holding at present

6. No Club will withdraw its notice to terminate membership without the concurrence of all the other Clubs

7. This Agreement has been signed by a duly authorised representative of each of the Clubs

ARSENAL F.C.
ASTON VILLA F.C.
CHELSEA F.C.
COVENTRY F.C.
CRYSTAL PALACE F.C.
EVERTON F.C.
LEEDS UNITED F.C.
LIVERPOOL F.C.
LUTON TOWN F.C.
MANCHESTER CITY F.C.
MANCHESTER UNITED F.C.
NORWICH CITY F.C.
NOTTS COUNTY F.C.
NOTTINGHAM FOREST F.C.
OLDHAM F.C.
QUEEN'S PARK RANGERS F.C.
SHEFFIELD UNITED F.C
SHEFFIELD WEDNESDAY F.C.
SOUTHAMPTON F.C.
TOTTENHAM HOTSPUR F.C.
WEST HAM F.C.
WIMBLEDON F.C.

16

The Deadliest Transfer

In my time at Manchester United, I was involved with many transfers, but there was only one which made me fear for my life.

It all started innocently enough with Alex Ferguson's search for a pacey player on the wide right, a player he considered essential if United were to finally win the league. The man he chose was Andrei Kanchelskis, a 22-year-old at Shakhtar Donetsk, one of the leading clubs in what was shortly to become the newly independent Ukraine.

Alex had been alerted to the player, who had pace and athleticism to spare, by Rune Hauge, who was then a youth development coach with FC Nuremberg and who was to become notorious for his role in the bung payments scandal that brought down George Graham at Arsenal.

Alex was impressed with the video Hauge sent and he and Martin Edwards – who had never heard of Kanchelskis – travelled to Ibrox in February 1991 to watch him play in one of the Soviet Union's last internationals – a 1–0 win over Scotland. The fee was £650,000, which Ferguson called 'a justifiable risk'.

Andrei Kanchelskis first came into my life a month later, when I attended a meeting at Old Trafford. Gathered in the boardroom were Martin Edwards, Alex and three gentlemen I had never met before. They turned out to be agents and all of them said they were working with the Kanchelskis deal. There was Hauge, a German agent, Wolfgang Vöge, who until recently had played centre-forward for Zurich, and Roland Klein, an agent based in Switzerland, who represented Shakhtar's interests.

Kanchelskis had agreed a three-year deal, with United having the option to renew the contract for a further two years. As Kanchelskis was from the Soviet Union – which unknown to us would collapse nine months later – and was therefore outside the European Union's free movement of labour, we needed a work permit. The FA operated a points system based on the standing of the player's national team and how many games he had played for them. Given that Kanchelskis was a regular starter for the Soviet Union, I had no worries about being able to obtain a permit.

The small print of the contract showed that, subject to playing the required number of games, Shakhtar would receive much more than £650,000. The payment terms were as follows:

- £650,000 on transfer
- £150,000 if Kanchelskis makes 40 appearances in first-team matches during the three-year period of the contract
- £250,000 if the player makes 80 appearances
- £150,000 if he signed a new contract.

This meant the full payment could amount to £1.2 million. There was also a sell-on clause under which Shakhtar would get a percentage of the profit we made when we sold Kanchelskis. It meant the total money they could get for the sale would be as much as £3 million. By then such clauses had become common, although I could not have anticipated the problems this one would create.

Just after we had concluded the agreement, one of Kanchelskis's team leaned over the table and said: 'Now what about the buses?' My immediate reaction was 'double or single deckers?' and that it was some sort of joke. However, it transpired that they thought as part of the deal United would provide two buses for Shakhtar Donetsk.

THE DEADLIEST TRANSFER

* * *

Andrei Kanchelskis made his Manchester United debut in May 1991 at Crystal Palace. Since it was a few days before the Cup Winners' Cup final against Barcelona, Alex Ferguson fielded a weakened team, and it showed. Crystal Palace, who finished third in the league, won 3–0.

Kanchelskis improved season by season. In his first full campaign, which was lost at the death to Leeds, he was substituted or came off the bench fifteen times. He was a peripheral figure when we finally won the league in 1993. Alex complained about the accuracy of Andrei's crossing and his lack of understanding of the English game. Kanchelskis came of age in the 1993/94 season, in which Manchester United won the Double for the first time in their history. He was even better the following year, scoring a hat-trick in the Manchester derby – the first United player to do so since 1960. Despite missing six weeks of the season with a hernia injury, Kanchelskis finished the season as Manchester United's leading scorer. Alex exercised the club's option to extend Kanchelskis's contract to June 1999.

The new contract not only increased his salary, it meant Andrei, as well as Shakhtar Donetsk, would profit from a sell-on clause. Kanchelskis, who had already been angered by United's failure to properly diagnose a hernia injury, now had a financial motive to move.

Kanchelskis had already aroused my suspicions. On 22 August 1994 I was travelling back on the team bus from a Monday night match at Nottingham Forest. Andrei had scored the equaliser in a 1–1 draw. The team bus always dropped people off at Old Trafford.

My car, however, was at the Four Seasons Hotel in Hale and Alex Ferguson had agreed to drop me off there as it was on his way home. I was sitting in his car waiting for him to drive off when I saw Kanchelskis's agent, Grigory Essaoulenko, approach the car with Andrei and speak to Alex. The conversation was a short one.

What had happened, as I was told the next morning, was Essaoulenko had told Alex he had a gift for him. When Alex had responded saying he would collect it in the morning, the Russian had replied he was leaving very early and would phone Alex shortly.

Almost as soon as Alex had dropped me off at the Four Seasons, Essaoulenko had rung his mobile and insisted that he come to the Excelsior Hotel at the airport that night and collect his gift. It was only a minor detour from his home in Wilmslow and when he arrived at the Excelsior, he found Essaoulenko at the entrance with a nicely wrapped parcel. 'This is a gift for you and your wife, I hope you like it.' It was only when he got home that Alex realised this was like no gift he had ever received before. He had thought it might be a samovar. Instead, it was a box with £40,000 in cash.

The next morning the club secretary Ken Merrett rang me. He said Alex Ferguson had brought a parcel containing £40,000 in cash and had emptied it on his desk. I could not work out why Essaoulenko should give this money to the manager and in such a furtive fashion. My concern was to make sure that Manchester United not only acted properly but was seen to do so. I told Merrett that the money should be secured in the club safe, all relevant personnel should be informed, including the auditors and Alex's solicitors. Although I was aware of it, I also made it clear that my firm, as the club's solicitors, should be formally told of what had happened. The money should be left in safe custody pending its return to Grigory Essaoulenko.

Andrei Kanchelskis was a man who could be difficult to manage. He was one of a number of Russian footballers who refused to play in the 1994 World Cup because they had no confidence in the manager, Pavel Sadyrin.

He had also had his spats with Alex which dated back to December 1992, when Alex told him he would have to train with the reserves. When he refused, Alex thundered that unless Kanchelskis kept fit, he would 'go to rot on the subs' bench and would not be ready if ever needed'. This seemed to do the trick. As Kanchelskis reflected in his autobiography: 'if the boss wanted to shake me up, he had done just that. It inspired me to train and work overtime to keep at the peak of my fitness.'[13] Nevertheless, he expressed a desire to move in April 1993 and repeated it a year later, which climaxed with the Old Trafford crowd chanting his name and pleading with him to stay. For the fans, the fact that he scored a hat-trick in a 5–0 thrashing of Manchester City on 10 November 1994 made him a hero to be cherished.

Relations, however, between player and manager began to sour. Kanchelskis had been left furious by Manchester United's failure to diagnose his hernia during the 1994/95 season; when it was diagnosed, Alex thought it less serious than it actually was. In June 1995 Grigory Essaoulenko wrote to Martin Edwards saying that Kanchelskis's relations with Ferguson had broken down and that he did not want to play another season for Manchester United – and that even if he did, he would not be an effective performer. He requested a meeting to discuss a transfer.

On 10 July Essaoulenko came to Old Trafford to confirm that Andrei could not work with Alex and wanted to move. During their conversation, Alex tried to return the £40,000. Essaoulenko refused, saying: 'Please, Alex, it is for you. It is a thank-you for all you have done for me.' Alex called Martin, who persuaded Essaoulenko to accept the money back, saying: 'Look, Grigory, Alex cannot accept this gift. It would reflect badly on his reputation.'

This was followed by a meeting between me, Esssoulenko, Martin, Alex and George Scanlan, a professor of modern languages at Liverpool University, who interpreted for Andrei and Eric Cantona. Grigory again made it clear that Andrei wanted to leave. He had no quarrels with Manchester United, but he could not play with Alex as manager. All the old recriminations came out again.

We made it quite clear that we wanted Andrei to stay and this was reiterated in a subsequent telephone conversation between Martin and

George Scanlan. We could not agree to Andrei going unless we could obtain a replacement at the same time and also secure a proper fee.

The only available replacement was Darren Anderton, but Tottenham Hotspur would not release him even though they were interested in Andrei. Interest had also been expressed by Everton and Middlesbrough. A move to the former would allow Andrei to continue living in Wilmslow. Boro were managed by Bryan Robson, who had got on well with Andrei at United – both their fathers had been lorry drivers.

We also made it clear that if we were to allow Andrei to go, then the sell-on fee payable to him and also to Shakhtar Donetsk would have to be waived.

This did not go down well. Grigory demanded that Andrei be transferred and at one stage he screamed at Martin: 'If you do not transfer him now, you will not be around much longer.'

After Grigory had departed, Martin turned to me: 'What are we going to do, Maurice?'

I didn't hesitate. 'Sell him!'

Two days later I continued these discussions with George Scanlan and Grigory. I also checked with the Tottenham chairman, Alan Sugar, on Darren Anderton's position but he was not available for transfer. I showed Grigory details of the sell-on clause in favour of Shakhtar. He said he would be in touch with them about this. Unknown to us, Essaoulenko was also in constant touch with Kanchelskis, urging him to agree to a transfer as quickly as possible.

On 13 July, United received a fax signed by Yuri Kolotsei, who described himself as the vice-president of Shakhtar Donetsk, stating that the club did not demand any payment from United under clause 4 of the transfer agreement of 24 March 1991.

Having received this letter, United permitted both Middlesbrough and Everton to speak to Kanchelskis. Eventually Everton came out as Andrei's preferred club and they were prepared to meet United's valuation, which meant paying £5 million. On 21 July Andrei agreed personal terms and signed a contract with Everton. At his press conference at Goodison Park he announced: 'My heart is with Manchester United, but I can't stay for one reason and that is the manager. Our personal problems are just too big.'

Six days later, United received a fax from Shakhtar Donetsk, this time signed by its president, Alexander Bragin. A businessman with close connections to the Ukrainian underworld, Bragin had taken over Shakhtar amid the chaos following the collapse of the Soviet Union. He was a keen pigeon fancier and the previous year had survived an assassination attempt when gunmen opened fire as he visited his coop.

Bragin reminded Manchester United of the terms of the March 1991 agreement and in particular clause 4, adding:

> We were informed that the negotiations on making changes to the mentioned conditions of the chapter 4 of the contract had been taking place between the board of the Manchester United Football Club and unknown for us persons.
>
> In connection with these, we would like to inform you that the board of the football club 'Shakhtar' has not discussed and submitted any changes and/or additions to the contract from March 24th 1991 and has not authorised any person on carrying out of such actions.
>
> Taking into account all above mentioned we confirm the validity and immutability of the text of the signed by us contract from March 24th 1991 . . .

Martin immediately notified the Everton chairman, Peter Johnson, that there might be serious problems with the deal, which we maintained was still at a 'subject to contract' stage –lawyer's jargon for saying it is not final. Martin also sent a fax to Bragin asking for an explanation of the volte face from Kolotsei's letter.

There was considerable publicity around the transfer, which led to me, as the club's spokesman – in 1995 Manchester United still did not yet run to a press office – making regular media statements. Everton were understandably anxious and on 6 August we held a meeting together with Rick Parry, the chief executive of the Premier League, at the Daresbury Park Hotel in Warrington. The hotel took as its theme *Alice in Wonderland*.

By this time, we had decided to take advice from Patrick Talbot QC on the two main issues. First, whether Shakhtar's first fax waiving their share of the sell-on clause was binding; and second, whether there was already a binding contract between Manchester United and Everton. On the first question, as we had originally suspected, Talbot said clause 4 was still binding on United because the first fax was effectively a promise without consideration – it was merely a one-sided offer.

As to the second question, Talbot's view was that there was a very reasonable argument that there was no agreement (as yet) for the transfer of Andrei's registration to Everton.

Everton had also been busy. They had requested that the Premier League establish an arbitration procedure to sort out the issue. The Premier League submitted an agreement for the arbitration to proceed, but both clubs had to consent. Given what Talbot had said, I advised United not to take part in the arbitration.

There was no question we faced a crisis. We had a player who wanted to leave and in his mind had already moved to Everton. There was also the urgent need to make sure Kanchelskis was registered with UEFA in time to take part in European competitions for Everton, who in May had beaten Manchester United in the FA Cup final to qualify for the Cup Winners' Cup.

It seemed to me and Martin that there needed to be a face-to-face meeting with Shakhtar. So on 10 August, after a telephone conversation, I sent a fax to the club requesting an immediate meeting.

The next day Bragin faxed to say that they would be ready to meet with me in Kyiv at the weekend. He also told me that a Mr Yuri Romanosov from the law firm B.I.M. would be acting for the club and that I would be receiving a letter of invitation from B.I.M. for the purposes of a visa application.

Given how Grigory Essaoulenko had threatened Martin, there was a question of how safe I might be in Kyiv. After a chat with Roland Smith, it was decided that I should be accompanied by United's head of security, Ned Kelly, who was ex-SAS.

We flew out on Sunday, 13 August. We had arrived at Kyiv's Boryspil Airport and were walking towards passport control when two young women, who spoke good English, approached us and said that for ten dollars each we could get our passports stamped without having to queue. The rouble had been swept away with the Soviet Union. The Ukrainian government issued a currency called the 'kupon' which was as worthless as it sounded. The only currency that counted was American.

Waiting for us was Yuri Romanosov. It had been decided that, though this was a Sunday, we would go straight from the airport to meet Shakhtar and were taken to the B.I.M. offices located at the Hotel Ukraine on Shevchenko Avenue – named after the Ukrainian poet, not the footballer.

It was a grey, old building which Ned thought looked like a hospital. When he told Yuri that it must once have been a KGB building, he agreed with a smile.

We were taken to a first-floor office which had a large oak table. Soon a blond man with slicked-back hair entered and he was introduced as Boris Mirdan, a club official. He did not speak English and Yuri translated. Intriguingly, also present was another man who was not named but identified as a vice-president of the legal firm.

I was told that Yuri Kolotsei was not a vice-president of Shakhtar and had no authority to sign the letter of 13 July. During the conversation, to my astonishment, it was even suggested that he may not even have been an employee.

If this was a shock, worse was to follow. Romanosov then alleged that Shakhtar had not received the second and third tranches of the monies due to it under the transfer agreement. But then, with a smile, he added that, if we agreed to pay the 30 per cent sell-on in accordance with clause 4, then no fuss would be made. He was not smiling when he said that if the money was not paid the matter would be reported to FIFA, who ultimately handle all international transfers.

I said that all payments had been made in accordance with the Shakhtar account instructions and, if Shakhtar's records were different, then that was a matter for them. I decided that this was the time to be bold and added that, in light of their letter of 13 July, one had to have serious concerns regarding anything Shakhtar said.

This did not go down well with Mirdan, who started banging the table and also shouting very loudly. When Ned told him to stop, he picked up a phone and shouted at whoever was at the other end of the line. Yuri did not translate what he said. He did, however, invite us to go to a football match, but we decided it was best not to.

What I was trying and failing to do was negotiate what we lawyers call a 'without prejudice' settlement of Shakhtar's claim. That meant that should the matter subsequently come to court, any settlement discussed would not be revealed to the judge nor be binding on the parties involved.

Ned and I were waiting on the pavement outside the former KGB building for our taxi when we were surrounded by armed police. Just for a moment even Ned looked uncomfortable. The police, however, were not there for us. They were there to protect the man described as the B.I.M. vice-president. He got into a large Mercedes with three policemen. There were police cars at the front and back of the Mercedes and this motorcade set off down Shevchenko Avenue. It was only later that I found out who the mystery lawyer was. He was the billionaire owner of another Russian football club who had made his fortune through post-Soviet capitalism, and counted among his business interests a firm of lawyers.

Ned and I then went to our hotel – the Kievskaya, another Soviet-style building. Ned, armed with the appropriate vouchers, handled all the issues relating to checking in. The hotel corridors did seem to be populated by what looked very much like security guards. There also appeared to be a certain amount of female activity. I managed to get some restless sleep before our return to Manchester.

By now press interest had reached a frenzy. I was handling calls from all the TV channels as well as the print media. There was also the position of Manchester United plc to consider and whether or not any announcements should be made to the Stock Exchange and in what form. The PFA also got involved, with Gordon Taylor, writing to the Premier League, stating that Andrei considered himself to be an Everton player and 'does not wish to return to Manchester United who have asked him to return and report to training'.

Everton, having failed to get the Premier League to arbitrate, turned to the FA and began pressing for an FA tribunal to determine the outstanding issues. Discussions were also ongoing between the clubs to agree a transfer linked to Kanchelskis turning down any sell-on fee he was entitled to.

However, all these proposals were subject to a revised deal being negotiated with Shakhtar in respect of the potential sum of £1.14 million due to them under the sell-on clause. Just then, a totally unexpected opportunity arose to try and resolve the issue – in Belfast.

On 18 August Manchester United received a letter from Derek Brooks, the secretary of Linfield Football and Athletic club in Belfast. Derek said Linfield were due to play Shakhtar Donetsk in the Cup Winners' Cup and had a suggestion: 'Your club might send a delegation to Belfast next Wednesday for discussions with officials of

Shakhtar.' To further help matters, a Ukrainian interpreter, Igor Koltun, who lived in London and had worked for Linfield when they visited Donetsk, would also be there. 'We would be willing to make Igor available to your delegation,' Brooks added.

I flew out to Northern Ireland on 23 August, accompanied by Rick Parry. We stayed in the Europa, which because of The Troubles was the most bombed hotel in Europe (amazingly, no one lost their life in the IRA's bombings of the Europa Hotel and only a handful of people sustained minor injuries). As I checked in, I thought how fitting that this was the place where we would try and resolve this football dispute.

There was yet another new face from Shakhtar for me to get to know: Ravil Safiullin, first vice-president of the club, who was later to become Ukraine's sports minister. After considerable toing and froing, it was agreed that Rick and I would meet him the following day. The indications were that Shakhtar were in no mood to compromise.

However, as always on these European occasions, the evening before the match saw the host club have a dinner for the visitors, and following the meal Rick and I met Safiullin. This was again what we lawyers call a 'without prejudice' meeting, which could not be referred to in court. With Igor Koltun interpreting, I explored what sort of deal might be struck. We could not agree, but I felt a bit more optimistic as we did discuss a reduced payment. Safiullin said he would have to speak to Alexander Bragin about it and come back to us.

Strangely, given we had been told he was not even an employee of the club, Yuri Kolotsei – who had supposedly sent the fax on 13 July – was also at the dinner. I was not given the chance to speak to him.

Despite my relative optimism following our meeting, by the next morning it was clear their position had changed. They were now back to the demand they had made in Kyiv that they had not received the second and third tranche of the transfer money. They were also now looking for £1.5 million as opposed to £1.14 million as part of their profit on the sell-on clause.

The Belfast visit resulted in a whole lot of letters and faxes flying between Manchester and Donetsk, with both sides sticking to their guns. The only thing that moved was that Shakhtar backed down from their Belfast demand of £1.5 million and went back to their original claim of £1.14 million.

We were also under pressure to resolve matters with Everton to enable Andrei Kanchelskis to move and begin playing football for his new club. Eventually, a deed of covenant was executed between the clubs whereby Everton agreed to United trying to settle Shakhtar's claim at a figure of £760,000. They also effectively agreed to indemnify United up to a maximum sum of £550,000 in respect of monies paid by United to Shakhtar arising from their claim.

Andrei Kanchelskis did not make his Everton debut until 26 August – the third game of their league season. He was not registered with UEFA in time to play in their opening Cup Winners' Cup fixture with KR Reykjavik, but he was able to be involved in the second round, against Feyenoord. Soon afterwards, however, matters in Donetsk took a sinister and bloody turn.

On Sunday, 15 October 1995, Shakhtar were due to play the Crimean team Tavria Simferopol. Alexander Bragin and his bodyguards were walking into the box reserved for guests when a remote-control bomb was exploded, killing Bragin and his guards. The match was naturally abandoned. *The Times* report quoted Yuri Kolotsei, the club's vice-president, denying the assassination was linked to the Kanchelskis transfer.

The more lurid sections of the tabloid press took a different view. The *Sunday Sport*'s headline ran: 'Man Utd Boss Has One Month To Live'. The article suggested that: 'Old Trafford chiefs would be the target for hitmen chasing a £½ million debt owed by them to the Ukrainians.'

The *Sunday Sport* claimed that their offices had received a call 'from a man purporting to have close links with the Ukrainian mafia'. The heavily accented caller warned that a hit team may move in on

Manchester United chiefs within a month, and chillingly he added: 'someone is going to pay.'

Not surprisingly the publicity engendered by Bragin's assassination led to United receiving offers of help from specialist agencies familiar with the workings of the former Soviet Union. It was eventually agreed that we would employ one such firm, General Commercial Services.

On 8 November I wrote to Safiullin expressing United's sincere condolences to Shakhtar Donetsk and to Bragin's family. I also suggested another meeting. We agreed on 23 January in Munich.

I flew out to Germany with Ned Kelly and Emma Griffiths, an interpreter. We did finally manage a decent hotel: the magnificent Bayerischer Hof. Safiullin was staying in the rather more soulless Novotel and we met there for two days of talks. Safiullin's opening gambit at our first meeting on Tuesday suggested things had not really moved and it would be difficult to do a deal. He was claiming Shakhtar had not received the second and third transfer instalments and asked for evidence of the payments already made.

I got Old Trafford to fax me the evidence, and armed with it I went to the meeting the next day. Now Safiullin acknowledged that the documents showed we had paid Shakhtar, that this would no longer be an issue and promised to take up himself the search for where the money had ultimately gone.

Nevertheless, we still had an impasse. Safiullin maintained that the sum of £1.14 million was still due. We insisted, as we had done all along, that the agreement had been changed by Kolotsei's letter.

Safiullin now upped the ante by saying the matter had been referred by Shakhtar to FIFA and UEFA, and he showed me letters written in November 1995 by both Associations noting the position and asking for further details. However, Safiullin said he was loath to pursue the matter through FIFA and UEFA or indeed through the courts and hoped a compromise could be reached between the parties. It was agreed we would both go back and reflect on the discussions.

A few days after my return to Manchester I received a fax from Safiullin which made me think this problem would never be resolved. Shakhtar insisted we pay them £1.14 million; but even worse, having in Munich conceded that the transfer moneys had been paid, they now claimed that payments had not been received.

The next meeting in this seemingly never-ending saga was held in London at the Royal Lancaster Hotel on 16 April 1996, and this was sufficiently promising for us to prepare a settlement agreement. However, we first had to obtain Everton's agreement to the figures negotiated and confirmation of their contribution to Shakhtar's sell-on clause. The action then moved to Manchester the next day when the formal agreement was signed by Martin Edwards for United and Ravil Safiullin for Shakhtar. Agreement was also received from Everton as to their contribution. Completion was, however, delayed until the next day in London, again at the Royal Lancaster Hotel, when formal confirmation was received from Shakhtar that Safiullin had the necessary authority to conclude terms and sign the agreement.

Under the terms of the agreement Shakhtar acknowledged that they had in fact received the earlier, disputed payments, and settled for a significantly reduced amount of the outstanding claim of £1.14 million.

Even then, the Kanchelskis saga was not yet done. In August 1999, Alex Ferguson published his autobiography, *Managing My Life*, in which he wrote about the £40,000 that Grigory Essaoulenko had offered him.

The book was serialised in *The Sun* and, as soon as the paper came out, there was a media frenzy, with the subtext that Manchester United had been caught up in a 'bung scandal'.

The Football Association had, in the wake of the bung scandals that had drawn in Terry Venables, Brian Clough and George Graham, appointed a compliance officer, Graham Bean. Two days after *The Sun* ran its story, he rang United to say he would be carrying out an investigation and requested permission to meet the club's representatives.

The United secretary, Ken Ramsden, passed on the request to me. I checked what the role of the compliance officer was and could find nothing in his terms of reference that would cover matters such as the Essaoulenko gift, but I agreed to meet him at my office with Ken.

I went through the story and told Bean how the £40,000 had been handed back.

Bean tried to draw an analogy between the payment and a bribe to influence the result of a football match. We quickly pointed out that this was an inappropriate analogy which did not recognise the circumstances of the event.

Some few weeks later we were asked by the FA if Bean could address a few questions to Alex Ferguson. Bean came up to Manchester where Alex and I met him. Alex dealt very well with the questions Bean asked. Bean said that he was going to have a word with Andrei Kanchelskis but we felt that this would be unlikely to produce anything further.

Sometime later we heard from the FA that no action was going to be taken and the FA considered the matter closed. It was suggested that if something similar happened again it should be reported to the FA. There were no more examples of samovars which turned out to be boxes stuffed with notes. At last, the Kanchelskis affair had finally been brought to a close.

By then Andrei had long left Everton and, following an £8 million move to Fiorentina, was playing for Glasgow Rangers in the stadium where Alex and Martin had first watched him all those years ago.

17

Of Sardines, Seagulls and Trawlers

Despite its rather homely layout, with a Sainsbury's superstore at one side, Selhurst Park was a ground I liked. On Wednesday, 25 January 1995, I travelled to Crystal Palace with considerable expectation.

Blackburn led the Premier League, but on the previous Sunday a late winner from Eric Cantona had cut the gap to two points. Blackburn had a game in hand but Manchester United had lost one league game in three months. We expected to overtake Kenny Dalglish's side.

I arrived at the Palace directors' box to find Paolo Taveggia, a former Italian Foreign Office official, who was then general manager of Inter Milan. A few days earlier he had rung Martin inquiring about Cantona, but his approach had been rebuffed. However, if Inter had offered more money we might have done a deal, who knows? As it happened, they came back later to buy Paul Ince. We had a nice chat, but he did not give any secrets away, nor did I expect him to.

The Crystal Palace chairman, Ron Noades, had unsuccessfully campaigned for a Premier League second division when the Premier League was formed. He stood for what was seen as the second-tier clubs of the Premier League who, unlike United, were always looking down the league table fearing relegation.

This was a greater worry that season as four teams were going down. Palace, who had been promoted in May, were only out of the relegation zone on goal difference, and Ron had even more reason to feel aggrieved that his Premier League second division idea had not been accepted. Crystal Palace would finish the season fourth bottom and be relegated with forty-five points.

The first half went much as expected: a battle between United's skill and Palace's physical attempts to stop Andy Cole, who had just made his debut for United following a club-record £7 million move from Newcastle, and Eric Cantona. Having resisted the drinks on offer in favour of a cup of tea and sandwich, I settled back for the second half in the section of the directors' box reserved for visitors hoping Cantona and Cole would get us the winner. Instead, I was about to experience possibly the most significant moment in my legal life.

It came in the 49th minute. A Palace attack was stopped, and the ball was kicked upfield from the United half. As it passed over the head of Cantona and Richard Shaw, they both gave chase. Shaw, the Crystal Palace full-back, had spent much of the first half pulling Cantona's jersey which, like all forwards, made Cantona mad.

Shaw's defensive partner, Chris Coleman, had earlier made a horrendous tackle on Cole, which had gone unpunished by referee Alan Wilkie. On this occasion Cantona, clearly riled by what had gone before, kicked the back of Shaw's leg. Wilkie immediately stopped the game and, as he put it in his official report, 'dismissed Cantona for his violent conduct'.

We all knew Eric could explode. He had a long history of doing so. Playing for Montpellier, upset by what a teammate had said, he had flung his boots at him, leading to a fight and six of his teammates calling for him to be sacked. Just ten months earlier, in March 1994, he had been sent off in two successive Premier League matches and in one of them he had stamped on the chest of Swindon's John Moncur, which led to Alex losing his temper with him.

As Alex put it in his memoir, Cantona 'was prominent in the creation of the team's lamentable disciplinary record over the second half of the 1993/94 season'.[14] The Palace sending off was his fifth red card as a Manchester United player.

It was what Eric did next that converted what is commonly called a walk of shame into the most famous common assault in the history of the English legal system. The walk to the Palace tunnel, which is at the far end of the pitch, is a long one, a good seventy yards. As Eric marched away slowly, his head sunk in gloom, Matthew Simmons, a Crystal Palace supporter, seated eleven rows from the front, ran down and verbally abused him. Eric's response, as the linesman's report put it, was to 'jump two-footed over the advertising hoarding into a spectator.'

Although I had seen the sending-off incident, I did not see the Simmons clash, but it was clearly serious from the way in which the players and fans were reacting. After the game, which had ended in a 1–1 draw with Gareth Southgate scoring a late equaliser for the home side, I made my way to the directors' room.

I had barely time to eat my sandwich when a member of Alex Ferguson's football staff came up and said Alex had been called to the referee's room and told by a police superintendent that there would be a full investigation. This was alarming and I quickly made my way to the away dressing room.

After a match it was usual for the directors to go to the dressing rooms to speak to Alex and others. This was a convention. If the team had had a poor game and Alex was giving the team a telling off, then the board members would wait outside until it was appropriate to go in. Now I was faced with a very different situation.

I arrived to find the dressing room very quiet. Eric sat in a corner saying nothing. Alex had been worried about Shaw and at half-time had warned Cantona not to get involved, advising him to keep the ball away from him. Ferguson was convinced Wilkie was a weak referee and, as he walked out for the second half, had complained to him about the Palace tackling. Wilkie reacted as if Alex had horns. Not that Alex condoned what Eric had done and at the end of the match had made his feelings known to Cantona in the only way Alex can.

I was aware of the enormous media storm Cantona's 'kung-fu kick' had generated. That was to be expected but what really concerned me was that, rather unusually, the police themselves were giving television interviews. Given what they had told Alex, my real worry was that the police might at any stage walk into the dressing room and arrest Eric. I would have had to go with him, and I had no desire for either Eric or myself to spend a night at South Norwood police station.

I decided I must make sure the entire Manchester United team got on the bus as soon as possible and headed for our charter flight at Gatwick before the police came knocking on the dressing-room door. That was not easy. After a normal match it can take an hour or so before players can get on the coach. There are media interviews with players and managers, both with the written press and television. It is also the custom in English football that the manager of the away side goes to the office of the home manager and they may have a drink. Alex was very proud of the wine he served visiting managers.

My main concern was to get all the players back to Gatwick and I felt a great sense of relief as I saw the team bus head out of Selhurst Park. I had travelled to London by train, but I flew back with the team to Manchester.

It seemed there was no other story but Cantona, with former players employed as pundits particularly critical of his behaviour. Cantona had always generated a great deal of media interest and some very critical comments. A year earlier, for instance, in a televised FA Cup tie against Norwich, Jimmy Hill had called him 'despicable' after Cantona had kicked the defender John Polston in the head. Ferguson retaliated, accusing Hill of being 'a prat'.

Gary Lineker, the former England striker, who was working as an analyst for the BBC, led the chorus of indignation in the wake of Eric's kung-fu kick saying: 'I think it is unbelievable and inexcusable. It doesn't matter what or how you are provoked by the crowd, whatever language they use to you, you've got to be above it.' Former England midfielder Alan Mullery, who had been at Selhurst Park working as a radio analyst, said the clash was 'the most amazing incident I have ever seen in thirty-five years in football'. Mullery likened the Manchester United striker's leap to something out of a Bruce Lee film. Alan Hansen urged Cantona to go back to France.

The media activities the following day were unprecedented, and I went into the office early as it had been decided that I would field any press and media calls. It was considered important I did so, given the possibility of criminal proceedings against Eric.

It was a particularly difficult first day for me. As a lawyer I had often spoken to the media on behalf of the club and have always found journalists to be good company, even if I did not always agree with what they wrote. But now, in various television and radio interviews, I was unable to say very much because the club had not yet taken a decision on how to deal with the matter. It gave the impression Manchester United were not being decisive and were trying to shield Cantona, but that was very far from the truth. This was not just a case of Manchester United coming to a decision; both the Professional Footballers' Association and the Football Association were also involved.

Fairly early in the day, a fax arrived at United addressed to Eric from the FA charging him with misconduct and asking for his response and whether he wanted a personal hearing. He was given fourteen days to respond. I knew it would come. This was standard stuff.

What I also knew was that Eric's misconduct would not be treated as a routine disciplinary affair. I had rung Graham Kelly, chief executive of the FA, and he made it clear that the game's governing body was looking for Manchester United to take prompt and decisive action. I had also spoken to the PFA's chief executive Gordon Taylor and learned that their lawyers George Davies & Co were representing Eric.

We held a special meeting of a board committee comprising Roland Smith, Martin Edwards, Alex Ferguson and me at the Alderley Edge Hotel, which was often used by the club for private meetings and for putting up potential signings.

It was agreed that Eric would be suspended for the rest of the season for an unprecedented twenty-one games and fined the maximum sum possible under his contract. I do not believe we could have done any more. Eric was our talismanic player. His arrival from Leeds had powered us to our first league title since the glory days of Matt Busby. We had gone on to win the Double in 1994. He had unlocked the door for us on the field. Not having him for the rest of the season could mean we might never catch up with Blackburn and win a third successive Premier League title. It could also damage the commercial appeal of United. Across the Channel, the French FA had also taken action and stripped Cantona of the national team's captaincy.

I worked closely with the lawyers of the PFA and they told me Cantona accepted our punishment. This also meant he was no longer in conflict with the club, so I could now represent him. This was important as Matthew Simmons had complained to the police, and it seemed Eric might be dragged into a criminal action. I knew we were entering uncharted waters. To complicate matters further, the police said they wanted to interview Paul Ince, who had allegedly been involved in a separate, unrelated, scuffle. What this did was portray Manchester United players as an unruly mob and coloured the background to the Cantona case in just the lurid terms I had hoped to avoid.

The morning after the meeting at the Alderley Edge Hotel, Eric and his wife, Isabelle, came to my offices in Chepstow Street in Manchester city centre. Eric had been a reasonably regular visitor to these offices.

There was a cinema nearby which showed French films, which Eric, who had a genuine interest in the arts – he painted and was a passionate reader of the poet Arthur Rimbaud – found a great attraction. He would sometimes pop in after the film.

As I made notes, I wondered why he had reacted in this fashion. Years later he would explain:

> Millions of times people say these things, and then one day you don't accept it. Why? It's not about the words. It's about how you feel at the moment. One day you react, but the words are exactly the same as those you have heard a million times.[15]

He was very close to Isabelle. She was a literature graduate from the University of Aix-en-Provence. Once, after spending time with Eric at his flat in Auxerre, Isabelle had jumped from a train taking her back to the south of France because she could not bear to be parted from him. I could see Isabelle's presence at my meetings with Eric clearly meant a lot.

His backstory was interesting. He was the grandson of a stonemason and grew up in a home formed partly out of a cave in the side of the Caillols hills above Marseilles. At the age of 12 he had missed out on winning the league because of an officious referee. In the crucial match that decided the league, Cantona, with an open goal to aim at, was about to shoot when the referee noticed his shoelaces were undone. He blew the whistle to get young Eric to tie up his laces first. I could see how from an early age Eric must have felt officials were there only to frustrate him.

I quickly prepared a document and, aware that we could be facing criminal proceedings, I engaged David Poole, a QC, to review it. David had played rugby for London Irish and in 2001 would be the judge in the trial of the Leeds footballers Lee Bowyer and Jonathan Woodgate, who had been accused of affray and grievous bodily harm. After two trials, Bowyer was acquitted, and Woodgate sentenced to serve 100 hours' community service. Woodgate was cleared of grievous bodily harm and convicted of a lesser charge of affray.

I then discovered that Nike were proposing to run an advert with the title 'Just Do It'. It featured Eric Cantona and Basile Boli, a black French footballer whom Eric had known from his early days with Auxerre and was now with Glasgow Rangers.

The dialogue went as follows:

What do you see? A black man? A Frenchman? Or a footballer? Is it okay to shout racial abuse at me just because I'm on a football pitch? Some people say we have to accept abuse as part of the game. Why? I know that violence is not acceptable in sport, so how can we accept hatred? We could spend a lifetime arguing about differences. But I'd rather play football.

I contacted Nike and explained it would not be helpful for the advert to be released before the FA hearing. They accepted my argument and pulled it.

Eric, Isabelle and their son Raphael decided to get away from it all and go for a break to the French West Indies. I informed South Norwood police station and thought for a few days there would be some respite. I was mistaken.

I had come to London on some work assignment and at about five that evening rang my office to check everything was all right. I learned that for the previous hour my PA had been deluged by calls from television, radio and newspapers wanting to know why Eric and I had not turned up at South Norwood for a pre-arranged interview.

The media was reacting to a statement put out by the Metropolitan Police press office. This was absolute misinformation as no such arrangement had been made and they knew where Eric was. They apologised but not before it triggered a press frenzy. Worse was to follow a few days later.

On the evening of Saturday, 11 February, I had just got home from Maine Road having watched United beat City 3–0 in the Manchester derby. I was in a good mood as United now topped the table by a point. I returned only to find that it was all over the TV that Eric had kicked off at an ITN reporter, Terry Lloyd, and his cameraman, who had tried to film him while he was on holiday in Guadeloupe.

Yet again, the matter was blown out of all proportion. The fact of the matter was that the cameraman, in breach of French privacy laws, had tried to film Eric and his family without permission. Isabelle Cantona was six months pregnant. The cameraman's film had been confiscated by the French police. I was upset how matters had been covered in the media, but all this did not help Eric with his case, either before the FA or with the pending criminal proceedings.

Now the question was when would the police interview with Eric take place. I had had a conversation with the DCI, Graham Panting, who was leading the case, and requested the interview be deferred until after the FA hearing.

The police were unwilling to agree to this and expressed surprise that the FA hearing was being held before theirs. In fact, I did not mind that. The view of our legal team was it would be better for the FA hearing to continue and be got out of the way before the criminal proceedings began. After further conversation with the police, it was agreed that Eric's interview would take place at South Norwood police station on Tuesday, 21 February. I made it clear we would need an interpreter.

David Poole and I worked out our strategy for Eric's police interview. We quickly agreed that this should be a 'no comment' interview. This made perfectly good legal sense. At that time the law regarding 'no comment' interviews was different from what it is now in that no adverse inference could be taken at trial from the fact that a defendant did not answer questions put to him at interview. We would, however, accompany this with a pre-prepared and signed statement from Eric handed in before the interview began.

The day before, I arranged a meeting with David Poole, Eric, Isabelle, Alex Ferguson and the interpreter George Scanlan. David and I explained to Eric what would happen at the police station when we arrived for the interview. We went through the statement with Eric that David and I had drafted for him, making sure he was happy about it.

Eric could be a firebrand on the field, but I was impressed with how quickly he understood what he needed to do, and he agreed and signed the statement. I explained to him that the police would not ask questions but, if they did, he should say 'no comment.' Eric smiled and said: 'Yes, no comment, Maurice.'

DCI Panting made it clear there would be an official Home Office interpreter, but I pointed out we needed our own. I was informed Eric would be charged with assault but was given no more details.

On 21 February I met up with George Scanlan and Eric in a suite at the Royal Lancaster Hotel. We then travelled over together to South Norwood. Entering the police station with Eric was like re-enacting a scene from a crime drama. The moment we announced ourselves, Eric was arrested and charged. As soon as the arrest formalities had been completed, we were taken to the interview room for the taped interview. It was conducted by two officers under DCI Panting.

The interview began in the classic fashion often seen in television police dramas. Eric and I sat on one side of a table, the two officers sat opposite us and then DCI Panting, pressing the tape recording, said: 'Interview with Eric Cantona' and gave the time the interview had started. But we did not get far before we were interrupted. The police asked for another copy of the agreed statement to be signed for police purposes, so we had an adjournment for Eric to sign it.

The next adjournment came because I could not stop Eric talking. Despite the fact that we had told the police that Eric had no comment to make, they still asked questions. I knew this could happen, it is a game the police play, luring the person questioned into their net. It would not have mattered had Eric done what I had told him to and refused to comment.

But to my surprise, he began to answer. I squeezed his knee to try and get him to stop but this had no effect. Eric, looking relaxed, had no problems with the English language and answered questions even before Scanlan had translated them. I had no option but to say to DCI Panting that I wanted an adjournment to consult my client. We retired to a room, and when I asked Eric why he was answering questions he said with a sweet smile: 'Maurice, the questions are easy to answer so I dealt with them.' I reminded Eric of why we had put in the pre-prepared statement and convinced him to keep to our 'no comment' strategy when the questioning resumed.

I felt the futility of Alex Ferguson telling Eric not to react to players who fouled him, but Eric nodded his head and promised to obey. We returned to the interview room and this time Eric followed orders.

The moment DCI Panting said the interview was over he charged Eric with common assault on Matthew Simmons contrary to Section 39 of the Criminal Justice Act 1988 and bailed him to appear at Croydon Magistrates' Court on 23 March.

I quickly wrote out a press statement and emerged on the forecourt of the South Norwood station to read it out. It was important to make it clear how co-operative Eric was being, and I began by emphasising that Eric had voluntarily come to the police station and given a statement. I had no desire to give media interviews and added no further comment would be made, but I knew that would not keep the media quiet.

As we drove back to central London, stopping on the way to eat, I knew we had barely reached half-time in the Cantona saga. The next stage would be the FA hearing against Eric for bringing the game into disrepute, that wonderful catch-all charge which over the years had been brought against so many players. Except these were very exceptional circumstances and the hearing would prove to be of the kind I had never before attended.

Even before Eric had been to South Norwood police station, David Poole and I had worked out Eric's response to the FA charge. I knew his would have to be carefully worded to express the remorse Eric felt and how, given the punishment United had already handed out, he should not be punished any further.

The statement went over Eric's version of what happened that night at Crystal Palace, how he understood he was losing the French captaincy, that he wanted to rehabilitate himself in English football and wanted the FA to take into account his regret, the severe punishment Manchester United had imposed and that he also faced a criminal court case.

The FA hearing was set for Friday, 24 February at Sopwell House Hotel, an elegant Georgian establishment near St Albans, where Lord Mountbatten had grown up. The FA had decided that its headquarters at Lancaster Gate, which insiders called the Old Curiosity Shop, could not cope with the media rush. They were right. By 9am Sopwell House was already surrounded by thirty photographers.

We had decided that Manchester United would field a strong team and travelled in two cars. United's security man, Ned Kelly, chauffeured Alex, Eric and me in the front car while in the second was Cantona's agent, Jean-Jacques Bertrand, and interpreter George Scanlan.

The members of the FA commission were well known to me: Geoff Thompson, the chairman of the FA's disciplinary commission; magistrate Gordon McKeag, who had been chairman of Newcastle and was now the president of the Football League; and Ian Stott, the chairman of Oldham Athletic.

Gordon Taylor, from the PFA, was also present as an observer. David Davies, a BBC presenter who was now the FA's director of communications, was also there but he sat in on all disciplinary hearings. The presence of the other observer showed what an unusual hearing this was. He was Graham Kelly, the FA's chief executive. In order to emphasise that the disciplinary commission was distinct from the hierarchy that ran the FA, Graham Kelly did not normally attend. However on this occasion he had asked to be present as a silent witness who would take no part in the proceedings.

As is usual at such hearings, the commission members sat at one end of a long table, with Kelly and Margaret O'Brien, the disciplinary secretary, at the far end of it. We sat opposite. It was a long hearing, lasting more than three hours, and I took my time to make a lengthy plea in mitigation based on our earlier submissions: I explained to the panel the financial consequences of United's twenty-one-game suspension, not just the maximum fine under the contract of two week's salary but missing out on the club's bonus schedule, a further financial penalty of over £25,000.

The suspension, I emphasised, was the most severe ever inflicted on an English league player other than expulsion from the game. Paul Davis of Arsenal had been given a nine-game suspension for punching and breaking Glenn Cockerill's jaw in a match between Arsenal and Southampton in 1988. The same year had seen Chris Kamara handed the same punishment for punching Jim Melrose at the end of a game between Swindon and Shrewsbury.

I explained to the panel:

In the light of the punishment already given, I would respectfully ask the commission members to resist any pressure they may feel that they have to do anything more by way of suspension to justify the holding of this hearing.

Eric's club acted promptly and severely in respect of the incident and it is to the player's credit that he has accepted his punishment with dignity and without rancour. I would suggest that, if the commission seeks to inflict further punishment on Eric Cantona by way of additional suspension, this will militate against other clubs acting promptly and decisively to situations which might involve FA disciplinary action and discourage them from doing so.

In this case the message which clearly came from the Football Association was a message calling for prompt and decisive action. That message was heeded with the punishment then imposed.

I also referred to the criminal proceedings, how the police had misinformed the media of the alleged failure of Eric to attend a police appointment, the hostile and critical publicity from the media laying all football ills at Eric's door, and the Guadeloupe incident.

I had thought long and hard about how to deal with the disgusting abuse Matthew Simmons had thrown at Eric. I did not want to repeat his words, so I decided to put them in a note; after I had finished speaking, I passed the commission members the note, explaining it was important for the commission to know exactly what had been said to Eric before he jumped into the crowd.

Jean-Jacques Bertrand spoke and so did Alex Ferguson.

There were a few questions from the panel members, one of which was most curious. Ian Stott asked Eric: 'Isn't it a fact that you are a kung-fu expert?' This made Alex and me laugh. Eric could make nothing of the question, and I stepped in to say: 'No, he is not a kung-fu expert.' Stott was clearly besotted with Eric because he wanted to get his autograph and had to be restrained by Thompson from doing so.

The hearing seemed to be coming to an end when Geoff Thompson said: 'We haven't heard from Mr Cantona. Would Mr Cantona like to add anything?' David Davies has said the idea of Eric saying anything filled him with dread as at a previous French hearing he had smacked an official in the face. But Eric could not have been more composed as he spoke.

Both Kelly and Davies have given an account of what Eric said. Let me quote the one in Graham Kelly's book, *Sweet FA*.

Mr Chairman, I do not want to say very much. You have heard my explanation through my representatives here today and you have read my letter. I just want to apologise to everyone concerned. I want to apologise to Manchester United Football Club; I want to apologise to my teammates; I want to apologise to the supporters of the club; I want to apologise to the Football Association. And I want to apologise to the prostitute who shared my bed last evening.[16]

Gordon McKeag misheard and turned to Geoff Thompson and said: 'What did he say? "He prostrates himself before the FA"?'

'Yes,' said Thompson, eager to get away from the subject.

Now I cannot comment with any certainty on what Kelly alleges Eric said in mitigation, but what I am going to comment on is what Kelly says in his book about my reaction to Eric's words.

He wrote: 'Maurice Watkins was also aware what was said as he was sitting next to Eric and because they were cramped, he was half-falling away from him when he spoke, Maurice turned, his mouth dropped open and he almost fell off his chair.'[17] The suggestion that any lawyer worth his salt would allow his demeanour to slip in such circumstances is surely a suggestion unworthy of any chief executive of the Football Association.

After Eric had finished speaking Thompson said: 'Thank you. Mr Cantona, you'd better retire now and let us consider our verdict.' Eric had been doodling on a blotter during the hearing. He left it behind, Stott picked it up and said he would take it home for his daughter.

It took the commission a long time to come to their decision and when they finally did, it was to extend the ban from all football activities from the end of the current season to the end of September 1995 and to impose a fine of £10,000.

The commission stated that it had taken into consideration (a) the previous misconduct record of the player, (b) the provocation he suffered, (c) the prompt action taken by Manchester United, (d) the apologies offered by the player to the commission, and (e) the assurances as to his future conduct.

Alex was understandably furious, and Graham Kelly took Alex, David Davies and me to a room in the hotel to talk things over. Alex felt the PFA should do something to contest it.

My immediate concern was the press statement the FA were planning to issue. The FA in their statement were proposing to express opinions which had not been tested at the hearing. I felt they were not only inappropriate for inclusion but also were, without doubt, prejudicial to Eric's forthcoming criminal hearing. The statement they had drafted spoke of Eric's 'disgraceful behaviour'.

I do not often lose my temper but on this occasion I did, and raising my voice warned Kelly and Davies: 'You give that out and you'll be in the High Court by Monday.' Gordon Taylor joined in this debate and eventually the FA gave way. We had to consider whether we should appeal Eric's punishment but decided it was best if we did not. I drafted our press statement which said: 'Whilst we are naturally disappointed that the FA have felt it necessary to increase the suspension, which was promptly meted out by Manchester United, the decision has been accepted in everyone's interest.'

Alex and I agreed that with a criminal case coming up, Eric could not say anything to the press and that I would take charge of answering the media questions. I knew we would get a lot of hostile comments. Many journalists had accused Manchester United of letting Eric off lightly, and, as often happens when people talk of the club, the name of Matt Busby was invoked. A common refrain was: 'Matt would never have tolerated this behaviour; he would have shown Eric the door.' This, of course, demonstrated how short public memory can be, completely forgetting Matt's often indulgent relationship with George Best.

The press conference was held at Sopwell House and went on for a long time. I dealt mainly with the questions as Alex did not want to answer them. I would answer questions which were genuine with as much information as I could give but would have no time for questions that I considered stupid and provocative.

And when one such question inevitably came from one of the tabloid papers I responded: 'I don't think I've got much time for that sort of question.' It proved an effective put-down. Much to my surprise I received a totally unexpected complimentary comment from United's fanzine *Red Issue*. In a piece headlined 'Maurice Watkins Unsung Hero' it said I looked and sounded imposing and had served the club well.

Eric's court hearing had been fixed for 23 March and I was working in my office on the criminal proceedings when my secretary put through a call. She said it was a lawyer in the special casework unit of the Crown Prosecution Service who was handling the case for the CPS.

It turned out to be Jeffrey McCann, a friend from the University College London law department to whom I had not spoken for many years. I was delighted I had someone on the other side whom I knew and could rely upon to deal with the matter in a fair and professional way. Jeffrey admitted that the case was somewhat of a light diversion from the kind of cases he normally dealt with such as the murder of Rachel Nickell on Wimbledon Common. I would remind him of that comment when the Eric case exploded for Jeffrey, and he had to defend himself physically in court.

Not long after talking to Jeffrey McCann, I met with Eric to discuss his plea. I told him that my advice and that of David Poole was that he should plead guilty and that if he did so the court would fix his punishment; I told him that the maximum punishment could be six months' imprisonment and a fine of up to £5,000, and what would be the likely result.

He agreed that he should plead guilty. I needed references and Eric mentioned we should approach Steve Bruce, the club captain, and also Alex Ferguson. He said he would let me know the telephone numbers of his friend Claude Boli, the brother of the French centre-half Basile Boli, and contacts at his previous club Leeds United.

By this time, I had received the witness statements from the police, and I discussed them with Eric. I read Matthew Simmons's statement, pointing out one or two paragraphs from it.

However, Eric's trial was not taking place in isolation, there were two other cases and a threat of a third one. Simmons had been charged with Public Order Act offences and his trial had been fixed for the day after Eric's. Paul Ince, meanwhile, had been bailed to return to South Norwood police station on 8 March. To cap it all a Mr Roy Edey (a self-styled 'People's Champion') was contemplating taking out a private prosecution against Eric arising from the Crystal Palace incident.

After a chat with David Poole, we decided to write to McCann asking the Director of Public Prosecutions to consider exercising his discretion to take over the conduct of such private proceedings. He issued Edey with a formal notice of discontinuance.

On 20 March, I went to David Poole's house in Heaton Mersey, Stockport. Eric came accompanied by his friend Claude Boli. We discussed the position generally, the likely outcome and compared our case with that of Dennis Wise, who had just been sentenced to three months' imprisonment for assaulting a taxi driver outside Terry Venables's Kensington nightclub. The jail sentence would be overturned on appeal, however Wise was ordered to pay over £1,000 in damages.

Claude spoke good English. He was writing a doctoral thesis for the University of Nantes and De Montford University, Leicester. The title was *Le Champ du Football Professionnel en Angleterre: Manchester United Football Club, un Modèle d'Excellence*.

Alex Ferguson would also be in London that day, but he would be at Buckingham Palace wearing a kilt while being awarded the CBE from Prince Charles. We had decided that for the court case the United team would be based at the Croydon Park Hotel and use the hotel's Barclay Suite. The hotel was only a hundred yards from the court, and I felt we could make a quick entry and exit avoiding the media scrum.

Before the hearing I had met with Ned Kelly, United's head of security, and agreed he would drive Eric to London the evening before and check him into the hotel. But, unknown to me, Eric had decided to travel down with Paul Ince, who faced two charges of assault for which he was ultimately found not guilty at trial.

The pair spent some time in Brown's, a nightclub in Covent Garden, and with the media constantly shadowing them this made the front page of the tabloids. The next morning when I met Ned, I asked him: 'Where's Eric?' When Kelly replied that he'd made his own way down with Paul Ince, I was not best pleased and showed the front page of the tabloids to Ned, saying: 'He made his own way to the front page of today's papers, too.' David Poole was also unhappy, predicting: 'That won't help his case.'

My mood was not lightened when I saw Eric. For the FA hearing he had been dressed in tie and jacket. Now he came wearing a brown collarless jacket over a grey T-shirt. He looked very smart, but that was not the point; David and I would have preferred a suit and tie. However, my efforts to get him into one of my shirts failed as his neck size was a few inches greater than mine.

If I thought the media pressure was considerable at the FA hearing, it was nothing compared with that at Croydon. The situation was exacerbated to some extent because Paul Ince was also appearing on the same day to plead not guilty to his assault charges.

In contrast to Eric, Paul, accompanied by his wife Claire and his solicitor, was dressed in suit and tie. The cameras and press filled the road, camera cranes in position to capture the best views. We had decided the best way of getting to the court was to walk with a police escort. That did not prove to be a good idea and I was almost knocked to the ground several times as I made my way to the court.

Unlike TV crime dramas, where the prosecutors and defence are always pulling rabbits from hats, real-life cases have few surprises. We each had our bundle of court papers and both sides knew what the bundles were made up of. After the case, I bought from ITV the court artist's painting of the court line-up.

Even before the start of the case we had agreed to the prosecution costs of £500 as reasonable. There was little that was unexpected in Jeffrey McCann's presentation of his case. He said Matthew Simmons had been seated eleven rows from the front. McCann said that he ran down to the front. He said Simmons disputed this and said he was going to the toilet. When Simmons was adjacent to Eric, he shouted abuse at him. He said a number of persons had made statements setting out what Simmons had shouted at Eric. Two examples were mentioned, the first that Simmons had shouted: 'You're a fucking dismal cunt, fuck off back to France, you don't deserve to be on the pitch.' The second statement said that Simmons shouted: 'Fuck off, wanker, motherfucker.' At this point, John Mannings, the magistrate's clerk, asked Eric, who had a court interpreter with him, whether he could follow what was being said. Eric, looking very composed, answered 'Yes.'

McCann continued with his description of the incident, saying that Eric had launched himself over the hoardings with a kung-fu type of kick at Simmons, striking him in the chest. Eric fell back, got on his feet and went to strike Simmons with his fist two or three times. Simmons defended himself by punching back. McCann said it was not clear whether or not the blows from the fist connected.

In his testimony, Simmons had claimed:

> As I reached the front row, I became aware of Eric Cantona on the touch line. I joined in with the rest of the crowd shouting 'Off, off, have an early shower'. He kicked my chest. I felt pain to the left side. I got hold of his legs and pushed him back. He started throwing punches in my direction.

McCann explained that from Simmons's own evidence it seemed that Eric had not connected with his fists.

Mr McCann then moved on to the statement that Eric had provided under caution at the police station. Eric said in his statement that he became aware of a man among a number of fans swearing and gesticulating. That man was abusive and insulting and used racist terms, telling Eric that he was 'a fucking cheating French cunt, bastard, wanker'. Eric said he was hurt and insulted but he regretted his actions. He said he should not have done it and was not seeking to justify his actions.

Eric said he had fallen over after he had jumped over the hoarding and that as he got up Simmons threw his fists at him, and Cantona swung his at Simmons. McCann said at this point that there had been widespread reports about Eric failing to keep his appointments with the police. This was not true and had been misrepresented.

McCann said that the injury to Simmons was minor. He had reddening and bruising around the left side of his chest. Simmons said that, after the incident, he began coughing, which hurt, and he also had a headache.

You never know what is going through the minds of judges or magistrates, but I was intrigued that as Jeffrey came to the end of his presentation the chair of the three-magistrate bench, Jean Pearch, who had been a music teacher, asked two questions. One was of the height of the barriers and the other was whether there were any studs on Eric's boots. Jeffrey had to turn for help to a police chief inspector who was in court and who, coincidentally, had attended the match as a spectator. The barriers were about four feet high. David Poole, after conferring with Eric, confirmed that the boots had a moulded rubber artificial surface on the sole. The studs were moulded in one place and there were no screw-in studs.

David Poole's defence of Eric emphasised his deep regret and that this was at the forefront of the mitigation. He had apologised to the court and to everyone affected by the incident. He had left the field immediately, albeit slowly and reluctantly, without protest or any inflammatory action, when he was sent off.

In contrast, Simmons had come from eleven rows back to the very front so Eric would have no alternative but to pass immediately in front of him and see and hear at close quarters the stream of abuse. The distance was two or three feet, almost touching distance. The spectator's right hand was gesturing in a way denoting sexual self-abuse.

This young man had put xenophobia before any love of soccer and expressed it in a way which black and overseas footballers have had to endure. Matthew Simmons's words were designed to taunt, goad, provoke and to hurt as deeply as possible, as were his gesticulations.

They had hurt Eric in three ways: as to his race and nationality; his own sexual integrity; and that of his closest and dearest relative, his mother. Simmons had suggested that the relationship between Eric and his mother was unnatural. Simmons succeeded in his determination to goad and provoke. Eric, said Poole, did not seek to justify his actions by the provocation, but it was a serious and severe provocation.

Poole asked the court to reject Simmons's explanation to the police that he was at the front because, by sheer chance, he was on his way to the toilet, and that Eric's action towards him was entirely unprovoked.

All the independent witness statements verified Eric's account as to what was done and said. What was also significant was that Eric's statement had been made before he or we had seen any of these statements which had been supplied subsequently by the prosecution.

Poole needed to tell the court something of Eric's background and this he did with great skill. That he had had an underprivileged upbringing. There had been deep family love but there was not much money about. He had always been of good character. He was known as a volatile and sometimes tempestuous footballer, but he was law abiding and had no convictions in this country or anywhere else.

Aware of the public image of high-earning footballers, Poole emphasised that Eric was not ostentatious off the field. He lived in a rented property with his wife and son, a second child was expected, and he drove a modest car. He gave unstintingly to charity. Poole read an extract from one character statement praising Eric for going out of his way to talk to the children and young people with a particular disability who had been invited to Manchester United's training ground.

Our case was that Eric had already been punished and Poole reminded the court of that. He had suffered a loss of £40,000 and this was assuming Manchester United didn't win either the League or the FA Cup.

Poole stressed that the court should treat Eric for what he is, an ordinary man. Had an ordinary man been before the court on such a charge and with such mitigation, Poole suggested to the court that they would be considering a conditional discharge, and this is the sentence he recommended.

As the bench retired, I felt we had presented our case well and, while there is never any way of telling how a verdict will go, I was confident. Poole and I went out to take a bit of air and forty-five minutes later we were summoned back.

Mrs Pearch's initial remarks were what we expected. That there would be no order for costs. Neither would they hear any application for compensation if one was being made, because of the provocation. It is what she said next that made me jolt:

> This is a serious offence on the facts. We have heard your deep regret as expressed by your counsel. We have taken this into account together with your previous good character and your guilty plea. Despite the seriousness of the offence, we are not asking for reports today because of the fulsome facts heard from both sides and the nature of the offence. We feel, however, that you are a high-profile public figure with undoubted gifts and as

such looked up to by many young people. For this reason, the only sentence appropriate is two weeks' imprisonment, forthwith, immediately.

You could have heard a pin drop. We were all totally amazed. David Poole was so surprised that he thought he had not heard correctly and asked: 'Could you kindly repeat that.' Mrs Pearch did. We had to appeal and Poole said that a notice of appeal would be lodged immediately and that he wanted to make application for bail pending the appeal.

Jeffrey did not object, but the court clerk intervened to remind the bench that other cases were waiting to be heard, and Mrs Pearch said that as other cases were in the list the magistrates would hear the application later.

While all this was going on, Eric had been whipped out of court and down into the cells. We then had to race up the street to the Crown Court, which was only a short distance away, and try to persuade the court office to put our application before a judge sitting in the Crown Court.

In the meantime, of course, there was media bedlam. Everybody wanted to know what was happening; we did what we could to keep people fully informed and also to see Eric as a client, and to explain what we were doing. I went down to the cells to see him.

Eventually we went before Judge Ian Davies, at Croydon Crown Court, who allowed bail and fixed the appeal for a week later. After a three-and-a-half-hour spell in the cells – where a prison officer having been his jailer came to his cell and asked for his autograph – we had secured Eric's release.

Bail was granted unconditionally subject to the provision of surety in the sum of £500, which I accepted responsibility for. During the course of the bail application Eric was advised of what might happen, including an increased sentence on appeal, which was fixed for 31 March.

Eric pondered submitting to imprisonment and serving his sentence as the few hours he had spent in custody counted as a day and you generally receive a remission of at least half the sentence. His decision to appeal, however, was the right one as there is a stigma attached to imprisonment, particularly in continental Europe where the courts tend not to send people to prison as much as they do in the UK.

The judgment had come as a shock and it meant there was now more work to be done to set matters right. We started off with a consultation at David Poole's house with Eric and Isabelle. David went through the possibilities that might result from the appeal, including the possibility that the sentence might be increased.

Both Eric and his wife wanted to continue with the appeal. It was also agreed that we should try to obtain an expedited pre-sentence/ community service report. It was explained to Eric that he should be prepared to undertake community service, but he was concerned as to what role he would have to play in this and whether there might be unsuitable objectives given to him which could cause him problems with the press.

On 29 March Eric and I attended the Eccles probation office for the purpose of a pre-sentence report. The next day Eric and I were driven by Ned Kelly to Croydon for the appeal. I did not wish to drive down too early as I had promised my son, Peter, that I would go to his Manchester Grammar School football presentation which was being held in the Manchester University premises at Owens Park in Fallowfield. When it was time to leave, Eric and Ned came into the hall to collect me. You can picture the amazement of the boys and their parents. Is that really Eric Cantona?

As I travelled down, I was getting more and more pain in my back, and by the time we reached the Croydon Park Hotel I could hardly move. The following morning, I just could not get up or get dressed. I tried to have a shower to ease the pain but getting dressed proved impossible. David Poole rang my room to see where I was as we had arranged an early meeting. I explained my predicament and he came up to help me get dressed.

We also asked the hotel to arrange for a doctor. The hotel doctor (a Dr Wilcock) came to the room and gave me an injection which certainly helped. We had arranged through the court administrator, Mr Malone, to get into a car at the back of the hotel and to drive into the court's underground car park and come in through the judge's entrance. This worked well and avoided the media crush we had had at the magistrates' court hearing.

The hearing before Judge Ian Davies, sitting with two lay magistrates, went according to expectations. The judge disagreed fundamentally with the decision of the magistrates and substituted 120 hours of community service for the prison sentence, saying that, whatever a defendant's status, he is entitled to be dealt with for the gravity of the offence and not to be made an example of as a public figure.

After the verdict had been given, we returned to the hotel for yet another press conference. I was sitting down at a table with Jean-Jacques Bertrand drafting what we wanted to say, while Eric was also putting pen to paper.

He did not want to attend the conference but said he would do so if he was able to say a few words. While he was writing away, he asked me: 'What's that big boat called that catches fish?'

'Do you mean a trawler?'

'And the big bird that flies over the sea?'

'You mean a seagull?'

He carried on and then showed me what he wanted to say. It read: 'When the seagulls follow the trawler, it is because they think that sardines will be thrown into the sea.'

He told me he wanted to read out these words. I was not sure he should, but I agreed. He also told me he did not want me to explain what these words meant.

At the press conference, Eric sipped a glass of water and then said his piece before getting up and leaving. When I was asked by the reporters what he meant, I said words to the effect of: 'You can see from that the extreme pressure Eric has been under.' In fact, after the conference was over, I was button-holed by a BBC TV reporter who told me that I should not have allowed it and the comment cocked a snook at everyone.

But it turned out fine. The media in the main loved it. There were lots of attempts to explain the meaning of the words and it had the effect of defusing the issue and bringing a very long saga to some kind of conclusion. It has gone into football folklore and is now included in almost any book of football quotations.

After the conference, I drafted a formal press release:

Eric Cantona's appeal against a custodial sentence of 14 days was allowed today and community service of 120 hours substituted. The Judge expressed the strong wish that he would be permitted during the community service to serve the community by training and encouraging young boys and girls to participate in and enjoy the game of football. This Eric is very willing to do.

In passing sentence, the Judge said that the provocation to which Eric was subjected would have provoked the most stoic and acknowledged that he acted out of character and would not have done so if he had not been provoked. The Judge accepted the argument that, whatever the defendant's status, he is entitled to be dealt with for the gravity of the offence for which he is convicted and not to make an example of a public figure.

I was staying in central London after the case and our barristers, who were heading back to Manchester, gave me a lift back to my hotel. As I got out of the taxi the junior counsel, trying to be helpful, slammed the cab door on my fingers which were still in the door. I had started the day off with an injection for my back and I finished it off with another doctor called out that night to put my fingers together again.

What lifted my spirits was a letter I received from a woman in London, written on the date of the hearing.

I have been following the events surrounding Eric Cantona with interest and concern. It is clear that he is an intriguing and charismatic man. I certainly find him so. It is those qualities that have led to his elevation to almost 'godlike' status by the press and, as usual with the British news media, to some unwarranted and vicious attempts to destroy him. Fortunately, it seems that the majority of the public in this country feel as I do – that he deserves a chance to make amends.

I am very pleased at the result of the appeal and I think the revised sentence is entirely appropriate and justified. I hope that Eric will decide that he can continue his career at Manchester United because I don't really believe life will be any easier for him elsewhere. Wherever he goes he taxes himself, we can none of us leave the worst aspects of our character behind us.

However, the reason I am writing to you is to express my admiration for the part you have played in this business. You have consistently represented a reasonable, considerate and altogether acceptable public face of Manchester United Football Club. I think you have been able to deflect even more criticism of Eric and the club through your unfaltering approachable and polite demeanour in standing in for Eric himself as he seems to have a genuine inability to 'play the game' for the press (I don't criticise him for this at all). I felt reassured each time I have seen you on television or heard you on the radio. If I were ever to need the help of a solicitor, I could do no better than to find someone like yourself to represent me.

Lastly, I want to applaud MUFC itself for the way the club has stood by Eric all through this time. It must have been tempting to see him as being more trouble than he is worth, but at a time when he has needed the Club behind him and backing him, that is what you have done consistently.

Whatever he chooses to do and wherever he decides his future lies I hope Eric will never forget or undervalue this aspect of his ordeal.

On Monday, 3 April at 6:30pm Eric, Ken Merrett and I attended the Greater Manchester Probation Services' offices at Redwood Street, Salford. Eric had an appraisal interview and we discussed how the community service would be dealt with and what involvement the club would have.

Insurance was obviously of some concern and Ken was given an indemnity form for consideration by the club's insurers. Eric was to be supervised by the probation service throughout his 120 hours' community service and the probation service said that suitable projects would be finalised taking into account Eric's footballing skills.

Eric began his 120 hours' community service on 15 April. It was a daily coaching programme for children at Manchester United's training ground, the Cliff.

The coaching programme had been devised by him and included a two-hour session for groups of around twelve children. He coached two groups per afternoon, working virtually every afternoon over the next two months. The children taking part in the coaching sessions were aged between nine and eleven from football teams and schools in the Salford area, and more than 700 young people benefited from the scheme.

This was, as assistant chief probation officer, Liz Calderbank, put it: 'No soft option. We have insisted that Eric Cantona devise the coaching programme himself, and we feel it very demanding in terms of the numbers of young people involved and the length of the coaching sessions. Four hours' coaching an afternoon will make considerable physical demands, and Mr Cantona will have to devote every weekday afternoon to this programme.'

The coaching took place indoors using a gym at the Cliff and both United and the probation service were very keen for a photocall with Eric and the youngsters he was coaching. But Eric was not.

While Eric was being punished, Matthew Simmons made his delayed appearance to face two offences contrary to Sections 4 and 5 of the Public Order Act 1986. At a preliminary hearing at Croydon Magistrates' Court, it was submitted on Simmons's behalf that he would not receive a fair trial because of extensive and prejudicial media coverage. The submission failed but the matter was then adjourned to enable Simmons to apply to the High Court for a judicial review.

Eventually, Simmons did come to trial. By then the 1995/96 season had started and I was dealing with other cases not related to football when suddenly I received a call. It was Jeffrey McCann ringing from court. 'Maurice,' he said, 'you will never believe this, but on being sentenced Simmons leapt from the witness box and attacked me'.

It happened after he was convicted for using threatening words and behaviour. Jeffrey had just got to his feet and had begun to argue for an order to exclude him from football grounds when Simmons leapt over a bench and appeared to kick Jeffrey in the chest.

Eventually, the police restored order and Simmons was led away in handcuffs. The chairman of the bench jailed Simmons for seven days for contempt of court. He was also fined £500 and ordered to pay £200 costs. The football exclusion order was for a period of twelve months. Jeffrey told the court he was content to accept Simmons's apology and had no intention of pressing charges. That did not surprise me as I remembered that Jeffrey had had a successful army career before he joined the law and could handle such things.

Cantona by then had returned to Manchester United colours, scoring against Liverpool on his comeback at Old Trafford. He would then score the only goal against them in the FA Cup final to secure the second Double in the club's history, both achieved in only the last three seasons.

A year later, he decided he wanted to board a different trawler chasing other sardines and departed. The Cantona case was a unique moment in my legal life. My only regret is I did not preserve the paper on which Eric wrote the famous words.

18

Racism and Lip Reading

Peter Schmeichel's arrival at Old Trafford was one of those chance encounters that nobody can legislate for.

In January 1991 Alex Ferguson had taken the players for a break to Spain and found that the Danish club, Brøndby, were also staying at the same hotel in Marbella. Ferguson, watching the Brøndby players train, was impressed with the tall, imposing Schmeichel.

His one problem was that, more than any other position, foreign goalkeepers can have problems adjusting to the special demands of the English game. But Alan Hodgkinson, the Manchester United goalkeeping coach, assured Alex the Dane had what it took to adjust. On his return, Alex made it very clear he wanted us to buy Schmeichel.

On 28 June Martin Edwards and I flew to Denmark to meet the Brøndby chairman, Per Bjerregaard, and his colleague, Benny Winthur, to secure the big Dane. Also present for part of the meeting was Rune Hauge, Peter's agent. Rune played no part in the negotiations other than an introductory capacity.

Brøndby, located in a garden city just outside Copenhagen, wanted a million. I suppose they felt the figure would sound good when they told their supporters what they had got for their much-valued 27-year-old who was a Danish international and had been part of the Brøndby side that had reached the semi-finals of the UEFA Cup.

That was much more than we were prepared to pay. The haggling took hours but eventually we managed to beat it down to £505,000. Both Martin and I were aware that Alex was desperate to get Schmeichel and we felt pleased that we had done the deal and also that we could have him for the start of the 1991/92 season, something they had been reluctant to agree to.

The transfer had an additional complication because with United being a public company and Brøndby also quoted, the respective British and Danish stock exchanges had to be kept informed. Per Bjerregaard impressed on me that the announcement had to be made simultaneously and I had no problems ensuring that.

There was a further meeting on 10 July at the Noga Hilton in Geneva with representatives of Brøndby which I and the club secretary, Ken Merrett, attended. This was also to discuss the detailed terms of a match at Old Trafford which was to be played as part of the agreement for the transfer. There was also discussion on Peter joining the club on a loan basis for United's pre-season training and matches.

I sent Per Bjerregaard his part of the agreement for signature, and he confirmed that he had been in touch with the Danish Football Association with regard to the release of the necessary international clearance certificate. There was also talk of bringing forward the completion date by a few days.

We had also bought Paul Parker, an England international full-back, for £1.75 million from Queens Park Rangers. These were the first transfers since flotation and it showed that, contrary to what some fans believed, being a plc did not preclude team strengthening.

It was then necessary to finalise the press release, which would be the first one we had done for players since flotation. It included the transfer of Paul Parker from Queens Park Rangers on 6 August, with £1 million payable immediately. Peter Schmeichel's transfer was completed the same day.

* * *

In the meantime, Manchester United had travelled for a pre-season tour to Norway, where Peter made his debut against Sanfrecce Hiroshima. The Japanese club won 2–1 and, to Schmeichel's embarrassment, one of their goals came from almost the halfway line. On the day the club arrived home from Norway, the team had to fly to Scotland to play Dumbarton and Aberdeen.

Eleven days later, on 17 August, Schmeichel made his league debut in a 2–0 win over Notts County. The atmosphere at Old Trafford gave him goose bumps and Manchester United did not concede in any of their first four matches.

Peter Schmeichel's biggest problem was his nationality. In joining Manchester United he became subject to the infamous 3+2 rule which prevented United fielding its best team for many years in European cup competitions. Under the rule, a club could only field in European competition three foreign players plus two 'assimilated players'. An assimilated player was one who had played for an uninterrupted period of five years in the country concerned, three years of which had to have been spent in youth football.

The difficulty for English clubs under this rule was that Scottish, Welsh and Northern Ireland players were considered foreign unless they could be treated as assimilated. On a number of occasions during his early years at Old Trafford Peter was stood down for this reason, most notably in the 4–0 Champions League defeat at Barcelona in November 1994. The rule continued to impair United and other Premier League clubs until it was swept away by the Bosman Ruling in December 1995.

The Bosman case is arguably the most important judicial ruling ever affecting football and had a dramatic impact on the game in all manner of ways. Not only was football covered by the ruling but all team sports across the European Union.

The background to the landmark case begins in 1990, when Jean-Marc Bosman reached the end of his playing contract with RFC Liège in the Belgian First Division. He had not been a particularly successful player and Liège offered him a one-season contract cutting his basic monthly salary by 60 per cent.

Needless to say, Bosman rejected the offer and was placed on the transfer list. Eventually, he accepted a position with the French club, Dunkerque. However, he was prevented from moving to France because of difficulties between the two clubs in arranging for the payment of the agreed transfer fee. These difficulties resulted in the French Football Federation not receiving the required transfer authorisation from the Belgium Football Union.

In view of the delay, Dunkerque rescinded its contract with Bosman and Bosman decided to take the matter initially to the Belgian courts. The case finally reached the European Court of Justice, and in its ground-breaking judgment on 15 December 1995, the Court decided two matters:

1. No transfer fee can be demanded at the end of a contract for a player who was a national of one European Union member state moving to a club in another member state.
2. Nationality clauses which limit the number of EU or EEA nationals playing in any national or European club competition are illegal.

UEFA did away with all restrictions on nationality for the 1996/97 season – whether or not players were citizens of the EU or the EEA, which included Norway and Switzerland. From that point onwards, Manchester United were able to field the same team that had won a league or cup competition that had qualified them for European competition.

A further result of the abolition of the 3+2 rule was the removal of the premium rating for English players. It was very unlikely that transfer fees paid for certain players would have been so high if there had been no 3+2 rule which artificially inflated the value of English players to English clubs likely to be playing in European competitions.

If Peter thought the new season would be a straightforward one, he was mistaken. He would soon encounter what he would describe as 'one of the most difficult and ugly periods in the whole of my footballing career'.

Under Arsène Wenger, Arsenal would become Manchester United's most sustained challengers. Although they were to become friends, in those days of great rivalry, Alex Ferguson disliked Wenger.

The two men met for the first time on Saturday, 16 November 1996 at Old Trafford. Towards the end of the first half, Ian Wright was attacking the United goal when the ball ran away from him and was collected by Peter advancing from his line. Although he had lost control of the ball, Wright challenged with his studs showing and caught Peter. Wright was booked and Schmeichel suffered bruising to his hand.

The following Sunday, the *News of the World* published an article in which Wright accused Schmeichel of racially abusing him. A fan, having seen a video of the incident, which was televised live, had gone to the police with information that Schmeichel could be seen mouthing the words: 'You fucking black bastard.'

Wright had been shown a video of the incident by the *News of the World* and said: 'To put it politely it is not nice. The powers that be in soccer say it's down to Arsenal or Ian Wright to bring charges. But I'm not in the habit of getting my fellow professionals into trouble. I've said things myself in the heat of the moment that have got me into trouble and I'm sure that's the case with Peter Schmeichel.' Wright said he was 'hurt and saddened' by Schmeichel's outburst at Old Trafford. And he launched a stinging attack on racists everywhere: 'They are ignorant, thick and stupid. What can you say about someone who has such a problem over something as trivial as the colour of someone's skin?'

A few days later Peter received a letter from the Football Association enclosing a copy of the article and asking for his observations.

Racism is abhorrent and there can be no truck with it. But the first thing that struck me was that Wright had not heard the abuse during the play but had seen it afterwards on video. So, it could not be claimed that, even if Peter had made these remarks, he had directed them specifically at Wright. And the remarks were based on lip reading, which is very far from an exact science. It is notoriously difficult to prove exactly what a player has said just by viewing television pictures.

Peter and I had to agree a response to the FA's letter. We met up to view the videos at my offices on Thursday, 12 December.

Peter had not viewed the incident with Wright, and it was fascinating to watch a match sitting alongside a player who had taken part in it. I felt like a coach reviewing how the play had gone except this was for a very different purpose. As we watched, Peter pointed out how strong Wright's tackle was. Peter also vehemently denied that he had made any racist remarks either directly at Wright or in general.

We wrote to the FA on 17 December and the last paragraph of it is worth quoting:

> Given therefore Peter Schmeichel's assertions that he did not make the comments alleged [by the *News of the World*], the evidence of the BBC tape, your own spokesman's comment allegedly made to the *News of the World* . . . Lip reading is not an exact science. It is very difficult to prove exactly what the player has said just by viewing television pictures, and in the apparent absence of any adverse report from the match official, I trust the contents of this letter will be adequate for your purposes and the matter may now be regarded as at an end.

It was not. The events at Highbury on Wednesday, 19 February, made sure of that. In the 76th minute, Wright made a horrendous, studs-up challenge on Schmeichel that left Peter with a swollen ankle. Alex Ferguson had to be physically restrained from running onto the pitch.

Manchester United won, 2–1, to go a point clear of Liverpool at the top of the Premier League. However, in the tunnel, there was a heated confrontation between Schmeichel and Wright, who reportedly shouted: 'Don't you dare make racist remarks to me.'

The following day, the squad was at a hotel in Burnham Beeches in the Buckinghamshire countryside, preparing for Saturday's game at Chelsea. Peter's fitness was the principal concern – until the FA's spokesman, Steve Double, gave an interview to a London radio station:

> There has been a long-running police investigation into the original incident at Old Trafford. As a result of police inquiries into the alleged racist remarks, a report has been compiled and is currently being considered by the Crown Prosecution Service. During the course of the inquiry the FA has co-operated fully with police officers into the investigation.

Peter was thunderstruck. I was flabbergasted that the FA would do something like this. The club had sent me a transcript of what had been broadcast on the radio and I immediately sent a copy of it to David Davies at the FA and asked him to contact me as a matter of urgency.

By now my phone was buzzing. The media wanted answers. I had to deal with Alex and the United plc chairman, Sir Roland Smith. Alex was due to give a BBC *Grandstand* television interview on Saturday which was to be recorded and the content agreed before it could be broadcast.

The following day, I had telephone conversations with Sir Roland Smith, Alex Ferguson, Peter Schmeichel and Andrew Clement of

Grandstand regarding Alex's interview. I heard the initial tape of the interview and asked for amendments. I also asked for the original interview and the edited version to be sent to the team hotel and for the edited version to be played over to me. The next day I had further telephone conversations with Andrew Clement and Roland Smith and confirmed the edited version of the interview could be broadcast.

By this time, I had had a discussion with Davies but that had proved unsatisfactory. He claimed that from the FA point of view the matter was already in the public domain. The FA was responding to calls it had received from the *Evening Standard* and the *Daily Mail*. However, he did express regret that Double had spoken before the United club secretary, Ken Merrett, had been notified.

I decided to write formally to the FA's chief executive Graham Kelly, asking for his responses to the questions I had raised with Davies. What I wanted to know was what the FA had meant when they said that they had helped the police with their inquiries. How had the FA helped? I also asked for copies of all correspondence between the FA and the police. Graham Kelly did reply to my letter. His response was:

Thank you for your letter earlier today.
1. Presumably our Public Affairs Department felt the need to respond to queries – I don't know.
2. I don't know – please ask David Davies.
3. I don't know – I haven't seen any documentation.

With two of its prominent members in a public dispute, the PFA naturally had got involved, and I had a chat over the phone with Gordon Taylor and his deputy, Brendon Batson. Gordon told me he wanted a peace summit between his two members where they would publicly declare a truce, bring an end to the bad blood that had developed between them, and thus avoid any punishment both from the courts and the FA.

I needed to work out our strategy and had a further meeting with Peter and this time his wife, Bente, also came along. Our meeting took place at my offices on the morning of 24 February. The meeting was a long one and beforehand I had a discussion with our counsel, a barrister called Tom Shields.

There were several issues to be discussed. I had already taken advice from counsel on whether we should sue certain newspapers for writing what I considered were defamatory articles. The larger question was to decide what was best for the Schmeichels and what they wanted to achieve. We also considered Taylor's peace initiative, went over the details of the racist comments Peter was alleged to have made, and any likely police action. Peter and his wife made it clear they wanted to be vindicated yet not get too embroiled in the 'politics of football'.

The FA suggested that Manchester United, Arsenal, the FA and PFA all gather on 28 February at the Excelsior Hotel at Manchester Airport. Graham Kelly and David Davies represented the FA, Gordon Taylor the PFA, and Arsenal's David Dein came up from London. I had a much shorter drive.

In the lead-up to the meeting, both the FA and the PFA had been busy. Taylor had spoken to Wright, following which he wrote a letter to Peter. Before the meeting, the FA had drafted a statement which David Davies dictated over the telephone to my PA, Marian Lynch, that formed the basis of our talks.

David Davies, clearly briefed by the FA's lawyers, began by saying this was a meeting 'without prejudice'; in other words, what would be said or proposed would be off the record should there be a court case.

The meeting, said Davies, had been organised in order to avoid the FA having to take any action. He did not want any further public comment by either Schmeichel or Wright and instead a single joint statement would be issued by the FA. He also wanted a suitable gesture on the part of both players. Davies presented the FA as acting altruistically for the good of the game. As he spoke, I thought the FA was not

RACISM AND LIP READING

being very altruistic when Steve Double spoke to the radio station in London without any advance notice to Peter or Manchester United.

I could see immediately that Peter would find it extremely difficult to agree to the statement as it went near enough to say he had made racist comments. After about an hour, I drove to the training ground to see Peter and it was clear he could not put his signature to this FA statement.

When I came back to the hotel to inform Dein and the FA, Dein turned on me and asked why, if Wright was prepared to make a compromise, Schmeichel was not. I had to remind him sharply that Peter could face criminal charges and that he was absolutely certain he had not racially abused Wright. The arguments went back and forth and over the next twenty-four hours I spoke to Peter – often considering some wholesale revisions to the document.

The next stage in the standoff came when United played Coventry City at Old Trafford on Saturday, 1 March. David Davies was also at the match and I had a chat with him. The FA were keen to have a Sunday morning 'reconciliation' between Peter Schmeichel and Ian Wright.

There was a reason for the FA's desire to hurry things along. The following week the FA expected to have its hands full with the Bruce Grobbelaar match-fixing controversy (for which Grobbelaar was ultimately acquitted), and so the sooner the Schmeichel and Wright issue was 'put to bed' the better.

After the match had ended (a 3–1 victory for United) and Alex Ferguson had finished his media duties, Alex, Peter and I met. Apart from not accepting in any way that he had made racist comments, Peter was not prepared to attend any press conference which the FA was trying to organise on the Sunday morning. Peter was very firm on this, and I rang Davies to tell him so.

That evening as I drove home mulling over the issues, I thought a way round this impasse would be for Peter and Ian to make their own statements with a third statement from the FA but no press conference. The next morning my phone lines were busy as I spoke to Davies, Dein, Ferguson and Schmeichel. Davies said that he would discuss the position with Kelly.

Kelly's response was to write to Peter, and he also decided to make sure the world knew what he had written as he felt this served the game's interests. It was clear that with more than the game's interest in mind, Kelly wanted to answer media criticism that the FA was sitting on its hands. Neil Harman in the *Daily Mail* had written that Kelly 'cannot raise himself to address the Wright-Schmeichel debacle'.

We had to respond, and I did so by reiterating that Peter was prepared to take any reasonable steps which would 'put an end to the present controversy'.

There was then much toing and froing between us and the FA, not helped by further inaccurate press comment with various spurious claims and allegations of Peter's standpoint. In the midst of this there was one comment which lightened the mood. Kelly had been suggested as a peacemaker, to which one columnist wrote: 'If so, to coincide with Comic Relief, would he wear a red nose and stand between the two players shaking hands? Graham Kelly apparently thinks this is quite a nice idea.'

On 14 March, Peter and Manchester United instructed me to write to the FA with a statement agreed by him and the club. The timing of the statement was to coincide with any statement issued by the FA and Ian Wright. We were to see any proposed FA statement prior to its release.

Unfortunately, this very positive step on Peter's part did not do the trick and the deadlock continued. By this time Peter was away playing for Denmark against Croatia but we spoke often on the phone as I kept him informed of the developments.

* * *

RACISM AND LIP READING

Matters finally came to a head on 10 April, when Graham Kelly wrote to Peter enclosing an FA press statement that was to be released to the media after 5pm.

The FA claimed that it had to bring the matter to a close – which required us to send a formal response reminding the FA, if it needed reminding, of the statement Peter had been prepared to issue some weeks previously. It is worth recording the terms of that statement:

> Peter Schmeichel is dismayed at the recent publicity which has been given to an alleged feud between him and Ian Wright. No such feud exists. Nothing that Peter Schmeichel has said or done has been intended to undermine the fair spirit in which professional football is played or to give offence, racially or otherwise. Peter Schmeichel is happy, at the request of the FA, to make his position clear and regrets if any other false impression has been given.

In his autobiography Peter wrote:

> I would not be a pawn in a political game and, irrespective of how much pressure was put on us, I stood my ground. I had not made racist remarks, and I am not, by any stretch of the imagination, a racist... Fortunately I received 100 per cent support from the club throughout this torrid time, and Maurice Watkins knew how to keep ice cool, which was a huge bonus. With his sharp legal brain he was able continually to undermine the arguments put forward in the FA's letters, to the point that eventually they began to run out of real evidence... In a concluding letter, Watkins pulled the FA's statement apart, and we thought it necessary to emphasise the following point. 'Peter Schmeichel intends to continue to behave as he has always done, as a responsible professional footballer. As far as he is concerned, he has not received any "bad marks" for his

conduct, and he intends, should it be necessary, to produce strong arguments against any allegations to the contrary.'[18]

There is support for his position from what might be an unlikely source: Graham Kelly. In *Sweet FA* Graham Kelly wrote:

> I received expressions of regret from both sides and a wider recognition of the wider interests of the game. Ian Wright was still deeply upset that what he insisted had been genuine attempts to win the ball were being misinterpreted. Manchester United had said Peter Schmeichel was not a racist and never would be. That was the best we could do. Neither would apologise.
>
> I was very disappointed. I learned a lesson that, if you become involved in something like that, you have to be confident that you are going to settle it, and quite clearly we had not been able to reach an agreed position to which both sides could put their signatures. It was our statement which came out and that was a watered-down version of what we had hoped to achieve when we first looked at the incident.
>
> I could quite clearly see that Ian Wright would have been prepared to apologise for being over exuberant or getting carried away, but the issue with Schmeichel was a much bigger one, going to the heart of a major national concern at a delicate time . . .
>
> As far as I was concerned, I was not going to charge Schmeichel on the evidence of a lip-reader's examination of the video recording of the incident. It would have been farcical, had I done so. It was one of the least satisfying results during my tenure at the FA and left more questions than answers.[19]

The Football Association did not commence any disciplinary proceedings against either party relating to the two incidents, nor were any criminal proceedings instituted.

19

A Transfer with a Twist

Karel Poborsky had much in common with Andrei Kanchelskis. Both were from eastern Europe, both were signed to bolster the right-hand side of Manchester United's attack, and I found myself dealing with their transfers long after they had left Old Trafford.

Kanchelskis would make a far greater impression on Manchester United, but Poborsky came to Old Trafford with a sizeable reputation after some excellent performances for the Czech Republic at Euro '96.

Alex Ferguson had been very impressed by Poborsky, watching Germany beat the Czech Republic in a group game at Old Trafford. The two teams would contest the final at Wembley. Since Poborsky had helped his club, Slavia Prague, reach the semi-finals of the UEFA Cup, he was a hot ticket. Liverpool were also interested.

The Israeli agent, Pini Zahavi, who had close ties to Manchester United, put me in touch with Poborsky's agent, Pavel Paska, and I met him in Geneva on 9 July. I was fascinated by Paska. He seemed to be acting for the whole of the Czech national team. He had secured such a hold over Czech football because he had looked after the players from an early stage and had nourished their development. Paska told me that he was so much part of their lives that he had paid the players' medical and dental bills.

Our talks went well. Poborsky was keen to move and it was clear we would have no problems agreeing a salary for him. But then an over-keen member of the United staff caused problems by getting ahead of himself and I had to step in to make sure we were not accused of a football offence. As the Czech Republic was then not part of the European Union there was no free movement of labour, so we needed a work permit from the Home Office.

Football had a points-based system for non-EU players. A panel composed of football experts evaluated whether the player was entitled to get the work permit based on such things as the FIFA football ranking of the country and how often the player has played for his country. This member of the United staff, no doubt trying to be helpful, wrote to Slavia Prague for details of Poborsky's playing career to help make the work permit application.

With terms not formally agreed, this was not something we were entitled to do, and we could have been seen as 'poaching' the player. Slavia Prague were not amused, and I quickly wrote to the Czech club to cool matters down. They understood and on 12 July I flew out to Prague to finalise the deal.

There was quite a party waiting for me as I arrived at the city's InterContinental Hotel. It included the Slavia Prague president, Vladimir Laska, his lawyer, Poborsky, Paska and also Poborsky's lawyer, Dr Jiri Suchauek.

As in all such negotiations the haggling was over the price, and our talks lasted all day before an agreement was reached and we shook hands on a deal. There was still the paperwork to be signed and it was, of course, subject to obtaining a work permit but I did not anticipate any problems regarding that.

I had every reason to think no one knew of my visit. Prague was not yet the place where the British went for cheap beer and stag nights and there was hardly a British face to be seen as I slipped in and out. But I had no sooner got back to Manchester, than the Press Association (PA), a news agency that did not deal in gossip, was running a story about my visit and suggesting that there might be a classic transfer heist.

A TRANSFER WITH A TWIST

PA described how, as I had flown home from Prague confident of concluding a £3.4 million deal, Roy Evans, the Liverpool manager, had made 'a top-secret dash to Prague' to take Poborsky 'from under the noses of Manchester United'. If PA knew about it, the dash was clearly not that secret.

If there was any interest from Liverpool, this soon cooled and Poborsky and Paska arrived in Manchester on 23 July and we put them up in the Crowne Plaza Hotel. The transfer seemed to be going without hassles. The medicals went well. We even agreed to play a match against Slavia Prague at Old Trafford. The Czechs were not asking for a lot of money for the fixture, £200,000 plus travel and accommodation expenses.

However, when I flew back to Prague six days later to finalise the financial agreement, Slavia Prague did ask for more money and I had to put my foot down. But I agreed that they could get a modest percentage of any sell-on fee over and above what we had paid them if and when we sold Poborsky. What I did not anticipate was how soon we would be selling Poborsky.

Karel Poborsky was paraded at Old Trafford as one of five summer signings – the others were Raimond van der Gouw, brought in as a back-up keeper to Peter Schmeichel; the Barcelona midfielder, Jordi Cruyff; and two Norwegians – Ronny Johnsen and Ole Gunnar Solskjær. The last two would play major roles in the 1999 Champions League final against Bayern Munich. But by then, Poborsky was long gone.

His first season had been reasonably successful. He had collected a Premier League title winner's medal, playing in twenty-two out of thirty-eight league games and scoring four goals, and helped United reach the Champions League semi-final which was lost to Borussia Dortmund.

However, Poborsky could hardly get in the side in the 1997/98 season. He started just six of United's matches in all competitions.

That brought us face to face with the work permit, as legislation laid down by the Department for Education and Employment stated that an imported player must appear in 75 per cent of the club's first-team matches if he is fully fit. The question was, who would buy him? Pini Zahavi, having helped us buy Poborsky, as so often, came up with the answer.

Pini had been in discussion with the Benfica president, Joao Vale e Azevedo, and he rang me to say we could do a deal with the Portuguese club. Pini did a great selling job on Azevedo, a lawyer with magnificent offices who was such a powerful man that he was being touted as the next prime minister of Portugal.

I must confess the more Pini sold Azevedo the more doubts rose in my mind, and the transfer would mean a loss of well over a million on the £3.5 million we had paid. However, Alex Ferguson had no further use for the player and the transaction moved quickly.

It was due to be concluded on 30 December 1997, with the transfer fee of £2 million, payable in three instalments supported by promissory notes and with a corporate guarantee. A promissory note is an unconditional promise to pay a sum of money on a particular date; the corporate guarantee was by way of additional security. Poborsky also waived his right to the balance of his signing-on fee. The transfer was completed at the FA's offices at Lancaster Gate, ensuring the speedy issue of the international clearance certificate to the Portuguese FA.

Just when it looked like it was all settled, we had a letter from Azevedo. Benfica were being incorporated as a public company and making a public share offer to raise £35 million. Azevedo told us: 'In order not to prejudice in any way this operation we have been advised that we should not issue any letters of credit or bank guarantees. If we did, it would weaken our position with regard to some of the banks which are backing this operation.'

A TRANSFER WITH A TWIST

Martin Edwards, Roland Smith and I had a chat about the quite dramatic changes Azevedo was proposing, but in the end we agreed to proceed with the amendments he wanted to make to the security provisions. We were soon to realise we were putting our trust in a man who could not be trusted.

Benfica failed to pay the first promissory note. Azevedo, however, was ready with an explanation – the flotation had been delayed. Therefore, it was not possible to make the payment of £1 million due on 1 February 1998. Azevedo said the first payment would come after Benfica's flotation, which he expected to be completed in two weeks' time.

Two weeks passed, and we did not receive the £1 million. I rang Azevedo and by now it was clear to me he was making excuses. We decided to make a complaint to FIFA.

New procedures had been laid down by the Players' Status Committee which imposed a process of three interventions. Interventions were a new procedure brought in by FIFA to deal with the ever-growing number of cases of clubs failing to fulfil their financial obligations. The interventions are imposed by FIFA. Offending clubs are given a deadline of payment of debt plus interest. In the event of non-payment, the defaulting club could receive a ban on international transfers. The case could be referred to the FIFA Disciplinary Committee, who could impose a ban on any involvement in future competitions.

I informed Azevedo of this and was bombarded with faxes and telephone calls from him. He spoke good English – my Portuguese is non-existent – and he assured me that the first promissory note would be paid and once again explained why we had not received the money.

The more phone calls I had with him the more I became convinced he was not going to pay, and I soon made it very clear to him that I did not believe he was a man of his word. That did not please him. My response was, what else could I say given his behaviour? However, what struck me as very curious, was that for a man whom I did not believe I could trust he never failed to take my calls or respond to my requests that he ring me back. He always rang back.

Convinced we would not get our money, I wrote to FIFA, asking that we now wanted the whole of the outstanding payments as there had been a failure to pay the first. The press got hold of this information and there was much written about the breakdown in the amicable relationships between the clubs which had been enjoyed since our two epic European Cup ties in 1966 and 1968.

Poborsky was back to the brilliant form he had displayed in the European Championships and his efforts had been largely instrumental in lifting Benfica into second place behind Porto in the Portuguese league.

Despite the fact that FIFA's circular had said we could approach them directly, FIFA held to its traditional position that clubs never approach them directly but should go through their own FAs. We decided not to get into a wrangle over this and I rang the relevant officials at our FA. The FA took it up directly with the Portuguese FA and we learned we were not the only potential victims of Azevedo: FIFA were already dealing with a similar case involving Brian Deane and his transfer from Sheffield United to Benfica.

Azevedo contested our claim with a raft of spurious arguments which were ultimately rejected by FIFA and its Players' Status Committee, which issued a ruling on 29 April 1998 that the full amount owed to Manchester United be paid within thirty days.

But still there was no money; only promises that we would be paid. This time Azevedo said it would be from a sale of part of Benfica's real estate. The property had to have been worth a lot as it soon emerged that Benfica also owed $1 million to Maccabi Haifa for the Ukrainian midfielder Serhiy Kandaurov.

FIFA warned the Portuguese League that, if the money was not paid by 23 June, the case would be sent to the FIFA Disciplinary Committee, where sanctions could be imposed on Benfica.

A TRANSFER WITH A TWIST

Four days before the deadline expired, my secretary, Marian, opened the post to find a letter from Azevedo with a cheque for £2 million. My suspicions were immediately aroused. This was not a Benfica cheque but a cheque from Sojifa Limited, a company I had never heard of. I was not surprised when it bounced. Sheffield United had also received a cheque from Sojifa Limited, for Brian Deane. Instead of a sum, it was made out to 'For what it's worth'. Not anything, of course.

There were yet more phone calls and letters, and Azevedo agreed to restructure the agreement and a new one was entered into. By this time substantial interest had accrued on the debt.

This new agreement included a provision under which Benfica agreed to assign to United any moneys which were due to Benfica for their participation in UEFA competitions in 1998/99. Benfica also paid us and Sheffield United £200,000 each.

UEFA had now taken over from FIFA to help us get the money. I had a meeting with Markus Studer, the UEFA deputy general secretary, in Manchester on 18 August. Finally, the Benfica safe was unlocked and on 21 December we were paid, including interest, costs and expenses incurred in pursuing the claim.

The only sour note in all this came when Marcel Benz, UEFA's head of the Professional Football Section, whom I also knew well, wrote to United, Benfica and the Portuguese FA saying that: 'We furthermore remind all parties that in the future UEFA will not be willing to undertake this kind of job anymore.'

Thankful as I was for UEFA's help, I felt very strongly that Benz's 'we shall not help anymore' was a wrong attitude and wrote to him saying:

> I think it would be a mistake if UEFA was unwilling to give effect to this kind of arrangement that was provided for in the MUFC/Benfica case as this helped to implement the arrangement for payment of overdue moneys from one European club to another and demonstrated the effectiveness of the 'footballing laws'. I think

that any example which proves those laws are a more effective remedy than proceedings through the national courts is in the interest of the game.

During this saga I had not thought that Azevedo was a crook but more of a chancer. In fact, he was utterly corrupt. There were a series of investigations into his siphoning-off of money from transfers.

He was forced out of the Benfica presidency in 2000, expelled from the club five years later, charged with various counts of embezzlement, sentenced to several prison terms in Portugal, and was eventually extradited from London in November 2012 after turning himself in at a police station in Belgravia, following the issuing of a European arrest warrant.

He was convicted of six criminal offences and sentenced to ten years in prison on 2 July 2013, and ordered to pay Benfica around €7 million for the money he had kept from the transfers of footballers Scott Minto, Gary Charles, Tahar El Khalej and Amaral. On 7 June 2016, Joao Vale e Azevedo was released from prison on parole.

20

The Boys from the Milan Tennis Club

It was called Operation Parsifal after the opera by Richard Wagner about a search for the Holy Grail. For the major clubs of Europe, the Grail was a European Super League that would guarantee vast revenues.

It all began innocently enough. In May 1998 Manchester United's chief executive, Peter Kenyon, and I were invited to Brazil to take part in a seminar on the management of sport business organised by the Getulio Vargas Foundation in Sao Paulo.

The foundation worked closely with Pele, who had been Minister of Sport in Brazil and was a good friend of Manchester United. It was agreed that I would speak on two subjects: first, 'Structuring for Success – the English Premier League Football', followed a day or so later with 'The Profitability of the Football Leagues – the Experience of the British and the Italian Football Leagues'. I was to combine the second talk with Rodolfo Hecht Lucari, the president of Media Partners. Media Partners was a Milan-based sports marketing consultancy that advised the Italian Serie A League on its television contracts, and which had a strong record in the sports rights business.

However, I did not arrive at the InterContinental until a few minutes before the conference was due to start, and I was the first speaker. I had a few minutes to change my shirt and then I was off to deliver my first contribution.

These conferences, bringing together as they do people who run football and many legal and media experts, are always full of intrigue and gossip but this one was even more so. Every now and again I could see people huddling in corners for confidential discussions. The catalyst for these was the presence of a number of representatives from Media Partners. They were in Sao Paulo to promote Project Parsifal: the codename for a new European club competition to replace the UEFA Champions League.

Kenyon knew Peter Ekelund, a Swedish executive with Media Partners, and the three of us met in the bar of the InterContinental where the project was outlined to us. What was proposed was the establishment of a midweek league made up of either twenty-four or thirty-two clubs whose membership would be partly determined by status and partly by merit.

The radical principle at the heart of the concept was that the founder clubs would enjoy permanent membership of the league by virtue of their size and wealth. AC Milan had just failed to qualify for the Champions League and for a club of its pedigree not to be in the top European competition was considered an outrage by its owner, Silvio Berlusconi. I was interested in what the men from Milan had to say, and Peter and I agreed to meet them in London to discuss their plans in detail.

On 3 June, Peter and I attended a meeting at the London offices of Media Partners' lawyers Slaughter & May. Peter Ekelund, accompanied by Slaughter & May, was about to go to Brussels to meet the European Commission to explain their ideas. We discussed the proposals for the European Super League and certain regulatory issues. In front of us was the document Media Partners would be taking to Brussels.

My problem was this could cause enormous problems for

Manchester United and the Premier League. At that very moment the Premier League and the Office of Fair Trading (OFT) were locked in a court battle, the outcome of which could have enormous implications for televised football in England.

The OFT had taken the Premier League to the Restrictive Practices Court, with John Bridgeman, director general of the OFT, saying that the League was acting illegally when it negotiated TV rights to its matches, rather than letting each Premiership club strike separate deals.

If United had the Super League document, then under the 'discovery' provisions of a court case this document would have to be disclosed to the OFT and could affect the outcome of the case. I consulted Patrick Talbot QC, and after further discussions with Slaughter & May it was agreed that there was no effective way the documentation could be passed to Manchester United without that documentation having to be disclosed to the OFT. The only way to avoid that would be for Peter and me to look at the documents, not make notes, and for me and Peter to advise the board orally.

We then realised this was a ridiculous way of dealing with a matter which could be of such commercial value. Litigation would not be welcome and would be costly but the commercial cost of not being involved in the Media Partners discussion would outweigh that.

It was clear to me and Peter that the European Super League (ESL) was a viable possibility. This meant that it was commercially essential that I should prepare a full report for the board. While I was doing this, Media Partners called a meeting of what were called the founder clubs – Juventus, AC Milan, Inter Milan, Bayern Munich, Borussia Dortmund, Manchester United, Liverpool, Arsenal, Real Madrid, Barcelona, Paris Saint-Germain, Olympique Marseille, Benfica, Ajax, Panathinaikos and Galatasaray.

Before the meeting I had a chat with Rick Parry, who had moved from being chief executive of the Premier League to take charge of Liverpool FC.

His view was that the project was politically flawed from a footballing sporting perspective, being built on a franchise as opposed to a merit basis. He had sounded out a number of clubs and the impression was that it was a device to get more money out of UEFA from their competitions. There was a nervousness about going to the meeting and no one wanted to be identified as being present. If there were twelve clubs to sign, then everyone wanted to be the twelfth club to sign up.

Liverpool did not attend, but we decided we should. The meeting took place at Slaughter & May on 2 July. Twelve of the founding clubs were present with another four who were not equal partners. There were at least fifty-two people in the room, including bankers and lawyers. By now the code name for the project was 'Gandalf'.

It turned out to be a very busy day. One meeting succeeded another as the pressure to get clubs to an agreement mounted. A second draft Founders Clubs' Agreement was circulated. There was a table of 'Market Value Points' which showed how the guaranteed minimum payment of $1.333 billion for the first season would be distributed to all the participating clubs. Six clubs had the highest 'market value' point: Juventus, AC Milan, Real Madrid, Barcelona, Manchester United and Bayern Munich. These clubs' share would be $8,333,330 each.

It was interesting to see what the principles were which were identified as being fundamental to the creation of the pan-European football competition. The pan-European club competition would be wholly owned by the participating clubs. The competition would lead to the creation of real market value. Clubs would also be able to predict how much they would earn, which would be very attractive. Apart from the big clubs, the competition would also have other clubs whose participation would depend on their performances the previous season. Project Gandalf also wanted all Super League clubs to continue to take part in their domestic competitions and to maintain strong, competitive and financially viable domestic football competitions.

The document explained that signature of the agreement would initially be nothing more than an indication of interest in the ESL. This would enable Media Partners to instruct JP Morgan to launch the formal bank syndication process. This would help put in place a bank facility of an aggregate of US $3.233 billion which would guarantee the clubs in the ESL minimum participation fees and prize money of that amount over the first three seasons of the competition.

Following the meeting, Peter and I were involved in a few days of lengthy conversations with a number of key individuals including Arsenal's vice-chairman David Dein, chief executive of the Premier League Peter Leaver, and Nic Coward of the FA.

By then the story of our meetings had leaked and, as was to be expected, UEFA reacted. Gerhard Aigner, the UEFA general secretary, dubbed Media Partners 'The boys from the Milan tennis club' and added: 'We are determined to defend the Champions League by all available means. We have to safeguard football for the future and for everyone.'

UEFA had support from its national associations, but I found it interesting that the English Football Association had accepted that change was necessary. Graham Kelly said, 'Generally speaking I would favour a re-structuring of the Champions League under the auspices of UEFA. I am not greatly in favour of breakaway situations of the kind envisaged. Whether or not UEFA can produce a format that will appease all the leading European clubs is the 64,000-dollar question.'

The meetings to set up the European Super League continued at the London offices of Slaughter & May. On 23–24 July we were updated on commercial rights, the regulatory position and the bank facility. The proposed agenda for the 24th was the availability of the franchise club agreement for signature, information from JP Morgan, and further discussions on the potential role for UEFA and the establishment of ESL Working Committees.

Manchester United had to play a very clever game. We were not the instigators of the project but press reports made it seem as if we were. United were always mentioned.

Behind the scenes, however, I was working with the finance director, David Gill, going through the latest draft of the Founder Clubs' Agreement and putting in our amendments. In addition, we were drafting marketing and intellectual property rights agreements.

I had spoken to Peter Leaver at the Premier League and was very surprised when, on 28 July, United, along with Liverpool and Arsenal, received a faxed letter from the lawyers Herbert Smith, acting for the Premier League.

This was a carefully drafted legal letter which held out various threats. The letter referred to discussions that were reported to have taken place regarding the establishment of a 'European Super League'. Also, that: 'there are financial incentives in favour of signing up to the proposal by this Friday, 31st July 1998 or shortly thereafter.'

Herbert Smith then listed the Rules of the Premier League and FA which bound the clubs. In essence this meant that clubs could only play in competitions which had been formed with the consent of the Premier League or the FA.

There was one other line in the letter which had great relevance to me personally. Herbert Smith also referred to the FA Premier League Chairmen's Charter which said: 'We will ensure that our clubs ... behave with the utmost good faith and honesty to each other.'

I could not help smiling as I read that. For I had drafted the charter for the Premier League at the request of Rick Parry. When I was asked to do it there was nowhere to look for a precedent for the drafting. So, I collected together a number of utility suppliers' agreements with gas and electricity customers and picked out some salient clauses from there. I sent the document over to Rick as a draft, expecting to receive a number of comments. I never heard anything back from him. Sometime later I was in Martin Edwards's office and there was a new framed document on his wall. It was the Chairmen's Charter. Rick had approved it without amendment, had it printed and framed and sent it to all Premier League chairmen with a request that it was put on their office wall. Now here was my own charter being quoted back at me.

The letter went on to request an undertaking from the clubs involved in the ESL that they would not continue discussions or sign up to the proposed Super League without first obtaining consent from the Premier League. They also asked for full details of the negotiation to date. Failing a satisfactory response by close of business on 29 July, Herbert Smith said they were instructed by the Premier League to issue High Court proceedings seeking an injunction.

The moment the news of this potential legal action broke, my phone never stopped ringing; other clubs, radio, television and the press were all wanting to talk.

I spent the remainder of 28 July and the next day at the offices of Slaughter & May with Patrick Talbot, representatives of Media Partners, Danny Fiszman and Ken Friar of Arsenal and their lawyer Michael Waugh. Danny had made his money in diamonds and was a director and major shareholder. Ken had started work in the box office at Highbury in 1950 and had risen through the ranks to become first company secretary and then managing director.

Every now and again I had to leave them in order to talk on the phone with Martin Edwards and David Gill. After several telephone conversations with Peter Leaver, it was agreed that the Premier League letter would be withdrawn and Arsenal and Manchester United would write to the Premier League. It was decided I would, as a director of Manchester United, write the letter to Peter Leaver.

Dear Peter

Following our conversation I confirm that we shall not sign up to any additional or alternative European competition before the Premier League members have had an opportunity to meet (on 20th August) to have a presentation on the 'European Super League'.

As agreed, however, in the meantime we shall be continuing to be involved in the discussions relating to the proposals and, in particular, the drafting of documentation.

Thank you, Peter, for confirming that the Herbert Smith letter is withdrawn and does not require a reply.

Ken Friar wrote a similar letter.

While this was going on, Gerhard Aigner of UEFA wrote to all the 'founder' clubs stating: 'May I advise you to refrain from committing yourself to this project launched by a private organisation and instead wait for the consultations to take place with UEFA in this matter.'

The letter was accompanied by a press release which contained the sting in its tail: 'UEFA takes it for granted that its clubs in question will not make any commitment to any such private party which would jeopardise their future participation in national and international competitions.'

An interesting comment from UEFA about 'national' competitions. For what is UEFA if nothing but a competition organiser?

For men in shorts to kick a ball you need men in suits with papers and briefcases working out rules and regulations. In that sense football is a trade whose trade body is the FA which licenses clubs; without an FA licence a club could not play competitive football in this country.

For the Premier League to be formed, the FA had to approve the First Division clubs breaking away from the old, united Football League. All clubs who belong to the FA agree to take part in the FA Cup – this was to cause Manchester United no end of a problem a few years later. The FA is also a regulatory body – although as Gordon Taylor, the long-standing chief executive of the PFA, has often said: the FA rarely exercises its regulatory powers.

Football has its own language. So, when football rules are broken such as a club poaching a player it is described as 'illegal', when it is not illegal as far as the law of the land is concerned, merely the law of the trade association run by the FA.

Player contracts are different to employment contracts as they cannot be terminated in the way employment contracts can. Also, players cannot decide to leave a club. They need the permission of the club they are playing for. Without the club granting a transfer, the player will not have a right to play for another club.

UEFA, however, was different from the FA. It comprises European football associations and they had come together to take part in competitions organised by UEFA. UEFA did not license the national associations, but you have to belong to UEFA to take part in their competitions.

Aigner was keen to maintain the public pressure on us and in a full-page interview in *The Times* on 1 August identified Silvio Berlusconi as having instigated the move towards a Super League:

> This is a serious threat. If the presence of Manchester United or Real Madrid is not guaranteed, you cannot pay some outsiders to launch such a venture but, as Europe's governing body, we cannot agree a concept that does not involve qualification.
>
> It goes against the credibility of all competition and, where we have to satisfy the grass roots of football, we must protect the national identities of the associations. We have to listen to the opinions and balance the needs for the good of the game. What we offer is continuity of integrity. We will not allow football to be torn apart with different fragments and I'm sorry to say that, after the European Commission rubbed the face of football into the dirt

(over the Bosman ruling) we have become quite hardened to our task.

In the past, UEFA had always shown a disdainful attitude to the clubs and talked only to the football associations. But now Aigner approached Ken Friar to arrange a meeting with Arsenal, Liverpool and Manchester United.

We could not meet at one of the clubs as the media attention would make it difficult to be kept secret. The obvious place was my offices in King Street, Manchester. It had a back door for vehicular access via a lift.

The advantage was that journalists would be watching the front door and not observing the rear, which was on a narrow, one-way street. The lift was in a garage, which had its own limitations with a series of pillars which needed careful negotiation. Alex Ferguson came unstuck on one occasion while driving me out, making a serious dent on the passenger side of his new Audi.

But while we wanted to keep the meeting a secret as far as the media was concerned, it was no secret to the Premier League as I had told Peter Leaver about it.

On the morning of Tuesday, 18 August, Aigner, accompanied by his number two, Markus Studer, came to my office using the back-door entrance. Arsenal were represented by Ken Friar and Danny Fiszman. To see Danny there but not David Dein confirmed that there had been a split in the Highbury board about Media Partners. Dein from the start had always been keen on the breakaway league, but Fiszman and Peter Hill-Wood, the Old Etonian chairman of Arsenal, were not and it was clear which camp had won.

Liverpool were represented by Peter Robinson, who had been club secretary at Anfield since 1965, and chief executive Rick Parry. I was well aware that their stance was cautious, although the cynic often said Liverpool came late to the party and drank all the champagne.

Manchester United had Martin Edwards, Peter Kenyon and me. Before Aigner arrived the three clubs had a chat to discuss our strategy.

The meeting was an amicable one. Aigner reiterated his view that the project was a 'pure' TV contract made by television not football people. He told us UEFA's experts had queried the TV figures and that our television income would be less than Media Partners envisaged.

He felt the project had been a 'raid' on European football to be used to facilitate the proposers' own purposes. The European Super League would involve a fight with domestic leagues. 'Gandalf' was a cartel.

Where was the judicial background for the project? There was no clear picture about what Media Partners and their backers were. Any signature by clubs to the agreement would weaken UEFA.

UEFA, he warned, would endeavour to block the project but that did not mean it was not possible to achieve the financial objectives of the clubs with something similar. It was necessary, however, to run competitions according to sporting principles with the normal need for qualification. UEFA's task was to keep the door open to all members. Movement of clubs was integral. With 'Gandalf' there would be no Dynamo Kyiv – who would make the Champions League semi-finals in 1999.

One point he did concede was that there needed to be a forum for clubs to talk directly to UEFA not through federations and national leagues. Tradition needed to deal with new business needs. He said UEFA were six weeks away from new sporting concepts, with the resulting contracts to run from the season 2000/01.

I had been appointed to the ESL's Shareholder Agreement Committee and had also become a spokesman for the clubs. Clubs like Chelsea, who had not been included, were opposed to Media Partners and made no secret of their dislike of the idea. Just before the Premier League's meeting with Media Partners on 3 September, I was asked to comment by journalists and said: 'We expect there to be a frank exchange of views. I expect a lot of things will become clearer after that.'

What I could not have anticipated was how Martin Edwards would behave. It would prove to be the major surprise of the meeting.

Much of the meeting went as you would expect. Media Partners, led by Rodolfo Hecht Lucari, their president, made their presentation, which went reasonably well. It was made clear that the ESL would be open and accountable. It would be wholly owned by the clubs.

Involvement in the ESL would be based solely on the performance of teams on the pitch ('sports merit'). The ESL would comprise two competitions – the Super League and the Pro Cup involving in total 132 clubs from all the territories covered by UEFA's associations. All matches would be played on Tuesday, Wednesday or Thursday, so the new competition would work with national leagues.

After Rodolfo departed, Aigner came in and told us about UEFA's plans to reorganise European competitions, which would be considered by UEFA's Executive Committee on 10–11 December. The Champions League would be expanded to thirty-two clubs while the UEFA Cup would move from a straight knockout competition to involve initial group stages.

Peter Leaver proposed that the clubs agree that all future discussions with Media Partners and any other body on the question of the organisation of European competitions should involve the Premier League board alone and no club should have any further involvement in such discussions.

The clubs sit in alphabetical order round the Premier League with the chief executive or chairman, or whoever is the lead representative of the club, in front and other representatives sat behind them.

Martin Edwards always occupied the premier seat that United had at the table and as Leaver went round, Martin voted in favour of the motion. Peter Kenyon and I looked at each other stunned and knew that this was a killer blow to Manchester United's efforts to remain involved. Did Martin realise what he had voted for? I am not so sure.

Perhaps he felt that things were going to change and the value of Media Partners as a 'stalking horse' was over. To be fair to him he had not been as involved in the new league as Peter and I had been. Maybe we should have briefed him before the meeting and agreed our line.

To complicate matters further, Peter Leaver made it clear that all future dialogue on any European competition should be conducted through him alone. I was not best pleased and made it clear that Manchester United should be on a working party in any further dialogue with Media Partners since we had been involved in all previous discussions on the subject.

One immediate issue involved what should happen to the meeting Peter Kenyon had arranged with the European Commission's Head of Competitions Karel van Miert on the EC's stance on the proposals. It was agreed with Leaver that Peter would go, and that I would attend a meeting of the clubs with Media Partners but report back not to the clubs but to the Premier League.

But could the Premier League's banning of Arsenal and Manchester United from taking part in Super League discussions with Media Partners be investigated by the Office of Fair Trading? The OFT met with Slaughter & May and it was decided that, if the ban constituted a 'new agreement' which should be registered under the Restrictive Trade Practices Act, then it would be declared void and unenforceable.

Media Partners had also formally complained to the European Commission about what they considered an infringement of competition rules. Media Partners claimed that UEFA was abusing their position by preventing new bodies from organising and marketing football competitions in Europe. The European Commission sent out questionnaires to us and a few other clubs involved in the Gandalf project. The Commission wanted to assess the compatibility of the agreement and practices in question with European Union rules on competition.

In the end, as was perhaps to be expected, it all petered out. A few days later Peter Kenyon and I reviewed this situation and concluded that it was not appropriate for us to attend meetings with our hands tied. Peter sent a fax on 7 September to Van Miert apologising to him for not being present in Brussels. I did not see any point in going to a meeting of the clubs with Media Partners and told Peter Leaver as much.

UEFA, having been caught unawares by Media Partners, revamped the Champions League. The expansion to a thirty-two-team group stage began a year early in 1999. Having seen off Media Partners, Aigner dismissed them, saying, UEFA 'is not particularly worried' about further pressure on the European body from the clubs in the future. 'It is not so much the clubs who have developed the ideas, it is the television market which has developed ideas. I think the clubs are very comfortable to stay with us.'

Aigner was rewriting history. Aigner and UEFA were very worried by the Media Partners project. Aigner not only attended and spoke at the Premier League meeting, he went to the meeting in my office with Manchester United, Arsenal and Liverpool. That was clearly indicative of his concern. It is unlikely that UEFA would have brought in the changes they did, with increased revenue for clubs, if there had not been the stimulus of Media Partners' attempted coup.

Media Partners – the boys from the Milan tennis club – had forced UEFA to change and deal fairly with the clubs. In fact, the Media Partners project was not a stalking horse, it was a serious challenge to the status quo. The financing was there, and considerable sums of money and effort were put into the project; but, in reality, it would only benefit a number of the bigger clubs and even many big clubs would have been left in their wake.

Certainly, the Premier League clubs, other than Manchester United, Liverpool and Arsenal, did not like the Media Partners proposals. So, the grand design fizzled out.

I had little time to dwell on these issues. For even as the Media Partners–UEFA battle was going on, in another part of the City of

Ian Wright's challenge on United's Peter Schmeichel at Highbury on 19 February 1997. Along with the incident on 16 November 1996, it embroiled me in legal issues with club and the FA.

The dressing room after lifting the Premier League title in 1997, with (from left to right) Bobby Charlton, David Beckham, Mike Edelson, Eric Cantona, Brian Kidd and Ryan Giggs.

Ole Gunnar Solskjær's last-minute winner sealed the treble for United, who were crowned European champions at the Nou Camp for the first time since 1968.

Above: With my friend Alex, a man I have much respect for.

Right: Representing Cyril the Swan, Swansea City's mischievous mascot, at his disciplinary hearing before the Welsh Football Association on 23 April 1999.

We did it again! Alex with his second Champions League trophy after beating Chelsea on penalties in Moscow, 21 May 2008.

When it all comes together: the elusive treble.

Above: Snapshot from the Old Trafford boardroom.

Right: Receiving my CBE in 2012 at Buckingham Palace from the (then) Prince of Wales for services to charity. A very proud moment.

Above: Parading the Premier League trophy through the streets of Manchester on 30 May 2011. Two days earlier we lost out on the Champions League trophy when we lost 3–1 to Barcelona at Wembley.

Left: Courtside in my role as Chair of the British Basketball Federation.

Right: Cheering on Team GB at the Rio Olympics 2016 with my partner Elaine.

Below: An audience with Pope Francis in his private quarters at the Vatican in 2018. As Chair of British Swimming, I presented His Holiness with a framed swimming cap. I wonder how often he's used it.

In the Royal Box at Wembley in my role as chairman of Barnsley FC at the League One play-off final, 29 May 2016. Barnsley beat Millwall 3–1 to gain promotion to the Championships.

Graduating all over again. Receiving an honorary doctorate for Law and Sports from the University of Bolton in 2017.

London a very different conflict had started. An attempted takeover of Manchester United.

Indeed, even as Peter and I were going to meetings at Slaughter & May, our presence was required at another City office – that of the HSBC Bank. On one occasion, when we were not at HSBC, my phone rang and it was an anxious David Gill asking: 'Where are you both?'

Rupert Murdoch had come calling. This battle, unlike the Media Partners one, would develop into a major war whose reverberations can still be felt.

21

The Bid

As we travelled on the train from Manchester to London, Martin Edwards and I had no inkling we were going to a meeting on entirely false pretences.

It was 1 July 1998 and we would be seeing Mark Booth, the chief executive of BSkyB, to discuss pay-per-view broadcasting. Halfway through lunch at the Sky offices in Isleworth, Booth suddenly made a confession.[20]

'Look, Martin. I have got you here under false pretences. When I rang to invite you for the lunch I said I wanted to talk to you about pay-per-view, but I have a bigger agenda, which I didn't want to say over the phone. What I really wanted to talk about is Sky buying Manchester United. We have looked at it and we would like to make an offer to buy your company.'

Martin and I tried to retain a calm exterior but underneath we were rapidly assessing what this could mean for the club, our own positions, the job of our fellow directors and the company shareholders. My overriding thought was that this could not be a good time with all we had on with the Media Partners project.

The lunch continued with Booth explaining what the attraction of Manchester United was to Sky, although we did not need any explanation for this. No money was mentioned but, as the lunch progressed, I was already moving on to next steps and what needed to be done.

When the lunch finished, Martin and I realised we needed to bring Roland Smith into the loop as quickly as we could. Clearly the plc chairman had to be told as soon as possible. We contacted Roland's offices in London and arranged to go in and see him straightaway.

Roland reacted positively to the news, but secrecy was essential and we agreed that it would be limited to the three of us for the moment. There were advantages in this. No price had been discussed. It was the height of the holiday season. We were all very busy and we had the proposed European Super League and all its constant meetings to deal with. Throughout the ESL negotiations, I found it difficult having to continuously absent myself to take calls. I started to run out of reasons and excuses for my somewhat bizarre conduct.

Martin had a meeting in early July with Mark Booth, and later in the month I met up with Martin Stewart, BSkyB's chief financial officer, at the Royal Lancaster Hotel. This was the first time a price was discussed. Stewart wanted to know how much United expected Sky to pay for the club, at which point I scribbled some calculation on a piece of paper and handed it over. Stewart's mouth dropped open when he saw the figure of 290p per share, which valued the club at nearly £750 million. No club on earth had a price tag like that. But at least it got the ball rolling.

Where did I get the figure from? Unfortunately, I cannot find the piece of paper with my workings on it, but how do you value Manchester United? It is the uniqueness of the asset that is the imponderable. In my view, usual valuation exercises fail to arrive at the right figure. No doubt I was also giving us some room for negotiation.

Martin and I met Mark Booth and other representatives of BSkyB on 4 August, again at the Royal Lancaster Hotel. My valuation came in for considerable comment, as you would expect, from the Sky side. They were looking at a figure of 190p.

By the time several hours of negotiation had elapsed, we were left with a figure of 217.5p per share, which Martin was prepared to put before the Manchester United plc board. I was supportive of this but believed there was still some considerable mileage to go on price.

On 6 August, the board met at Old Trafford and all the board members were present – Sir Roland Smith, Martin Edwards, Peter Kenyon, David Gill, Maurice Watkins, Amer Al Midani, Greg Dyke, who had joined the board in 1997, and secretary David Beswitherick.

Roland Smith reported that two separate approaches had been received for the company: BSkyB's was a cash offer of 217.5p per share; the one from Interpublic Group of Companies, an American advertising business, was a cash offer of 210p per share.

The offers were discussed at considerable length before it was agreed that the company's financial advisors, HSBC Investment Bank, should be asked to prepare a valuation and assess the two potential bids. It was also agreed that a consultant should be appointed to assess the value of television rights to the company.

The board met again on 28 August, but focused only on the BSkyB offer as Interpublic would not, as Martin Edwards reported, go above 210p per share.

HSBC's assessment was that an offer price between 200p and 230p made Sky's offer recommendable. The board could decide to remain independent but there may be some negative reaction from shareholders.

Unable to reach a decision, the board also received advice from their lawyers, Freshfields, on how a referral to the Monopolies and Mergers Commission worked and the likelihood of this outcome. It had been a condition of the BSkyB bid that the takeover had to have the unanimous recommendation of the Manchester United plc board. A further meeting was convened for 2 September at HSBC's offices; but again, no unanimous decision was reached.

By now speculation was rife about a BSkyB takeover and United had to release a short statement on 6 September. That sparked a strong reaction from the Independent Manchester United Supporters' Association, who wrote to me (and presumably the other board members) in the following terms:

Dear Mr Watkins

Following the speculation in today's newspapers we would like to express our horror at the prospect of Rupert Murdoch buying a stake in Manchester United. We would ask that the views of ordinary fans are considered. As supporters we would call upon the directors to carefully weigh the implications of News International having a stake in our club and to reject outright any approaches from this quarter.

Yours sincerely,

Andy Walsh (chairman)

Another meeting took place at HSBC's offices on 7 September with an evening start. It went past midnight as we debated the news that BSkyB were prepared to make a revised offer of 230p. The board also had the benefit of considering a report prepared by Merrill Lynch. No unanimous agreement could be reached, so the meeting finally closed with a decision made to reconvene in the morning.

On the same day, Manchester United made another Stock Exchange announcement about expanding Old Trafford. An application for planning permission to add another 12,400 seats, which would increase the present capacity of 55,000 to 67,400, had been submitted to Trafford Council. The likely cost was reported as approximately £30 million with the project financed from the club's own resources and from existing bank facilities.

The plc board met again the next day. When the meeting opened, HSBC's managing director, Rupert Faure Walker, circulated a letter from Mark Booth confirming a revised offer of 230p per share with a full cash alternative.

It was Sky's 'best and final offer', which required a majority board recommendation and the majority had to include Sir Roland Smith, Martin Edwards, myself and Peter Kenyon. The letter pointed out that the premium was approximately 45 per cent over the closing United share price of 159p on 4 September.

There was much toing and froing. Martin Edwards left the meeting to speak to Mark Booth to see if there was any possibility of BSkyB raising the offer price.

Finally, at 5:30pm Rupert Faure Walker announced that BSkyB had increased their offer to 240p per share including a full cash alternative. Shortly afterwards the board unanimously agreed to recommend to shareholders acceptance of BSkyB's 240p per share offer (being 50 per cent cash and 50 per cent new BSkyB shares with a full cash alternative).

In getting to this position the board had already considered in detail the pros and cons of the preceding 230p offer and the importance of unanimity on the board's part despite the 230p not being BSkyB's final position. Greg Dyke's views were obviously of considerable importance as the only independent director with specialist knowledge of the television marketplace.* Was the final offer a knockout bid?

How did I feel about the deal? I would have preferred it not to happen, but one has to be a realist. Once you float a company it comes 'into play'. It can always be taken over. In the case of BSkyB, from a corporate perspective United would be ahead of the game, it would unlock rights, the merger would make United more dynamic, more

---

* In his memoirs, Greg Dyke states he thought the credibility of the bid suffered when the BSkyB chief executive, Mark Booth, could not name Manchester United's left-back when asked at a press conference. He argued that being owned by a television company would severely compromise United if they wanted to sell their broadcast rights to their matches as an individual club if the collective deal with the Premier League ended. He did not consider Rupert Murdoch an appropriate person to be in ultimate charge of Manchester United.

resources would be made available and management would get a stimulus.

From the personal side I would continue as a non-executive director of United, James Chapman & Co would continue to do the legal work and 240p per share was a reasonable return for my shares. In fact, 240p was getting closer to my original figure that I had put forward as an opening gambit and which had been considered 'far too rich'. Clearly there would be supporter hostility and the presence of Rupert Murdoch would fan that.

Later that evening, the Manchester United plc board, with the exception of Amer Midani, went over to the Freshfields offices for a formal board meeting at 10:30pm to confirm that the BSkyB offer was reasonable, that the shareholders should be given the opportunity to consider whether or not to sell their shares under the offer, and that it was appropriate for the directors to recommend it.

Amer's absence did not mean he was opposed to the deal; he had previously spoken to Freshfields on the telephone to notify his agreement. Martin Edwards had been offered a position on the BSkyB board should the offer become unconditional. David Gill and I proposed to contact BSkyB concerning future employment with the company.

After the meeting, and despite it being well after midnight, the United board moved into a separate room where Mark Booth and his representatives were waiting. It was a strange moment. I was already very tired as I looked down the line in front of me and wondered what the future would hold from an individual perspective. It was interesting how the individuals aligned themselves at the table. To me it was reminiscent of Field Marshal Montgomery accepting the German surrender on Lüneburg Heath in May 1945. I had always been enthralled by Montgomery ever since I had met him at Manchester Grammar School when he spoke to the sixth form before embarking on a visit to China in 1961 to meet Chairman Mao Zedong, who took him swimming in the Yangtze River. I had asked him a question about his upcoming visit and he spent some time answering it.

Once it was announced, the fury at the deal was unleashed. Matt Lawton in the *Daily Express* speculated that two of the seven plc directors were opposed to the takeover and quoted Andy Walsh, the chairman of the Independent Manchester United Supporters' Association:

> We will fight this deal and call upon all shareholders who have the interests of Manchester United and football in general at heart to reject any overtures from Rupert Murdoch. We call upon United fans to show their vocal opposition to this train of events at the Charlton match this evening.

On the morning of 9 September there was a press conference in London, directed mainly at the City. Manchester United were playing Charlton at Old Trafford that evening and it had been arranged for the United party of Martin, Peter Kenyon, David Gill and me to fly back to Manchester for the match in the plane hired by Sky on which Mark Booth and the rest of the BSkyB team were travelling. A further press conference had been arranged at Old Trafford, this time mainly directed at the fans. It was here that Mark Booth was asked: 'Who plays left-back for Manchester United?' and his inability to answer that it was Denis Irwin received enormous publicity. United beat Charlton 4–1 on the night.

The City pages of the next morning's press made for more uncomfortable reading than the sports pages. 'The Unmagnificent Seven' was the headline in the *Daily Express* article by John Cassy:

> They were football's untouchables. Seven men who transformed Manchester United into the richest sports club in the world. Their visions and strict financial management helped United's value soar

THE BID

from less than £50 million when they floated on the Stock Exchange in 1991 to an agreed sale price of £623.4* million yesterday.

Yet for all their boardroom savvy and the millions they brought into the club, there was a growing feeling last night that United's seemingly invincible plc board sold the club down the river. Some experts believe that had United waited for digital TV to establish itself in Britain, they could have got at least £300 million more.

Despite directors' insistence that the deal was voted through unanimously, two directors, Greg Dyke and Maurice Watkins, were adamant that the club was worth more and that there was no need to sell now. Watkins, the straight-laced, straight-talking club solicitor, will make £16 million. The 55-year-old has almost seven million shares and has been a director for seven years.

One of the major opponents of the deal was journalist and broadcaster Michael Crick, who was an old boy of Manchester Grammar School. Michael had recounted to the journalist Mihir Bose that I had encountered him at the London press conference and asked if he had contributed to the MGS bursary appeal which I was chairing.

Michael had replied that if he was forced to sell his shares, he would donate a quarter of his profits to the school appeal, but as he said to Mihir:

[I]t was some cheek on Watkins's part to ask me if I had contributed to the school appeal. I did not have the presence of mind to say to him: 'in that case will you agree to donate a quarter of your profits, and if you do, the appeal fund will have reached its objective and nobody else will have to pay!'[21]

---

* Note from editor: Corrected from a typo in the original which put the figure at £632.4m.

The size of my shareholding and likely payout attracted interest, particularly in the legal and business press, which also helped to bolster the James Chapman sports team's profile.

Under the headline 'Rich Devil', *The Law Society Gazette* stated I would become one of the country's wealthiest lawyers if the BSkyB deal went through. The report said that my 2 per cent shareholding was worth up to £16 million. The article added: 'Reports identified Mr Watkins as one of the minority of directors who maintained that the £623.4 million deal undervalued the club.'

Insider Magazine carried the headline 'Red Devils' Profits to Tempt the Saints', went on to enumerate the financial gains of all involved and, talking of my share, opined: 'Director Maurice Watkins, senior partner at James Chapman, stands to make £16 million. The cunning lawyer's experience at United has given the traditional insurance firm a new string to its bow in the fashionable arena of sports law. Once Watkins' ties to the club are severed, they will be free to market these skills more widely. Unless of course, he decides to give up his day job.'

A *Sunday Telegraph* scoop on the story on 6 September had been followed by other scoops. Roland Smith was very exercised that some of these stories were emanating from the Manchester United board. He was at great pains to remind us as directors of our responsibilities during the offer period – no statements should be made to members of the media regarding the BSkyB offer or other potential offers that may be in the wings.

He was very keen to track down the source of a piece in the *Financial Times* of 16 September headlined 'Dyke Offered to Resign over United Sale', pointing out that articles of this kind did not make the work of the board and its advisors any easier.

The situation became more formal when the Takeover Panel got involved and said that they were investigating the circumstances surrounding the leaks of information (i) of the talks to the *Sunday Telegraph* prior to its 6 September article, and (ii) of the terms of the deal to the press ahead of the formal announcement on 9 September.

I and all other directors were asked to confirm to Roland Smith in writing (a) whether I had had contact with the *Sunday Telegraph* prior to 6 September, and/or with journalists concerning the offer talks prior to 9 September; and if so (b) what was the substance of the relevant contact with these journalists (by way of a brief note of the conversations held). I responded I had no contact with the *Sunday Telegraph* nor with any journalists concerning the offer terms.

During that time I also received a handwritten note from Mark Booth:

> Dear Maurice
>
> Thanks for all your support the past couple of months – especially the past week.
>
> We're looking forward to a great relationship with the group.
>
> Mark

Less friendly letters came from individual shareholders and fans, the Independent Manchester United Supporters' Association (IMUSA) and Shareholders United Against Murdoch (SUAM), who threatened: 'Don't assume the Murdoch takeover is bound to happen. BSkyB have numerous obstacles to overcome, and we plan to throw more in their way!'

The letter outlined the case against Murdoch, pointing out major upheaval the fans would cause at Old Trafford, and continued:

> Don't think the takeover will enable United to 'buy Ronaldo'*, there are serious competition problems posed by the acquisition, the price is too low, there is no passion for football (Mark Booth

---

* The Brazilian Ronaldo, not the Portuguese. Ronaldo Nazario had moved from Barcelona to Inter Milan in 1997 for a then world-record fee of $27 million.

couldn't name United's left back) and there were no links with Manchester, nor any understanding of the local community.

The shareholders were told by SUAM what they should do, including writing to their MPs and the director general of Fair Trading. They were also told the consequences of sufficient shareholders rejecting the offer and that 'only if BSkyB gets more than 90 per cent acceptances can dissident shareholders be forced to sell their shares'. And they pointed out that:

> 23.4 per cent of United shares are owned by ordinary individuals – fans mostly – so this target is well within our grasp. That means we could remain part owners of the club we all love and carry on receiving annual reports and exercising our rights to attend Annual General Meetings and still take all dividends that are received. The bigger the minority – both in total shares held and numbers of people – then the harder it will be for BSkyB to delist United shares from the Stock Exchange and the more attention they will have to pay us.

Granada Television also got into the act, disclosing it had sold its £429 million stake in BSkyB. This led to speculation that the move could lead to a rival Granada bid. Granada said the decision to sell would help reduce borrowing and was logical because the two companies were competing for a share of the digital market.

On 29 October 1998, the Secretary of State for Trade and Industry, Peter Mandelson, finally referred BSkyB's offer to the Monopolies and Mergers Commission (MMC) on the advice of John Bridgeman, director general of the OFT.

He stated that the takeover 'raises competition issues in respect of the broadcasting of premium English football and may have implications more generally for competition in the broadcasting market'. There were also public interest concerns and the MMC was given until 12 March 1999 to report. Both companies issued a joint statement confirming that, under the conditions of the offer, BSkyB's offer for Manchester United had now lapsed and previous acceptances had no further effect.

In a joint statement, Mark Booth and Martin Edwards set out the two companies' position:

> BSkyB and Manchester United will put their case strongly to the Monopolies and Mergers Commission that the purported transaction would not operate against the public interest and should be allowed to proceed.
>
> The boards of both companies firmly believe that the acquisition of Manchester United by BSkyB would be good for the Club, the players and the fans and would bring together two companies whose skills complement each other and who have demonstrated their commitment to football.

Mark Booth added: 'Sky wishes to co-operate fully and we are very confident that ultimately this transaction will be cleared.'

22

Stopping Murdoch

Although he was awarded the Freedom of Hartlepool on the same day as Sky Sports presenter Jeff Stelling, Peter Mandelson was not a football man. Stelling may have been devoted to Hartlepool United, but the town's MP made headlines when he allegedly went into a fish and chip shop in the town and asked for 'some of that guacamole dip', not realising it was mushy peas.

That did not matter. Mandelson's judgement had to be made on business rather than football grounds. Dr Derek Morris, the chairman of the Monopolies and Mergers Commission, would head the inquiry into the takeover and would report back by 12 March 1999.

Mandelson hoped to let the world know what he had decided within twenty days of receiving the report. The big question for him was the public-interest angle of the bid. He would have to decide whether, in taking over Manchester United, BSkyB would have such power that it would prevent proper competition.

We at Manchester United had to work out our defence strategy and on 2 November 1998 Roland Smith, Peter Kenyon, David Gill and I had a meeting at HSBC with our advisors including Freshfields. Not only did we discuss how our case should be put but what the relationship with Sky should be during the process. It was agreed that in principle United, as the target company, should be seen to be independent from Sky. Sky would do their own thing; United needed to tell its story in its own way but it would be stupid not to have liaisons with Sky.

We also agreed that we should keep a low profile and not respond to the tremendous public criticism of the bid. We needed to be aware of our friends and our enemies and what they were saying about us. We decided that we needed advice on government relations. And that we should take a very rational, calm and informed approach, and not be influenced by publicity.

A few days later we received notification of who the panel members were in addition to Dr Derek Morris. They were Nicholas Finney, chairman and managing director of the Waterfront Partnership, a UK ports consultancy. Finney was an active supporter of the Conservative Party. As general secretary of the Welsh TUC, David Jenkins was politically on the other side. Roger Munson was a former partner of chartered accountants Coopers & Lybrand, and Dr Gill Owen an energy and environmental consultant and chair of the Public Utilities Access Forum.

Our meeting with the panel was set for Thursday, 17 December in London and both us and BSkyB were asked for additional information, including annual reports and management accounts. We also requested from our advisors a summary of press and other comments on the bid both positive and negative. The negatives easily won this match, with their team including the entire football establishment. It certainly was a strong team. This is how I saw them take their positions on the field:

- Gordon Taylor, general secretary of the PFA, in goal
- Ken Bates, chairman of Chelsea, centre-forward
- David Mellor, the former minister, Chelsea fan but voicing his opinion as chairman of the Football Task Force in what may be called a false No 9, although then this position had not yet been invented
- David Sheepshanks, chairman of the Football League, and Keith Wiseman, chairman of the FA, as the central defenders

- And a whole host of journalists led by Michael Crick, Paul Hayward, David Conn, David Brookes, as the wing-backs ready to supply the crosses that Bates, as the quicksilver No 9, would put into the back of the net. Some analysts also opposed the bid and I could see them as midfield enforcers making sure we did not get anywhere near their goal.

Compared with this giant we looked like minnows from non-league football hoping to cause a Cup upset, but, having decided to back the bid, we had every intention of making a fight of it.

The first thing to explore was where the Premier League stood on the issue. On 9 November David Gill had a meeting with Peter Leaver, chief executive of the Premier League, who said that the only points he had made to the Office of Fair Trading were that takeovers are a part of corporate life and he did not see any particular issues that should make it any different for football clubs.

He also thought that this was probably the first of many investments by media companies in football clubs. He was relaxed as long as there was a mechanism in place to cover the potential conflicts-of-interest scenario with BSkyB now being on both sides of the negotiating table.

Leaver was going to ask for a meeting with the MMC after the early December Premier League meeting so that he could impart the views of the clubs. He assured us that there would be no opposition to the bid from him or the Premier League unless there was a desire to break away from the Premier League.

The next day, following a meeting at Bell Pottinger, Sky's PR advisor, Mark Booth, Vic Wakeling, head of Sky Sports, Martin Edwards, David Gill and I attended a meeting of the All-Party Football Group in the House of Commons. The omens were not good. This was a 120-strong all-party parliamentary football group and it strongly opposed the bid.

The Labour MP, Joe Ashton – a Sheffield Wednesday director who chaired the group – had, in a letter to Peter Mandelson, demanded a change in policy to force pay-television and sport to receive government approval before embarking on new initiatives. He wrote:

> Rupert Murdoch's pay satellite television is now an unfair competitor to both ITV and BBC. ITV companies have to be awarded franchises and satisfy the adjudicators to ensure they will act in the public interest. The BBC Charter insists on this too.

Ashton had told the press:

> The only alternative is to handicap those small number of clubs that will be far richer than all the others. Football's regulators will have to ensure that some clubs start the season five points behind everyone else.

I felt we were going into the lions' den.

We had decided that Mark Booth would be the first sacrificial lamb. I must say he spoke well, quashing any idea that the transaction would operate against the public interest and argued persuasively that the bid should be allowed to proceed.

Since our opponents were always arguing that everyone was against the bid, Booth made the point that more than 7,000 Manchester United small shareholders had voted in favour of the proposal, far greater than the number of people who had turned up to protest against the offer at an anti-Sky rally.

If the offer was allowed to proceed, it would bring together two companies whose skills complemented each other, and who had demonstrated their commitment to football. Manchester United's record spoke for itself and the hundreds of millions of pounds that BSkyB had invested in its broadcasting rights had, in turn, been invested in the game from ground improvements to exciting foreign talent.

He also dealt very competently with issues of BSkyB being on both sides of the TV negotiating table, which much had been made of; essentially, that this marriage would make Manchester United unassailable and that this was a prelude to the formation of a European Super League.

The United team had prepared questions and answers trying to anticipate what might come from the Parliamentary Group. Much of our argument echoed Booth, who liked to stress how football had changed since Sky had become a player. Ten years previously, viewers had seen fewer than twenty live First Division games each year and football received £3.1 million annually from the BBC and ITV. Now there were sixty live games from the Premier League, each club was live at least three times each season, and annual income from TV rights was around £160 million.

At the start of the Premier League, many had feared such television coverage would mean fewer people would go to football. They had been proved wrong at the turnstiles. At the close of the 1997/98 season Premier League attendances were up 38 per cent in six years and Football League attendances had also risen over twelve consecutive seasons.

I felt our meeting with the All-Party Football Group went reasonably well and, although it was initially somewhat nerve-wracking, we were well prepared. We were shown respect and allowed to make our points. It had not been as testing as I had feared.

After the meeting in the House of Commons, I went over to the Football League's London offices. It was a chance to meet Peter Middleton, who had just taken over from David Sheepshanks as chairman of the Football League. Middleton was a remarkable man, who had been a monk, a building-site worker and chairman of Lloyd's. He rode motorcycles.

I wanted to know whether the Football League had put in a submission to the OFT and, if so, whether Manchester United could get a copy. Middleton did not know, but what was really interesting was, unlike Sheepshanks, he did not oppose the merger.

His view of business was that assets are neutral and one should remain unemotional. He said there was no particular sign that the government was concerned and, if it was, then it would be opening a 'Pandora's box'. In his opinion there were no business grounds for objecting, and he did not intend to make any public statements. This was normal commercial life. It was reassuring to hear that the Football League did not have any objection to the merger.

I was back in London on 13 November at White's Hotel on the Bayswater Road, a regular FA haunt, meeting FA officials Keith Wiseman, Graham Kelly and company secretary Nic Coward.

I wanted to raise three points with them. Had the FA made any submissions to the OFT, and if so could we see a copy of these? What were their concerns, and could we discuss these directly with them? And could they see how all the parties might find a satisfactory way through all this?

Nic Coward stated that a ten-page submission had been lodged with the OFT and that he saw no reason why United should not be supplied with a copy of this. He revealed that the FA, together with the Premier League and the Football League, had already met the MMC and they were now in the process of fleshing out their concerns, which were primarily competition based. This was a case of a merger between the dominant football broadcaster and the dominant football club. There were competition issues both in broadcasting and football. The FA felt that the reference to the MMC was warranted.

As Coward saw it, the MMC would have to make a decision in an uncertain market. In the FA's view, television negotiations should only be handled collectively. He said that the BSkyB acquisition left the FA greatly concerned that there would be a loosening of the collective position. There were also worries about the FA Cup and, so far as the Football League was concerned, the League Cup. I reminded Wiseman of the comments he had made in the *Daily Telegraph* opposing the bid. Wiseman's defence was that there were no serious rivals to BSkyB.

Around this time the MMC had written to individual Premier League clubs to ask whether they wanted to make any representations regarding the merger in addition to any they may already have expressed to the OFT. Martin wrote to all clubs asking for their support for the merger by the deadline of Friday, 20 November.

By now we were having several meetings. David Gill and I had separate ones on 20 November with the chief executives of the Premier League and Football League. Peter Leaver confirmed that his opinion on the merger had not changed since it was first announced. He said more complex competition issues might arise if collective bargaining for television rights went. He also told us he had appointed two advisors to assist on TV matters. They were Sam Chisholm and David Chance.

Richard Scudamore, the chief executive of the Football League, said he favoured the merger provided collective TV negotiations would continue and that the clubs were given assurances that the status of all competitions would remain unaltered.

The big date was when the MMC would meet Manchester United. This had been fixed for Thursday, 17 December. In the lead-up came a series of meetings, a bit like the debates and rallies held in the run-up to polling day. The most crucial one was Sunday, 29 November, when the MMC came to Old Trafford. United were at home to Leeds, and we on the board planned for the MMC visit with the sort of military precision with which Alex Ferguson prepared his team.

Its main point was to give the visitors the best possible insight into what the club was all about. There would be opportunities to meet key executives before the game with a buffet lunch during which discussions would continue until our guests were escorted to their seats at 1:45pm. It was also a good opportunity to make sure the commission members had an overall view of the way the whole enterprise worked.

Twelve members of the commission and its staff came for the visit, arriving between 10am and 10:30am. They were ushered into the Directors' Private Room. After a short welcome and introduction from Roland and Martin the tour began with visits to the Club Museum, Red Café, Platinum Suite and seating, the Manchester Suite, the Megastore, the Stretford Suite, and finishing up with a presentation back in the Directors' Private Room. Not all stayed for the game and those that did paid for their tickets. Those that paid saw a thrilling match that Manchester United came from behind to win 3–2.

With hindsight it would have been better if the MMC visit had been held later and not on a match day. That might have allowed a more detailed appraisal of the business rather than be tied up on matchday activity with a timetable that was affected by all that was going on. Also, it may not have been a good idea for the visit to be publicised by a formal press release which sparked controversy from fans who speculated how the commission members had obtained tickets when home games were always sold out.

Another crucial meeting was with the PFA, who opposed the bid. The PFA had not yet put in a submission but would be doing so in the next few days. They would also be meeting with the MMC.

On 9 November, following an informal meeting between certain members of the United board and Gordon Taylor, the chief executive of the PFA, David Gill and I had a meeting with Taylor and his solicitor, John Hewison, at the PFA's Manchester offices in Oxford Court.

Taylor referred to competition in broadcasting and sporting terms, and raised the question of collective bargaining over freedom for clubs to negotiate their own TV deals. Manchester United, he said, was the 'jewel in the crown' and, if BSkyB owned the club, then why would it distribute money to others? Effectively, it would be sitting as a spider in the middle of the web.

Our defence was that if BSkyB only acquired rights for Manchester

United matches, it would only effectively be showing nineteen home games; that is, only 5 per cent of Premier League matches. What about the other attractions? Manchester United had to play someone and there needed to be an effective competition.

Taylor was also worried that domestic football would be diluted by European competition – the strong would get stronger. The club that paid the best wages would end up with the best team. Taylor saw his job as ensuring that football attracted investment, but he was not concerned with increases in shareholder value.

We had set aside two days for rehearsals before our meeting with the MMC. On 15 December we had a rehearsal meeting at Old Trafford with our legal representatives, Roland Smith, Martin Edwards, David Gill and myself, plus our expert, Professor George Yarrow of Oxford University. We went through how the meeting might go and the questions we would face. The next day we set out for London.

At the beginning of January 1999, Manchester United made its second submission to the MMC. This followed up on a few points left outstanding at the end of the first hearing and particularly Manchester United's account of the Premier League bidding competitions for television rights. There was then a meeting on 15 January before the MMC to deal with the second submission.

By this stage we were confident we would win. The first doubts came on the morning of 24 January when I opened the *Mail on Sunday* to find an exclusive by Rob Draper, which began:

The Premier League is ready to ask the MMC to block BSkyB's £623 million takeover of Manchester United.

In a sensational development, Premier League chief executive, Peter Leaver, has compiled his responses to MMC enquiries. In the draft document, which has been passed to Sportsmail, he calls for the 'prohibition of the merger'.

Leaver's bombshell comes at the end of a 19-page report. He tells the MMC of his concern at the consequences of the takeover by the television wing of Rupert Murdoch's media empire if collective bargaining by the League regarding a television deal is outlawed.

Leaver writes that in the absence of collective licensing, the Premier League finds it difficult to see how any remedy other than prohibition of the merger would address the adverse effects.

I could not believe what I was reading. In none of my meetings with Leaver had I heard any hint that the Premier League was going to oppose the bid. Of course, it was possible the story was not accurate. But we could not take that chance. The next day, United wrote to Derek Morris at the MMC rejecting Leaver's suggestions as reported by the *Mail on Sunday*. The MMC was to submit its report to Stephen Byers, who had taken over from Mandelson as Secretary of State on 23 December. Advised by our PR team, we decided to issue a press release as to why the bid should be allowed to proceed.

Despite the opposition, we were confident the deal would go through, but on 9 April Byers announced he had blocked the Sky bid. It was clear from the MMC's 254-page report that they were dead against the merger, finding both public interest and competition grounds for opposing it.

I must say I was not surprised the bid was stopped. Notwithstanding the strong opinion of the Sky and United legal team, I always had a niggling doubt that it would not go through.

To me it was clear from the beginning that all the commission members had a lack of knowledge of the football industry. Time frames for comment were very tight; pressure to report on time and rushing things appeared to be the maxim rather than getting to the nub of the issues and identifying what really did concern the commission.

A more focused debate would have been more meaningful and given more appropriate time for dealing with arguably flawed analyses.

How important in the rejection of the merger was News International and its owner Rupert Murdoch? This was not explored by the commission despite the concerns and comments of other parties that, if Murdoch had got hold of Manchester United, prices and season tickets would have gone up, pay per view would have come in – and no players would have been purchased.

The deal and merger work involved considerable effort and it corresponded with some very big footballing issues going on at the same time in which I was involved – in particular the European Super League. It was a draining time. Like Martin Edwards, I had not enjoyed being described as a greedy bastard for being ready to take Murdoch's money, but nor did the decision cause me any loss of sleep. I just think the merger would have been a good thing for the club and it would have been good for me as a United board member and legal representative; but as Martin said, 'you move on'.

The board member who was really disappointed was David Gill, who had worked so hard on the project. He firmly believed the decision should be with the shareholders. He could see major benefits in Sky taking over. Afterwards, he said there was lots of opportunity ahead of the club if it could stay independent. But could it stay independent?

As events were to prove just six years later, United did not stay independent. The club went to the Glazers, and can it really be argued that they have been better owners than Murdoch would have been? I am writing this after two decades when any number of owners have taken over Premier League and Football League clubs, some mysterious, some dubious. Compared with them, Sky looks like a knight in shining armour.

But this being the first bid of its kind, it generated the sort of opposition that now sounds amazing. So much of the landscape of football has changed that the events of 1998–99 now seem to belong to another age.

23

Cyril the Swan

In the midst of the failed twin attempts to introduce a European Super League and BSkyB's bid for Manchester United and hence some of the most intense legal work of my life, I came across Cyril the Swan.

Cyril – a man dressed as a swan – was the mascot of Swansea City FC. In November 1998 Cyril the Swan, or rather his club, had been hauled before 'the beak', in this case the Welsh FA, for bringing the game into disrepute.

The misconduct was alleged to have been committed on 13 November when Swansea played Millwall in the FA Cup. In his referee's report, Steve Dunn detailed a catalogue of offences that this 'twelve-foot-high character dressed in Swansea City colours' was alleged to have committed.

They included: inciting trouble with the visiting supporters by running up and down the touchline to drum up support from the home crowd; kicking the ball aggressively at the opposition players; entering the field of play; and interfering with the visitors' substitutes who were warming up.

Cyril, it must be said, had 'form'. In a Football Association of Wales (FAW) Premier Cup game against Barry Town some weeks earlier, the match referee had complained that the club mascot's behaviour and antics were of concern and that his interference in the game was of an unacceptable nature and should stop immediately.

The Swansea board had approved the introduction of a club mascot in May. Cyril the Swan's first game at the Vetch Field saw him perched at the top of a floodlight pylon for forty minutes before abseiling down to the pitch just before kick-off. Swansea beat Exeter 2–0.

This rather macho introduction endeared him to the home fans, and from that moment on he became a hero across Swansea's fanbase. Cyril was voted the 1998 Personality of the Year by the *South Wales Evening Post*. Although he had not attended many away games despite receiving invitations to do so, he was a regular attender at local schools and the local hospital.

The story was gold dust for the media. With reports suggesting that Cyril's activities could result in him being banned from matches, *The Sun* decided to put its campaigning hat on and wanted the charges dropped, under the slogan 'Don't Put Cyril Up Before the Beak'.

The club's chief executive, Peter Day, requested a personal hearing. Day, who had previously been club secretary at Tottenham, then rang me to ask whether I would represent Swansea at the hearing. I was intrigued by the case and had no hesitation in agreeing.

Cyril was not my first case for Swansea. I had represented them at a number of disciplinary hearings and had started to run out of original reasons in my pleadings on behalf of the club. In view of this, I had thought it might be a good idea to get someone else from James Chapman & Co to represent the club and had sent my assistant Scott Duxbury to attend a previous hearing. This clearly pleased the FAW as he received a fulsome welcome from the chairman of the Disciplinary Committee, who admitted that it was nice to meet someone else other than Mr Watkins. Scott subsequently became chief executive of West Ham and is now chairman of Watford.

I also knew Neil McClure, Swansea's owner and major shareholder, quite well, having represented the club in a defamation case against the Welsh broadcaster S4C which we settled in the club's favour with an appropriate apology. I had sent it to Neil for approval, who was happy with the wording but asked me to check what language it would be published in. The answer was Welsh. We ensured that it was also presented in English.

I went to the Vetch in January to see Swansea, managed by John Hollins, overcome West Ham in an FA Cup replay. Later that month Peter Day told the FAW I would be representing his club. The *News of the World* wrote on 24 January 1999: 'Swansea have called upon one of the hottest legal eagles in football to defend Cyril the Swan.'

Interest in the case was not just confined to Wales; Manchester United TV was keen to interview me about the case, and Swansea, who had clearly decided the more publicity this case received the better, had no objection to my talking to them. Cyril had become a marketing manager's dream ticket and the club's commercial manager, Mike Lewis, was making the most of it. There were 'Cyril Is Innocent' car stickers, T-shirts, dolls, lunch boxes and cushions on sale as well as Cyril's debut single 'Nice Swan Cyril', which filled thousands of Christmas stockings that year.

A hearing was agreed for Friday, 23 April 1999 at the Posthouse Hotel in Cardiff. The matter was further complicated, however, by the FAW deciding to have two other charges dealt with on the same date. These were pitch encroachment by fans celebrating the winning goal in the FA Cup game against West Ham United, and racial abuse and throwing of missiles against Brighton & Hove Albion on 5 February 1999. The FAW said the three charges would be heard separately, with one hour allocated for each hearing.

The club was not happy about this, and I wrote to the FAW complaining about the scheduling of the three cases in one afternoon. The charges were serious, the one alleging racial abuse was a very grave one, I would be calling a number of witnesses and there was also the prejudicial nature of three charges being heard by the same commission on the same day.

I also referred to seemingly prejudicial comments attributable to the FAW that had appeared in several newspapers stating that: 'it is very unfortunate that all these incidents have occurred so close together and it is certainly within the power of the FAW Commission to close the Vetch Field.'

The FAW refused to relent and insisted that all cases should be heard on the same afternoon. They argued that extra time for each case was available and that there was an appeals process.

I decided that I would go down to Swansea the day before the case and spend the night there before travelling to Cardiff for the 2pm hearing. The club booked me into the Norton House Hotel in Swansea where I found McClure, who was a London businessman, was also staying at the same hotel. That evening we had a nice chat in the bar followed by dinner discussing the case and wider football issues.

The next morning over my hotel breakfast, I was surprised to hear BBC Radio 4's John Humphrys conducting a learned discussion on the *Today* programme about Cyril the Swan and the fact that Swansea had engaged the services of 'a well-known legal eagle, Maurice Watkins'. I did not know whether to feel flattered or concerned that I had now made the national broadcaster's flagship radio news show, one which Margaret Thatcher told her ministers to always listen to and which opinion-makers and journalists never missed.

Soon after breakfast I went to the club and started interviewing our witnesses and carried out necessary briefings. I was hoping that, given the time that would be taken in dealing with Cyril, there would be insufficient time in the afternoon to deal with the other two cases. This, of course, was what we wanted as it was considered very important that they should not be heard on the same day.

However, just in case the other two cases were also heard, I watched the videos of all three incidents and briefed witnesses that I planned to call for all three cases. For the hearing, the secretary general of the FAW, David Collins, was to call as his witnesses the referee, Steve Dunn, the assistant referee, Russell Maynard, Chief Inspector Thomas and a PC Phillips. I had decided to call among others Don Goss, the club safety officer, and produce Cyril in costume for the benefit of the commission.

I had met Cyril at the briefing meeting on the morning of the hearing. I quickly realised we would be under some considerable difficulty if we had as a witness the man behind Cyril's costume. In any event, his identity was a closely guarded secret.

I suggested to Swansea that we keep Cyril well away from the proceedings. This almost caused Mike Lewis, the club's commercial manager, to have apoplexy, given the case had already generated huge sales of Cyril memorabilia. Mike had just commissioned the purchase of thousands of additional Cyril statuettes. Neil McClure was also keen that we generate as much publicity as possible for the club. Neil, Peter and I had a long and very serious discussion, and I agreed that we would compromise. The Swan would be available as an exhibit but would not give evidence.

After the meetings at Swansea, we travelled to Cardiff for the hearing. We arrived in good time but one of the commission members had misjudged how long it would take to reach the Posthouse and so we started forty-five minutes late.

Cyril attended the hearing in his costume as planned, and although the commission asked if they might question him, I made it clear that they could not as he was only attending the hearing as an exhibit. Cyril remained a mute swan.

I had decided, however, that I would question the right of the FAW to even hold the hearings. I thought I had a very good argument for this. The incident had taken place in an FA Cup match. This meant it should have been an FA case not a FAW case. The panel had not expected my challenge and this led to some serious discussions. The chairman of the commission, Alun Evans, who said he was an historian, then said the right to try the case stemmed from an accord entered into in 1922 between the FA and the FAW. The lawyer in me was immediately aroused and I asked Evans if he could let me have a copy of this accord.

I thought the hearings went well, with the witnesses keeping to their brief. However, we had mixed success with the commission's decisions. Swansea were held to be in breach of two of the rules, and after a plea of mitigation fined £1,000 for each. Several other charges were dismissed or found not proven.

The commission also ruled that:

> The club mascot, Cyril the Swan, will not be permitted to remain within the playing area after the start of the match and thereafter while player and match officials are on the field of play. This shall remain in force pending a code of conduct to be drawn up by the FAW with respect to the activities of club mascots.

By this time, it was nearly 7pm and the commission still wanted to proceed with the other two charges. We strongly opposed this, and the commission eventually accepted the force of the argument and the cases were held over to a later date.

Given the media interest and the number of journalists and cameramen present, we decided that Neil McClure and I would hold a press conference. Cyril also was present, playing the mute swan to perfection and not performing any of his tricks. Neil confirmed that there would be no appeal.

As was only to be expected, the papers had a great deal of fun with this story which also saw my name in the headlines: 'Mascot swan gets bird from FA', 'Nice Swan Maurice', 'A pitch evasion proves to be Cyril's swansong', 'Fowl play', and 'Cyril the Swan banished to the stands'.

There was no doubt this whole case was all good publicity for the club, and I am sure that sales of Cyril memorabilia continued to take off.

I, of course, know the true identity of Cyril the Swan – but under client privilege, I could not possibly disclose his name.

24

Football Versus the European Union

One of the most serious but, arguably, one of the least understood issues faced by the game was the European Commission's attack on the transfer system.

The problem started as a result of a complaint in July 1997 to the European Commission by an obscure Belgian trade union. The European Commission issued a Statement of Objections against FIFA, attacking the FIFA rules which govern the international transfer of players. The Commission wanted a professional footballer to be treated in the same as any other worker for the purposes of EU law. Hence, a player's contract could not be unilaterally terminated without compensation. Accordingly, damages payable for the breach of a contract should be governed by national labour laws and once a player had paid any damages due under his national labour law, he must be free to move to any new club in the EU/EEA area.

In football language, therefore, the crucial issue was that the release of an international clearance certificate could not be withheld, and the player must be allowed to work. Where international transfers were concerned, a player could not move from one national association to another unless this clearance certificate (which is like a passport or car logbook) was released, and this did not happen unless the player's current club agreed to the move.

The Commission noted that transfer fees which were 'agreed' between all the parties concerned (selling club, buying club, player) were also contrary to EU competition laws if the amount of the transfer fee did not correspond to objective criteria such as the real costs incurred by the selling club in developing the player.

The view of the Commission was that 'very high' transfer fees (even if agreed by all parties concerned) were anti-competitive and impeded the free movement of professional players in the EU/EEA area.

FIFA received these objections in December 1998 but did not come up with any meaningful proposals. This led to a threat from the Commission that they planned to issue a negative decision which would have resulted in the whole transfer system being declared illegal. The deadline was 20 September 2000.

With only a few weeks to go, the football world was in a state of panic. There was much lobbying of politicians (which quickly resulted in an extension of the deadline); prime minister Tony Blair and the German chancellor, Gerhard Schröder, expressed their support for football.

Europe's football associations, leagues, clubs, players and players' representatives lobbied the EU Competition Commissioner, Mario Monti. There were fears that the proposals would lead to the breakup of teams that had taken years to build if players were allowed to breach their contracts, pay damages and move on to more lucrative employment elsewhere. Clubs worried about all the money which was being invested in training grounds and football academies: What incentive would there be if transfer fees ceased to exist and players had no value?

Then there was the question of the effect on those clubs which had been floated on stock exchanges, some of whose players appeared on the balance sheets as intangible assets. Their values would have been written off at a stroke. In the case of Manchester United, the club would lose £32 million. Banks would withdraw their support and funding would be even more difficult to obtain.

In the United Kingdom, the position was complicated by our national accounting rules. Players for whom a transfer fee has been paid have to be shown in the balance sheet as intangible assets and the transfer fee amortised (paid off in instalments) over the period of the player's contract.

Players who are 'home-grown', such as Manchester United's David Beckham and Paul Scholes, are not included in the balance sheet because no transfer fee has been paid. However, financial analysts clearly attribute value to these players when reviewing the worth of a football club, and there was no doubt that the uncertainty over the continuance of the transfer system caused by the sudden and unexpected intervention of the EU had seriously affected football club values.

But not all clubs believed that to be the case. Leeds United, for example, clearly thought that the system was going to continue, for in the middle of all this uncertainty they paid £18 million to sign Rio Ferdinand from West Ham in November 2000. On the other hand, West Ham were happy to take the money because their chairman, Terry Brown, thought transfer fees would soon be abolished.

In order to investigate the issues, FIFA, in conjunction with UEFA, set up a task force which in its turn established three sub-committees. I was made chairman of the legal or juridical committee. There was also an economic consequences committee and a committee to examine the specific characteristics of sport, aimed at trying to obtain a sporting protocol which would be annexed to the European Treaty.

Our first step was to carry out a detailed survey of the national labour laws covering ten of the European leagues. We found that in nearly all of the countries concerned, a contract between a professional player and his club was one of employment, though there were crucial differences between them.

Spain, for instance, had a specific law allowing large buyout sums to be paid for the transfer of a player. The result was Luis Figo's transfer from Barcelona to Real Madrid at an exorbitant fee of €62 million in July 2000. Belgium, meanwhile, had a law providing for the payment of a relatively small amount of compensation on the basis of a statutory formula.

In the UK, Germany and Italy, courts determined compensation for breach of contract in accordance with standard employment law principles. Heads of damages could include loss of opportunity to win games, replacement costs, loss of commercial revenues and training costs for young players.

However, the total amount of damages to be paid was often extremely difficult to quantify and it could often take a long time to establish if each case of breach of contract had to be decided in the relevant national courts. But this system did mean that in respect of claims in most of the European countries under their national employment laws one would be looking at serious amounts of money. This contrasted sharply with the Commission's view that compensation or transfer fees should equate to training costs.

The findings of the economic sub-committee demonstrated that another plank of the Commission's case – that the transfer system reinforced the position of the large clubs and leagues to the detriment of the small ones – was also seriously flawed. The existing system, the sub-committee found, did provide an effective redistribution of money within the football system.

In the English Football League over a five-year period, transfer receipts allowed Crewe Alexandra to cover its operating losses by 200 per cent. Oldham Athletic's figure in the same period was 98 per cent. At a national level the majority of European countries were shown to be net receivers of transfer fees. Only England, Spain, Italy, Scotland, France and Germany were net payers.

Nevertheless, my legal sub-committee came to the conclusion that it would be difficult to defend the current FIFA system from a legal point of view. This was partly because of the competition rules in the EU Treaty but also because a player might at any time challenge the current system before a national court as an obstacle to the free movement of workers. All of us on the committee agreed that, if such a legal challenge were made, the player would probably win the case.

It is notable that there had only been one serious threat to the current system in England, when Vinnie Jones had fronted a campaign in 1997 for the Bosman Ruling to be applied to transfers between British clubs rather than just internationally.

The reason why there had not been more cases is because there was a very strong collective agreement between the Premier League and Football League on the one hand, and the PFA on the other. This agreement had worked well to preserve contract stability in English football.

Our recommendation was for a new regime aimed at preserving as much as possible of the current system, and which it was hoped would stand up if challenged before the national courts or the European Commission.

We proposed what was essentially a sport arbitration system to regulate the international transfer of players. The tribunal would apply objective criteria to determine compensation to be paid for the transfer of a player who breached his contract, and these criteria would include, for example, the length of time remaining on a contract, the terms offered by a new club, and the number of first-team or international appearances. This new tribunal would have to respect relevant principles of national law, but it was hoped that over time it would move towards generally accepted common principles to regulate the transfer of players in Europe.

Linked to the compensation tribunal, there would also need to be sport disciplinary sanctions as a deterrent to unethical behaviour; for example, sanctioning a club for inducing a player to breach his contract.

It was very rare for players to break their contracts and stay at home cutting the grass; they generally did not break their contracts unless they had another club to move to.

One important issue was the continuance of agreed transfers. There were seen to be no legal obstacles to preserving the situation where both clubs and the player agreed terms for a player's move. We felt that a compensation tribunal linked with disciplinary sanctions might well persuade parties to simply agree a transfer fee on a mutual basis, because otherwise the clearance certificate issued by FIFA – and essential for an international transfer – would not be released to enable the player to join his new club.

There were also proposals governing the establishment of a formula to calculate training compensation for the transfer of players under the age of 23.

I was by now wearing a number of legal hats and the result of all this was that I was involved in one presentation and meeting after another with the Commission, FIFA and UEFA, FIFPro – the world players' union – numerous ministers of sport, as well as regularly communicating with the Premier League and its clubs. I spent so little time at home that by the time we had reached a deal on the transfer system, I was the proud holder of three airline gold cards.

Travel was exhausting but I always flew business class, and UEFA and FIFA made excellent chauffeuring arrangements. There was always a man waiting for me at whichever airport I arrived and took me to the meeting I was due to attend. These organisations can often be slow and bureaucratic, but they certainly know how to get people to meetings. This may be because they always have so many of them.

Working on the future of the transfer system made me aware of the constant struggle between the world body and the European body. UEFA felt that FIFA had not kept its much-talked-about 'football family' aware of the problem with the Commission when it first emerged. The statements of the FIFA president, Sepp Blatter, seemed prepared to abandon the system without a fight.

I was working mainly with the UEFA team, particularly Gianni Infantino (now president of FIFA) and lawyer Alasdair Bell, and had a wonderful insight into how UEFA (based in the small Swiss town of Nyon) saw Blatter's FIFA (based in Switzerland's largest city, Zürich) as always trying to undermine the Europeans.

While the players' union agreed with a number of proposals in the task force document, FIFPro were hoping to maximise their opportunities in relation to unilateral termination of contract and appeared only willing to accept a one-year unbreakable period. They were also not happy with the assessment of compensation.

Nor did Gordon Taylor – who besides being chief executive of the English PFA was also president of FIFPro – miss a chance to hear his own voice. Indeed, he even outdid Blatter, who also liked to hog the microphone.

At a meeting at FIFA headquarters, Sepp Blatter was complaining to a large gathering of football representatives that he could not make progress with FIFPro or understand its motivations. He suddenly looked up from the podium and saw Gordon Taylor entering the conference room at the back. He waved the microphone at Gordon and said: 'Perhaps Mr Taylor will explain his position to us?' I knew Gordon could not resist the temptation to speak at length if circumstances permitted, but what he did next surprised me. Not only did he move resolutely and, with speed, to the podium, taking the microphone from Sepp, but he went on to speak for over an hour despite several attempts by Blatter's FIFA staff to bring his contribution to an end by seizing the microphone. Then to cap it all, as he eventually left the stage, Gordon saw me and said: 'That was unexpected.' I could not help but wonder how long he would have spoken for had he been expecting to speak.

Despite the problems between FIFA and UEFA, I got on reasonably well with both organisations, which explained my appointment as chairman of the FIFA/UEFA juridical committee. It must have helped that I did not have any ties with either of the governing bodies. The Premier League was pleased with the appointment, and I was told to make sure that I was fully in the picture on what steps were being taken to head off the threat from the Commission and come up with an appropriate solution, and what those steps might mean so far as English football was concerned.

But while I was always careful to tread a fine line between UEFA and FIFA and not upset either side, I must have done so on one occasion for it led to a bizarre standoff between the two. A meeting with UEFA had been organised only to find that I was the only one present and the UEFA representatives were meeting separately elsewhere. A sharp call to Mike Lee, the UEFA director of communications, who had previously worked at the Premier League, brought things in line and the meeting duly took place albeit with a few hours' delay.

Our submission to the EU had to be made by 31 October 2000 and the days leading up to it were spent in committee rooms drafting the proposals for the Commission. But while UEFA and FIFA could set aside their problems, despite our best efforts we could not get the players on our side. So when on deadline day FIFA general secretary, Michel Zen-Ruffinen, lodged the 'negotiating document' with European Commissioner Mario Monti, he had to admit, 'FIFA regrets that the player representatives decided to remain absent from the final meeting on 27th October and not to take part in the discussion on that day.'

Blatter always made much of 'the football family', but in this case one child was definitely not playing ball.

Submitting the document was only the first step. Long months of negotiations lay ahead. This clearly needed another committee. After a little delay, FIFA established a small negotiation committee comprising the chairman, a Norwegian called Per Omdal, the general secretaries of FIFA and UEFA, and the head of FIFA's Players' Status Committee.

Attached to the four negotiators was a small legal committee which I was on, comprising also competition lawyers from FIFA and UEFA and lawyers from the Italian and Portuguese leagues.

Perhaps not unexpectedly, matters did not proceed as constructively as hoped, and there was a falling out between FIFA and UEFA with FIFA putting forward proposals without consultation. The other legal experts and I were anxious to get on with the technical discussions as the proposed deadline of 31 December had long passed. Relations were eventually restored, and progress was made with the preparation of a FIFA/UEFA updated proposal document.

However, there would be no reconciliation with FIFPro. Their position seemed to be more extreme than ever.

In mid-February 2001, I flew to Brussels for a meeting between the Commission and the presidents of FIFA and UEFA followed by further technical meetings dealing with outstanding issues involving the legal team.

The settlement meeting was arranged for 5 March at the European Commission. Just before the meeting started, FIFA chief Sepp Blatter, the president of UEFA Lennart Johansson and Per Omdal congregated outside the door with all the lawyers. When it was opened to start the meeting, Blatter, Johansson and Omdal entered. The lawyers held back, cautious as to whether they were invited.

Very much mindful of Richard Scudamore's instructions to make sure I attended and got to know everything, I went in and settled myself into a chair. The other lawyers did not follow. We sat round a table and the meeting was friendly but business-like. I was glad that I went for it as I had the opportunity to make a number of telling interventions, particularly on stability of contracts.

No one queried my presence, but my legal colleagues outside were surprised and asked me how I had managed that. I did not let on that it was the Mancunian 'get your foot in the door' way of thinking.

The meeting ended in an agreement with FIFA. As Blatter in his letter to Monti put it: 'This regime can be improved to better reflect the interests of the family of football.' In return the EU had agreed to withdraw the pending infringement proceedings against FIFA concerning the transfer regulations.

The one big change the new regulations brought in were transfer 'windows'. The introduction of these windows was the 'quid pro quo' for the European Commission agreement that there would be no breach of contract during a season. Before this new system, clubs in Britain could buy and sell players throughout the year, except for a period just towards the end of the season, usually in late March, which was meant to stop clubs looking to win the championship or avoid relegation by buying players.

The new transfer windows specified the periods during which players could be bought and sold. The first transfer window operated from the end of one season to 31 August in the following season, and the second, shorter window occurred in the middle of the season, normally the month of January, and lasted four weeks.

As often happens in Britain when change is introduced, this was fiercely resisted, but now it is so much part of the landscape that Sky has even made it a television spectacle with its own dramatic countdown clock to the end of the transfer window.

That evening there was much celebration in the FIFA and UEFA ranks at a drinks and dinner party held at the Conrad International. Messrs Blatter and Johansson looked as though they were the best of buddies and it was a very convivial occasion.

A few days later I received a nice little note from Marco Bronckers, the FIFA lawyer:

> It was indeed a pleasure to resolve this matter with you. I have been impressed with your persistence on a variety of points, not in the least the Famous Five Words 'and/or end of contract'.

The arrangement looks good, also after a refreshing night's sleep.

Following the conclusion of the agreement, UEFA was quickly off the mark organising a conference for the presidents and general secretaries of the UEFA member associations together with representatives of the European Professional Football Leagues. I was also invited to a preparation meeting of the technical group. This group comprised Alasdair Bell of UEFA, me, and Mario Gallavotti of Italy.

Gianni Infantino, in his capacity as UEFA's Senior Manager of Professional Football and League Services, produced an early paper of how compensation for producing a player should be calculated, which it was hoped would be acceptable to the EU as it took account in his examples of actual training costs and benefit to the training club.

Now the challenge was the conversion of the principles into actual rules, and I was much involved in this.

This led to the creation of a court, the FIFA Dispute Resolution Chamber (DRC) to which I was appointed as an employer representative. The DRC was to judge international disputes between players and clubs relating to contractual stability, sporting sanctions or contractual penalties. The decisions made by this body did have potentially serious repercussions for clubs and players, and the new members of the DRC were invited to Zurich to be appointed officially by Blatter.

It was an enjoyable occasion, and the members were all photographed being welcomed individually by the FIFA president. Unfortunately, on subsequent enquiry as to the whereabouts of the photographs we found out that there had been a problem with the camera, so the historic event had not actually been recorded. I would have liked that photograph as a fitting reminder of a lot of hard work.

Membership of the DRC involved a number of visits to Zurich to hear a plethora of cases on a multitude of different topics. Generally, the meetings involved an overnight stay which gave me a good opportunity of getting to know the players' representatives on the DRC.

Appeals from decisions of the DRC went to the Court of Arbitration for Sport (CAS) in Lausanne. This arrangement involved a considerable increase to the business of CAS as there were many footballing cases referred to them.

The transfer saga took up much of my time, my normal work suffered, and I did not even get a chance to watch Manchester United's Champions League games with the club defending the trophy it had won so dramatically in 1999.

That season would see it lose in the quarter-final to Real Madrid. But I am not complaining. This was a once in a lifetime chance to operate at the top level of European football administration and I made a considerable number of significant contacts in the game. The negotiations I had been involved in had changed football, and I look back to the time with great fondness.

25

A Pawn in Their Game

Critics have often presented Manchester United as an arrogant club, always obsessed with their own fortunes and who never think of the national game.

In fact there have been many examples where Manchester United's actions have benefited their fellow clubs. By defying the Football League and entering the European Cup in 1956, United paved the way for others to join. Wolverhampton Wanderers followed suit in 1958, followed by Burnley and Tottenham.

In 2000, Manchester United, aware of how the country had not staged the World Cup since winning it in 1966, stepped in to help England in its attempt to win the right to stage the 2006 World Cup. It was a huge sacrifice on the club's part and made it very unpopular in many parts of the country without any justification.

England were bidding against Germany, South Africa, Morocco and Brazil – although Brazil withdrew just before the vote was held and backed South Africa. England's bid was opposed by UEFA which claimed that there was a gentleman's agreement that England would get Euro '96 in return for supporting Germany's bid in 2006. England denied there was any such undertaking.

With eight votes, UEFA was the most powerful block in the twenty-four-man FIFA executive that decided the World Cup. One of those was David Will of Scotland, and England was assured of his support. But the other seven would vote for Germany.

If England's argument was that they had not staged the World Cup since 1966, many were swayed by the counterclaim that this would be the first World Cup staged in Germany since reunification.

With the odds stacked against England, they needed every vote to win. This is where Manchester United came in.

FIFA had decided to launch the FIFA Club World Championship, to be held in Brazil in January 2000, six months before the FIFA executive met in Zurich to decide the venue for the 2006 World Cup.

This was a tournament for clubs that had won their continental championships and was the brainchild of the FIFA president, Sepp Blatter. It was seen by Blatter as a tournament to clip UEFA's wings, whose immensely popular Champions League had begun to emerge as a world league followed by millions around the globe, some of whom had never seen Europe. UEFA was run by Blatter's great rival, the Swede Lennart Johansson, a man Blatter had beaten to become FIFA president, and the Swiss was determined to curb what he saw as UEFA's growing might.

As winners of the 1999 Champions League, United had been invited to represent Europe in this inaugural competition. For the FA it was important that United take part. If England's champions did not go to Brazil, this would be seen as a snub by Blatter, further reinforcing the image of English arrogance.

The FA had cosied up to Blatter and in 1998 had even voted for him to become president of FIFA, turning their back on their fellow European, Johansson. There was no way they could now upset him. But for United, this created a huge problem. The eight-team tournament was due to take place over two weeks in January 2000, thereby clashing with the FA Cup fourth round and making it impossible for United to take part in the new competition. From the moment Manchester United won in Barcelona, the pressure was on us to go to Brazil.

The FA were not the only body pressing United to go to Brazil. So was Tony Banks, a diehard Chelsea supporter and a somewhat surprising choice as sports minister by Tony Blair – they were on opposite wings of the Labour Party. After United had initially told the FA they could not send a team to Brazil, Banks wrote on 10 June 1999 to Sir Roland Smith, stating:

> . . . whilst I understand fully the fixture demands being made upon the club, a refusal could have serious ramifications for England's 2006 World Cup bid. I have been informed personally by three FIFA Executive Members, all of whom have previously committed themselves to England's cause, that they will not vote for us in the event of Manchester United's non-appearance.
>
> I can appreciate how unfair it is to put such a burden upon you. But it is clearly in the national interest for your club to compete in the FIFA Championship.

This led to urgent meetings between United, the FA, the director of England's World Cup bid Alex McGiven, the Premier League and Tony Banks. The question was how could United's fixture load be reduced to both go to Brazil and play in the FA Cup?

Here it should be stressed that taking part in the FA Cup is a requirement of all clubs that belong to the FA, and this had been re-emphasised when the FA sanctioned the formation of the Premier League. There were various suggestions mooted: a bye until the fifth round; an extension to the 1999/2000 Premier League season; the 1999 Charity Shield match between Manchester United and Arsenal should be treated as a league game; and that United players should not be chosen for England friendlies.

The story broke in the *Daily Telegraph* on 12 June, with Mihir Bose writing that, if Manchester United did not take part, Bayern Munich, the losing Champions League finalists, would go instead, taking advantage of the Bundesliga's midwinter break. The report added:

The FA, however, are believed to be offering two carrots if they agree to Blatter's request – the season will be extended to accommodate the rearranged fixtures and United will be allowed to field a weakened team in the FA Cup without fear of penalty.

The Premier League made it clear that it would not agree to extending the season. In the end it was Martin Edwards who proposed the solution that if United had to go to Brazil the club should be allowed to withdraw from the FA Cup in its entirety.

That would be an unprecedented step. In May Manchester United had beaten Newcastle to win the FA Cup, and for the holders not to defend the Cup would make a statement that was certain to go down badly with the fans. But given the circumstances, that was the only way to square the circle.

United also had to consider the financial consequences and risks which might arise with potential claims from sponsors, partners, executive seat holders and box holders.

On 29 June, I had a discussion with Michael Cunnah, the finance director of the FA. This followed upon my request to Dave Richards, the Sheffield Wednesday chairman who had become chairman of the Premier League, in relation to the deed of guarantee and indemnity which we were looking for from the FA. This would enable Manchester United to withdraw from its commitment to the FA – in other words, to play in the FA Cup – without penalty and with compensation for the lost fixtures. We were looking for £1.2 million.

Nic Coward, the FA's in-house lawyer, had told Martin Edwards earlier in the day that this could not be arranged. I explained to Michael Cunnah, however, the thinking behind the need for the cover from the deed and the fact that it was one thing for a club not to play significant games as a result of lack of success, but it was quite another thing for it unilaterally to reduce its chances of playing games by withdrawing from a competition.

I arranged to see Dave Richards and the FA's David Davies at White's Hotel that night. They were finishing off their meal in the restaurant, and I joined them for coffee to run through what I had said earlier to Michael Cunnah.

David Davies said that he needed to make a telephone call to the Minister for Sport as he felt the government would give the indemnity. He left the table and returned some short while later. He then rang Tony Banks from the table and put the sports minister on to me. I explained our thinking and the extent of the indemnity required. Banks said that the amount of indemnity sought should not prevent United from taking part in the tournament but that it was difficult for him to speak to anyone at this late hour (it was around 11pm), but he would stick his neck out and say that he would provide the necessary guarantee. I asked for this to be confirmed in writing.

The next day I spoke to Roland Smith and Martin Edwards to update them on developments and the assurances of a guarantee given by Tony Banks. Clearly confidentiality was essential.

I also spoke to Davies and asked if he could help us get something in writing from Banks. He gave me Banks's various telephone numbers. I tried all these but could not contact him, and in the end left a message for him on his pager. He rang me back some time after 10:15am. He first of all asked why the FA itself was not giving the guarantee and I explained that the FA had been placed with other difficulties, namely with AXA, who sponsored the FA Cup. He then asked me what would happen if United made a profit on the World Club Championship over and above what they had earned from their winning run in the FA Cup the previous season.

He thought in that scenario the guarantees should be reduced accordingly. I said that based on last year's figures, initial indications were that we would not benefit as much as we would have done if we won the FA Cup. I also said that the difficulty we were faced with was that we were having to make a decision on coming out of the Cup in the summer of 1999 and there was no way of knowing how much we would have earned. Hence the reason we had asked for the guarantee.

Banks kept asking various questions, but he was at great pains to make it clear that he was not going back on what he had said the previous evening – he had stuck his neck out – but it was necessary for him to speak to the appropriate person in the government and he thought this was the Chief Whip, Ann Taylor. He had been trying to speak to her but had not been able to get through.

He also asked me to clarify that the guarantee did not involve the government paying any money at this stage to Manchester United and I confirmed that this was the case. The indemnity would only come into play if and when a claim was made and United would obviously do its best to deal strongly with any claims that came in.

It might well be that some box or executive seat holders would decide right at the beginning of the season that the basis on which they had bought their seats had been misrepresented and seek payment at that stage. I assumed that we would be able to deal with those claims and re-sell those seats. The main difficulty was that the majority would in fact wait and see how the season went because there might be a good run in Europe which would provide the necessary home games without needing any FA Cup matches.

I spoke to Martin about a press conference that was taking place at 3pm. We would say that we would be taking part in the tournament subject to clearing certain outstanding legal and contractual issues.

At around 2:30pm Banks rang me on my mobile. He said he had spoken about the matter at senior level in Cabinet. It was a Treasury issue. He was confident that, if required, the government would deliver the required guarantee, but they had to decide which contingency pot it would come from. It had to be a pot that did not have to be approved by Parliament.

He said that he was satisfied it would be done, but he was unwilling to put it in writing. The matter could leak – that, he said, would be 'suicide'.

What he was prepared to do was give his personal assurances, backed up by senior members of the Cabinet, that the necessary funds would be paid when called upon. And that, if anything went wrong in relation to that, then it would be a resignation issue.

I told him that I was concerned that if anything happened to him or to me then there would be no evidence available to establish the fact that the guarantee for the £1.2 million had been given. I insisted that something be put in writing, as a guarantee must be effective. Banks agreed and said he would send a handwritten letter by fax to me at the Premier League and he wanted me to stand by the fax machine.

We discussed the terms of the letter that he was going to send, and I agreed the wording with the additional sentence that Manchester United's requirement would be honoured, not merely that its requirements were acceptable.

I then went over to the fax machine, having given Banks the number. There were two abortive attempts to fax through the letter before the complete version arrived. At his request, I then shredded the two incomplete copies.

The handwritten letter, dated 30 June 1999, on Department for Culture, Media and Sport notepaper, stated:

To: Maurice Watkins, Manchester United FC

Further to our telephone conversations on 29&30 June, this is to confirm that the requirement made by Manchester United FC is acceptable to HM Government and will be honoured, if required.

Tony Banks

The confirmation that Manchester United would be going to Brazil was made by Martin Edwards at the 3pm press conference. Alex Ferguson and David Davies were also on the top table for the announcement. Martin's statement raised a storm of protest.

All kinds of solutions were put forward, including one by AXA, the FA Cup sponsor, who proposed that our FA Cup opposition should be flown to Rio de Janeiro and the Cup tie should take place there. I had telephone conversations on this with the AXA chief executive, Mark Wood. Apparently, AXA also proposed to fly two jumbo jets full of supporters out to Brazil for the matches.

Supporter criticism also mounted, with allegations of breach of contract. Members of Parliament had their say. The Competition Commission became involved. The *Daily Mirror* became particularly involved, launching their 'Save the FA Cup' campaign.

Martin was approached by the *Mirror* editor, Piers Morgan, for an interview which he agreed to do despite warnings from Roland Smith. Not surprisingly, the ensuing exclusive articles were hardly flattering for Martin and seriously condemnatory of the club. The *Mirror* edition which published Edwards's interview contained an 'apology' in the following terms:

> The Mirror would like to apologise to all our readers and every football fan in Britain for failing to win our campaign to save the FA Cup.
>
> Manchester United last night confirmed we'd lost the fight by announcing they will NOT re-enter the competition and defend their title.
>
> You can't say we didn't try. We fought one of the biggest campaigns in the Mirror's long history.

By this time, Tony Banks had been succeeded as sports minister by Kate Hoey. As she left Downing Street having met Tony Blair and taken her dream job – she had been Northern Ireland high-jump champion – the government's director of communications, Alastair Campbell, pulled her to one side: 'Don't say anything to the press about Manchester United pulling out of the FA Cup to play in Brazil.' Hoey did not approve of the decision and thought it a mistake.

In terms of results, she was right. Manchester United did not make it out of the group stage of the World Club Championship. The only side they managed to beat was South Melbourne from Australia. I had intended to go to Brazil if we reached the semi-finals. I did not need to pack a bag.

England lost the bid to stage the 2006 World Cup, which went to Germany. But one consequence of Manchester United's involvement with the bid was that I was asked by the FA to join teams working on overseas missions.

One was to the Ivory Coast. This was a country where there was a Foreign Office directive against any non-essential travel. I commented on this when checking in at the airport to the FA chef de mission, Jane Bateman. I also mentioned that I had heard that rabies incurred from bat bites was a significant hazard.

'Oh, that's interesting,' was the reply. 'There are thousands of bats roosting in the trees next to the hotel.' I did not ask any more questions and got on the plane. She was right about the bats, however; there were thousands of them.

Much has changed in FIFA and the running of world football following exposure of corruption in the organisation and an almost wholesale change in personnel. However, one thing has not changed. England have not won a bid to stage the World Cup, losing out to Russia for the 2018 tournament. I can only hope no club will ever go through what Manchester United had to endure at the turn of the millennium when England once again bid to stage the competition.

Looking back, I feel strongly that Manchester United was made a pawn in a bid that did not have any chance, and led to us being unfairly castigated by fans, both inside and outside of Old Trafford, as a self-seeking club that only looked after its own commercial interests. Had the bid been better led, United would have been spared this unnecessary public censure.

26

Gordon and Me

I am something of a hoarder and, amid the vast amount of documents and cuttings I have acquired over the years, there is one little note which I much treasure. It reads:

> Dear Maurice,
> Just a quick note to thank you personally for all your help and support during the latter stages of the PFA saga. The story will never be written – despite Gordon's attempts on Sunday – of what really happened. Nobody would ever believe it!
> Thanks again, it was a good outcome for the whole of football.
> Kind regards

It was written by Richard Scudamore, now chief executive of the Premier League, and referred to my part in averting a players' strike in the winter of 2001.

The saga involved intense talks with Gordon Taylor of the PFA, and I shall never forget how fraught it was and how often it seemed we were on the brink of collapse. To understand it, let us look into the PFA. The back cover of *Behind the Glory*, the authorised history of the PFA, has a comment by the journalist Mihir Bose: 'The Professional Footballers' Association is one of the most extraordinary trade unions in the country.'

This was even more emphatically emphasised during 2021 with the departure from the PFA of Gordon Taylor – one of the longest-serving and the highest-paid trade unionist in the country, reportedly earning £2 million a year. Gary Neville compared his final days at the union with Arsène Wenger's at Arsenal.

Twenty years earlier, Taylor was in his pomp with no fear he would be elbowed out. The PFA was anxious to flex its muscles and portray the Premier League as a money-making machine which had no concern for the 'football family'. Like Sepp Blatter, Taylor loved using those words, and during the players' dispute he would never miss a chance to talk about this 'family' to which we were all supposed to belong.

The dispute centred round the PFA's share of the Premier League's television revenues. The PFA had been getting a share of this long before the Premier League was even an idea; since 1956, roughly 7½ per cent, with players receiving five guineas 'appearance money' per televised match.

The formation of the Premier League meant a lot more money was available and in 1992/93, the first year of the Premier League deal, the PFA had received £2.5 million from the Premier League and £500,000 from the Football League.

I had been involved in discussions in 1996 when the Football League wanted to make the payment discretionary. The Premier League made no such formal move, but we watched what the Football League was doing carefully, and I advised the then chief executive Rick Parry on the issue. The PFA issued a strike ballot – and with 91.8 per cent in favour the matter was settled. The Premier League and the Football League agreed that the PFA should receive five per cent of their television money.

Two years later, in 1998, there was another huge television deal, then the biggest in UK sports history, and the PFA received £7.5 million from the Premier League which, with the money from the Football League, meant its coffers were richer by almost £9 million.

It was the deal that Parry's successor Richard Scudamore negotiated in June 2000 to bring in £1.5 billion that lit the fuse. The Football League had done a separate deal under which ITV Digital agreed to pay them £315 million.

It was another year before the PFA went to war when the 1998 agreement with the Premier League expired at the end of the 2000/01 season. Gordon, seeing how well the Premier League had done, could sense an opportunity.

The Premier League's initial offer was £150,000 on top of the previous offer. This incensed Taylor, who said:

> We have just received what can only be described as a derisory offer from the Premiership and the Football League. It is substantially less than last year even though they have far more TV revenues. In fact, I will go so far as to say it is an insult and can only surmise this is an attempt at a show of strength on their part.

Taylor, having stressed that the money received went to the PFA's schemes to help current and former players, threatened a players' strike if, as he put it, the Premier League did not offer a sum 'that respected previous agreements'.

Richard Scudamore briefed clubs on the state of the negotiations. Scudamore pointed out that in addition to the grant aid for the PFA, the Premier League had also chosen to support the Football League Youth Development Programme and the Football Foundation grassroots facilities from the increased television income.

This clearly did not worry Taylor. At an emergency meeting on Sunday, 23 September 2001 the PFA executive gave the go-ahead for strike ballot papers to be distributed to its 3,500 members.

In essence, what Taylor wanted was 5 per cent of the new deal. However, as Scudamore made clear in a letter to Taylor:

... percentages of TV income are irrelevant as they create a false premise for these negotiations. Under the 1998 Agreement, as you know, it was agreed that a simple and straightforward amount would be paid by the FAPL to the PFA and this was not tied to any percentage of TV income.

As for the threatened strike action, Scudamore also pointed out that the PFA was not in a trade dispute as defined by the employment legislation. It was a dispute merely about provisions for a benefit fund distinct from the contracts of employment of its members.

Scudamore warned Taylor that, if the PFA went on strike, the Premier League might go to court to seek an immediate injunction to stop it. The threatened action did not please the clubs, and Arsenal and Leeds warned their players that if they came out on strike they would not be paid.

David Dein, the Arsenal vice-chairman who effectively ran the club, compared how well off the PFA was compared with equivalent unions in other European leagues: 'In Germany their union gets nothing, in Italy likewise they get nothing, in Spain about £500,000 and in France just over £1 million.'

Ken Bates, the Chelsea chairman, had his own view, suggesting that as the PFA had just paid £1.9 million for LS Lowry's painting, *Going to the Match*, they did not noticeably need any more money.

There were further concessions. The Premier League and the Football League clubs would fund the payment of a cash benefit retirement income scheme for professional footballers. This was a non-contributory scheme that provided a benefit to Football League and Premier League players once they reached the age of 35.

But Taylor wanted more for his members. Further talks between Scudamore and Taylor led nowhere and on 15 October Taylor wrote to the clubs saying that he would ballot his members about going on strike.

It was at this stage I was starting to get more and more involved, having discussions with Dave Richards, the Premier League chairman, Scudamore and the Legal Working Party. My involvement led to media speculation that I had been brought in because Scudamore was not getting on with Taylor. The media ran a story saying Scudamore had been 'dumped' and that Richards and I were part of a new negotiating team which would be better equipped to deal with Taylor.

This did not please Scudamore, and when he briefed the clubs on 13 November his report included the following note:

> One of the unsavoury aspects of the coverage was the fabrication of the stories around Sky exerting pressure and my personal 'exclusion' from talks. Sky have been kept fully informed and, although concerned as we all are, have exerted no pressure whatsoever.
>
> There is also no truth in the suggestion that a new negotiation team of Dave Richards and Maurice Watkins has been put in place. Dave and I had discussed and agreed that he would talk to Gordon in an effort to influence him into accepting the 2nd November offer and specifically ask him to show some restraint when announcing the ballot.
>
> Their meeting was unable to be convened prior to the ballot announcement and so now this phase has passed we are re-engaging with the negotiations. The press were fully briefed on my being 'dumped' [. . .] I can assure you that we remain committed to resolving this matter and, despite attempts by the press to convince people otherwise, Gordon Taylor and I have retained a professional relationship throughout.

To me it was clear that one of the problems was that Taylor and Scudamore did not gel. While Taylor also denied their personal relationship was an issue, he did say: 'In the past we've been dealing with those with respect for the history of the game – and that has not been happening of late.' He went on:

We come from different backgrounds. I have been in football for a long time, but Richard is not the same. He is a businessman and he didn't want to talk about any of the history of our agreements or the situation of the PFA, so I am not quite sure he fully understood in the beginning.[22]

As far as Taylor was concerned, Scudamore was new to football. He had been in his job for two years, following two years in the Football League. Before that he had worked for the Thompson Corporation in America and this, as *Behind the Glory* puts it, meant he had come 'to the job largely unencumbered with any sense of football history' and not much aware of the football family.

On my part I put all this to one side and was happy with the PFA solicitor, John Hewison, who happened to be a good friend. However fraught the negotiations may be, when solicitors on opposite sides get along it can make a huge difference, as these talks would prove. By this time the FA and its chief executive, Adam Crozier, were also involved as it was important that there be a coordinated approach from all those who ran the game.

On 15 November, Scudamore called a general meeting of the Premier League and it was agreed:

1. The board be given authority to continue talks with the PFA on the basis that a final offer of £52.5m to be paid over three years would be made, the money coming from the Premier League, Football League and FA.
2. A sum equivalent to the first year's funding would be placed into a separate escrow account* as a sign of good faith.

---

* An account in which money is held by a third party on behalf of two or more contracting parties that are in the process of completing a transaction; the money is released when the agreed contractual conditions for this have been met.

3. In the event of talks failing and the PFA calling a strike, the board of the Premier League would go to court to get injunctive relief.

The next day, Adam Crozier, the Football League's chief executive David Burns, Premier League lawyer Peter McCormick and I met Taylor and his team, which included Mick McGuire, Barry Horne, Brendon Batson and John Hewison. The meeting lasted all day and made some progress, but there was no final resolution and it was agreed we would meet again the following week.

On 19 November, Scudamore and I met Taylor and Hewison at my offices. We also met the next day with talks finishing at around 7pm. Taylor wanted more than £52.5 million and various amounts of money were discussed 'without prejudice'– meaning that, if not accepted by both parties, the various offers could not be referred to in court. It was clear we were no nearer a solution.

We had further discussions the following day, but by 7pm it was clear we could not agree on a settlement with the PFA. Richard and I were under the impression that the strike notices were going to go out the following day (the 21st) but, after we had adjourned, I received a call from Hewison in which he confirmed that the strike notices *had gone out that evening*. As Taylor would make clear in a statement to football supporters, the strike meant that:

> we are only asking our members to refuse to play in front of television cameras. Normal league matches; cup matches and European matches are not affected. If your club is prepared to send us an undertaking that cameras will be switched off for matches at your ground until such time as our dispute is settled, then we shall of course inform our members accordingly and your matches will be unaffected.

Richard and I were both thunderstruck at this development, which left Richard extremely upset. We both decided to go to the Midland

Hotel in Manchester to consider how we should react to this unexpected development. Clearly, the clubs had to be told and I drafted a fax which Richard sent expressing our surprise at this turn of events.

I had to go to Zurich for a FIFA meeting, but Richard and his team held a press conference which revealed the £52.5 million offer and emphasised that this was a two-thirds increase and represented an annual contribution of £17.5 million.

The Premier League had to respond to the strike action, and on 22 November the clubs were told that the Premier League was issuing proceedings in the Queen's Bench Division of the High Court and that these would be served on the PFA's solicitors the following day. That evening I had a telephone call with Taylor and it was agreed to hold make or break talks on the morning of the 23rd at the Hilton at Manchester Airport. I also went through matters with Scudamore.

The meeting at the Hilton started at 8:30am. Four rooms had been hired. I was joined by Scudamore and McCormick in one room; next door was the PFA team of Batson, McGuire, Horne, Nick Cusack and Hewison. In a third room was Crozier and Burns. There was also a fourth room, which was reserved for me and Taylor to talk in private with no one else present. We had an initial meeting when we all met together. Then, as had been arranged, I went off with Taylor into the fourth room.

The Premier League's offer of £52.5 million for three years could be extended by a further three. Taylor made it clear he wanted a ten-year deal. And every 1 per cent increase in the television deal would see the PFA receive an extra 0.75 per cent. But if the television income fell, the PFA's share would reduce by only 0.5 per cent.

Taylor also made it clear that the Premier League and the football authorities could not tell the PFA how it should spend this money. He saw it as important to assert the independence of the union.

I went back to Scudamore, Crozier and company but they were not prepared to accept those terms. When I went back to Taylor, he told me that this would mean a strike. I went back to my team and for forty minutes we discussed our options.

In the end we agreed the PFA would receive £52.5 million for each of the two three-year cycles with an option to increase to ten years and without any conditions attached as to how it would spend the money. However, each Football League club would receive £10,000 for player-related benefits.

By 11a.m, Taylor and I had agreed the deal. Now was the time for smiles and the photograph of Scudamore shaking Taylor's hand with Crozier standing in the middle looking like a referee. While Taylor looks ebullient, Scudamore's lips are tightly drawn, expressing the strain the whole thing had been.

It had been a stressful few weeks, and I know it had not been easy for Scudamore. There is no doubt that my relationship with Taylor and Hewison helped to bring a satisfactory conclusion to a potentially very damaging conflict.

Gordon Taylor subsequently sent me a copy of the authorised history of the PFA, writing in the flyleaf:

To Maurice: A brilliant lawyer, a great football man and a trusted colleague!

Every good wish
Gordon

PS: Thank you for all your help and for all your work for the New Children's Hospital

These comments were much appreciated by me, as was the £1 million donation from the PFA towards the Manchester New Children's Hospital Appeal from the PFA centenary celebration.

Gordon led the players union for the past four decades, following a career in which he played at every level of the Football League. During his tenure, the PFA has spent nearly £1 billion on supporting its members. As Gordon has pointed out, it has not always been easy or uncontroversial, but he has been fiercely proud of the support the PFA gives its members day in, day out.

The PFA's collective bargaining agreement is the envy of the sports world. As well as fighting on pay and conditions, education and medical support, the PFA has taken stands on issues as difficult and important as mental health and racism in football.

The PFA has helped to lead the way on ground-breaking dementia research, funding FIELD (Football's Influence on Lifelong Health and Dementia Risk study), which provided the first significant insights into lifelong health outcomes in former professional footballers.

The chapter is closing on Gordon's forty-year career, and the PFA has concluded a competitive and exhaustive recruitment process in its search for its next chief executive, Maheta Molango – a trained lawyer who has played for Brighton, Lincoln and Oldham and had been chief executive of the Spanish club, Mallorca.* The baton is being passed on, and Gordon is in no doubt that the PFA will continue to be the best and strongest sports union in the world.

---

* Note from editor: Gordon Taylor stepped down as chief executive of the PFA in June 2021.

27

The Fall of the Plc

The board of Manchester United was never so ham-fisted as when it tried to deal with the Irish horse-racing magnates, John Magnier and JP McManus. How they could have allowed their biggest shareholders to fall out with their most important employee, Sir Alex Ferguson, seemed bewildering.

You have to think the plc chairman, Professor Sir Roland Smith, that veteran of so many boardroom disputes and skirmishes, would have seen this one coming and stopped it in its tracks. He insisted the dispute was a personal matter, but the arguments over a racehorse fired the starting gun in a breakdown between the club and its main shareholders that would fatally undermine the plc.

Magnier and McManus represented a formidable partnership. Magnier had founded the Coolmore Stud in County Tipperary, which was to become the most successful in the world – in 2018 it was valued at £3.5 billion.

John Patrick McManus had set up the Martinstown Stud in County Limerick and had moved to Switzerland in 1994, becoming a highly successful currency trader. In London, a suite at the Dorchester was kept permanently at his disposal.

Between them, Magnier and McManus owned 28.4 per cent of Manchester United.

They became close to Ferguson and invited him to become co-owner of one of their stallions, Rock of Gibraltar. Magnier's wife, Sue, the

THE FALL OF THE PLC

daughter of the great racehorse trainer Vincent O'Brien, owned the other half.

Rock of Gibraltar's racing career was a triumph. He became the first northern-hemisphere horse since Mill Reef in 1970 to win seven consecutive group-one races. He would win both the Irish and the English 2,000 Guineas.

By 2003, he was ready to be retired to stud, which is where the problems began. Alex claimed he was entitled to half of Rock of Gibraltar's stud fees. In 2004, his fee to cover a mare was around £44,200. Magnier and McManus disagreed. Ferguson employed solicitors.

The club itself had no involvement in the claim – but should it have taken a more interested role and been more active in trying to manoeuvre a settlement? Particularly, as lawyers specialising in bloodstock affairs had let it be known that Manchester United's manager had little chance of success. According to one piece of legal advice I have read:

> Because of the absence of a written contract between him and Magnier, Ferguson will have everything weighted against him. I don't believe the judge will award him half the horse's stud fees as compensation. I think he will lose and, if I were advising him, I'd tell him not to proceed. The Irish Court have only heard one similar case in modern times, over 30 years ago, which produced victory for the defendant.[23]

Matters worsened when in January 2004 Magnier and McManus published their '99 Questions' they wanted Manchester United to answer. They covered, among other things, the transfers of Jaap Stam, Juan Sebastián Verón, Tim Howard, David Bellion, Cristiano Ronaldo and José Kléberson. Action was threatened if the answers were not satisfactory.

In a letter accompanying the questions, Magnier and McManus wrote:

> There is insufficient detail about certain transactions and there is a lack of transparency in relation to a number of material payments of significant sums.
>
> What we cannot understand is the necessity for the relative secrecy in which agents conduct their role and the astonishing fees that have been charged to the company on completion of the transfers.

They highlighted a conflict of interest. One of the agencies that did significant business with Manchester United was Elite, who employed Alex's son, Jason Ferguson.

Issues also arose about the distressing experience suffered by Jason and reports from Alex in an MUTV interview that he had had to call the police on account of people hiding in his garden and stealing his mail and bin bags. Magnier's case was that Ferguson appeared to have implicated him, indirectly or not, in alleged criminal behaviour. Lawyers for the two Irishmen had contacted United's board to demand tapes and written transcripts of various newspaper, television and radio interviews.

Manchester United responded through David Gill – who had become chief executive when Peter Kenyon left for Chelsea in September 2003 – with a full statement to the Stock Exchange. The statement indicated the club's approach to transfer dealings; what the manager does and what the off-the-field team does.

Manchester United believed those procedures were rigorous, but as a result of the unsubstantiated allegations, the club felt that it could not let the matter rest. Accordingly, an internal review was started by the finance director, Nick Humby, to look at them and any changes or improvements to come out of it. The review was to be implemented immediately and to be completed as quickly as possible.

Before his action reached Dublin's High Court, the manager began talks on 5 March 2004 to reach a settlement. Despite Ferguson receiving an out-of-court settlement, it was a fraction of the entitlement for stud fees that he initially sought and can be seen only as a victory for Magnier and his associates.

What involvement did I have with the Irishmen? Little or none, I had been at the odd social event with Sir Alex Ferguson where he had invited JP McManus but I had never met John Magnier – until a chance encounter.

I had gone to the Villa Tiberio Restaurant in Marbella for lunch when I was stopped by the owner, Sandro Morelli, as I was being shown to my seat. Sandro said: 'We have some friends of yours here today.'

'Oh yes', I responded. 'Who?'

'John Magnier,' Sandro said.

'I have never met him,' I said.

'We should do something about that,' was Sandro's response, and he took me over to John's table where he was lunching with some friends. Nearly two hours later, I was still talking to John and my own guests had given up on me and ordered their lunch.

It was not an unfriendly encounter and when we finally broke up, John indicated that relationships between Cubic Expression (the investment vehicle controlled by him and JP McManus) and the club would improve.

Coincidentally, the next evening, I found myself sitting next to John Magnier at a table in another restaurant, the Marbella Club Café, which I subsequently discovered was a regular haunt of his. We exchanged a few pleasantries and, shortly afterwards, he sent over a rather nice bottle of champagne.

While all this was going on, the Glazer family – who owned the Tampa Bay Buccaneers American football franchise – were beginning their takeover of Manchester United through their investment vehicle, Red Football.

They had begun buying shares in September 2003. Within five months, they owned 16.3 per cent of Manchester United, which was then valued at £741 million. By the time of the club's AGM on 12

November 2004, their stake was nearing 30 per cent. Once it passed that threshold, the Glazers would have to launch a formal takeover bid.

The Manchester United board refused the Glazers permission to perform due diligence (an audit of the company before a takeover). The Glazers informed the club they would be voting against all resolutions at the AGM, although their shareholding of 28.1 per cent would only guarantee the defeat of special resolutions that required approval by three-quarters of the shareholders. The key factor on the ordinary resolutions would be the decisions of Cubic Expression.

Three directors were up for re-election – Andy Anson, Philip Yea (who had been finance director at Guinness) and me. If the resolution reappointing us was not passed, each of those three United directors would be deemed, in accordance with Article 108 of Manchester United's articles of associations, to have retired from office at the close of the AGM.

I suppose I was a little slow in grasping the significance of the Glazers' threat to vote against all resolutions. Was I thinking of the consequences for myself? With little time remaining, I thought I should try and speak to John Magnier (whose contact details he had given to me) and see whether he would be prepared to cast the Cubic Expression vote in favour of the board re-elections.

By the time I managed to get hold of John it was too late to do anything effectively. He was on his way back from Barbados, and I was on my way off the United board.

That soon became academic as the whole plc board would be swept away. In May 2005, Cubic Expression sold the Magnier and McManus shareholding to the Glazers. The following month, with the Glazers having upped their stake to beyond 75 per cent, Manchester United was delisted from the Stock Exchange and became, once more, a private company.

28

Goodbye Old Trafford, Hello World

My time at Old Trafford came to a close on a soggy, all too typical Manchester day in 2012 over a lunch that I had been invited to but which I ended up paying for.

The plc board was no more but I was still part of the football club board when I had a call from David Gill inviting me to lunch. Invitations from David were not frequent, so I did wonder what the reason behind it was. I did not have to wait long for all to be revealed. We met at Rosso, the Italian restaurant at the top of King Street in which Rio Ferdinand had a financial interest.

We had barely ordered our drinks and food, when David said: 'Maurice, you are close to reaching the age of 70 and the Glazers feel that your board tenure should come to an end at that point.'

'All a bit sudden' was my immediate reaction, and I suggested that there should be a lead into this and that I should have at least one further full year. I was not the only board member who was close to the age of 70, and in the timespan being considered, I wondered why there was the urgency.

For somebody who had been on the board for such a long time and been part of so much change at Old Trafford, it seemed extraordinary that I should be asked to leave with such abruptness.

But my suggestion of an additional year was not greeted with much enthusiasm by David, and I was left with the feeling that he had been given a brief by the Glazers and that's what he had to stick with. As our lunch progressed, it became clear that there would not be any room for manoeuvre to change the Glazers' minds. I brought lunch to an early close and even paid for it. Sacked over a lunch which you have paid for must be a first of sorts.

As events turned out, I was the only person to whom the age element was applied. It was not applied to Bobby Charlton, who was then 73, or Mike Edelson, who remained on the board after turning 70. I wonder why not? The Glazers must have had their own reasons but what surprised me was the lack of support from my fellow board members.

They do say that as one door closes another opens. For me, it was more a case of several doors opening, providing me opportunities to work in various sports that I had not previously been involved with.

The first opportunity on leaving Old Trafford arrived in December 2012 when I was appointed chairman of British Swimming.

The process involved a number of interviews, and I thought I had missed the boat and had already asked my PA whether or not I should file my papers as I had heard nothing definite. She was told that it was still very possible I would get the job. Eventually, I was invited to a meeting at Heathrow Terminal 5 followed by one at Birmingham Airport, culminating in an offer for an initial four-year term that I was very pleased to accept.

Little did I realise the opportunities which would open up to me from taking on the role, which involved chairing British Para Swimming as well as able-bodied swimming. The role involved responsibility for swimming, diving, high diving, water polo and artistic swimming.

The main focus was the 2016 Olympics in Rio de Janeiro. Both the main Games and the Paralympics were wonderful experiences. In

London, four years earlier, we had finished 15th in the swimming medal table. In Rio we were sixth, above China (who were seventh).

Rio was a great success for Team GB. We finished second in the overall medal tables for both the Olympics and Paralympics – we came away with 147 medals altogether, including 64 gold, which was a fantastic performance.

Swimming also took me to worlds I had heard and read about but never seen. This included an audience with Pope Francis in his private quarters in July 2018. Before I met him my colleagues and I had a great deal of discussion as to what I should present him with. We decided on a framed swimming cap, which he much appreciated.

My tenure as chair or British Swimming was renewed for a further four-year term and there was a further extension to cope with the impact of Covid-19 for the Tokyo Olympics. It was a huge disappointment not to take part actively in Tokyo, but I have to be grateful for having had the opportunity of attending the Rio Games.

While I was on the board of Manchester United, I had been appointed to the board of the Rugby Football League (RFL). The chair of the RFL was Richard Lewis and when he was appointed as chief executive of Wimbledon I took over as interim chair.

The Rugby Football League had become one of the most respected national governing bodies in the UK. The sport had built a positive reputation for good governance based upon the two fundamental ideas of an independent board and a unified structure for the whole of the sport.

I decided we should review the structure, which was called the Watkins Review of Rugby League Governance, to ensure that the governance model for Rugby League maintained best practice; we also undertook a consultation process with all relevant stakeholders to ascertain whether further improvements could be made. It was also the case that all UK national governing bodies in receipt of

Sport England funding would have to demonstrate continued adherence to the governance principles as set out in the Whole Sport Plan funding agreement, which required each sport to devise a five-year plan.

During my time as interim chair I also played a full part in hosting the 2013 Rugby League World Cup. This involved speeches and presentations at the Houses of Parliament, the Welsh Assembly and the City of Manchester Town Hall.

Rugby League was the only reason I returned to Old Trafford after I ceased being a director of Manchester United. In 2012, I presented the Leeds Rhinos' captain, Kevin Sinfield. with the Super League Grand Final trophy after Leeds had beaten Warrington Wolves.

The 2013 World Cup final at Old Trafford gave the sport the opportunity to renew its relationship with the Royal Family. The Queen's grandson, Peter Phillips, whom I had got to know, was presented to the Australia and New Zealand players before the game and then awarded the players their medals at the conclusion of the game, which Australia won 34–2.

Although I thought I had made it clear to Peter what his role would entail, he was a little surprised that he was so front of stage, but his attendance was much appreciated by the sport. He brought along, as a guest, the singer Alfie Boe.

In 2013 the chance presented itself to return to football management with my appointment by Patrick Cryne, the owner of Barnsley FC, to the position of chairman of his club. This was a very interesting opportunity to experience non-Premier League football across the Pennines.

It was not without its successes. In 2016 Barnsley made two Wembley appearances: the first saw them win the Johnstone's Paint Trophy; the second was the League One play-off final where Barnsley beat Millwall 3–1.

In September 2017, Patrick Cryne, who was very ill with cancer, was keen to dispose of the club to a new ownership group headed by the Chinese businessman Chien Lee and the US businessman Paul Conway.

Also involved in the deal was Billy Beane, the vice-president of the Oakland Athletics baseball club, whose use of data to build a winning team at a relatively low cost had made him the subject of the *Moneyball* book and film. At this stage I decided it was time for me to stand down from my role as chairman. *Inside World Football*'s comment on this development was that with my departure also went a wealth of football experience and contacts that could not be replaced by data alone, even with the newest of the AI algorithms.

For Lee and his co-investors, Barnsley was their second European club, having taken over at Nice in France's League 1. That takeover had generally been viewed as a success. It was clear the punt on Barnsley depended on whether they could take that giant step into the Premier League. As things turned out, the giant step was nearly made with Barnsley qualifying for the Premier League play-offs in 2021, before losing out to Swansea in the semis.

The broader question of how the data-driven approach can deliver performance goals in football, a game with a greater set of variables than baseball where Billy Beane made his name with Oakland, still remains to be answered.

In August 2018, I renewed my involvement with basketball when I was appointed chair of the British Basketball Federation.

In the 1980s I had been a director of Manchester United Basketball Club and we had also been one of the principal architects of the formation of the original English Basketball League.

Christmas 1984 had been a busy time for some of us at Manchester United with the club having decided to purchase the Warrington Vikings basketball club. We wanted to copy the multi-sport approach being taken by Real Madrid and Barcelona.

Manchester United wanted to build a sports hall next to Old Trafford where the basketball team would play. There was no Christmas dinner for me as we raced to conclude the deal and sign up the players all over a matter of days.

I began my career as a basketball director in style. Our first game was the National Basketball Cup Final at the Royal Albert Hall in London. Unfortunately, we lost in overtime to Kingston, but it was a fantastic inaugural experience.

The game was, however, overshadowed by controversy. The cup games were televised by Channel 4 and, just before the final, the television company dropped the bombshell that, instead of using the team's new name of Manchester United, the commentators were to continue to call the team Warrington Vikings. The reason given was that otherwise the viewers could be confused.

This seemed completely ludicrous. The arrival of Manchester United on the basketball scene had created considerable interest. All basketball fans knew about it. Why not recognise this from the start of the biggest game of the basketball season?

I was instructed to do something about it. So, armed with a court injunction, I presented myself at the Royal Albert Hall, where Channel 4 was carrying out the pre-match preparations, and told the producer that if he did not agree to use the team's current name I would serve him with the injunction I had in my pocket and then there would be no game.

Would we have carried out this threat? I will keep that to myself, but with good British compromise, we agreed that the name could be gradually introduced into the commentary so that by half-time the team would only be called Manchester United. In fact, it worked out much earlier than that and we were soon using our new name.

The financial impact of the Heysel tragedy, which resulted in all English clubs being banned from European competitions, brought the shutters down on United's visions for the sports hall. In 1988 the basketball club was sold, bringing an end to my interest in the game for three decades.

My chairmanship of the British Basketball Federation lasted for two years from 2018 to 2020, when I brought it to an end by resigning from the role. My involvement was acknowledged by the chair of UK Sport, Dame Katherine Grainger, as follows:

> I understand that you have left your role as chair of the British Basketball Federation. I wanted to write to you on behalf of UK Sport to thank you very much for your commitment to the sport during this period. I know that you have overseen the organisation during a period which has seen some funding and governance challenges, but you have also helped to drive pivotal progress in areas such as the relationship with the International Federation, securing crucial Aspirational Funding and supporting the great progress in the elite women's game – who fell just short of qualification for the Tokyo Games. I hope you are proud of your contribution . . .

When I look back on my long career in sport, the failure of the women's basketball team to qualify for the Tokyo Olympics was probably the most disappointing sporting result I ever experienced. In a four-nation group qualifier in Belgrade, Great Britain were drawn with China, the European champions Spain, and South Korea.

Qualifying for Tokyo came down to the final match, which Korea won 82–79.

If I go back to my school days, I was interested in a number of different sports but cricket was the most important to me. I was delighted to be invited in 2013 to join the Lancashire County Cricket Club board and to chair its Remuneration Committee.

In that capacity, I was able to invite John Bercow, the Speaker of the House of Commons, as my guest to an Old Trafford Test match against Australia.

John had never seen an elite game live and had a very enjoyable experience. It started with him being asked to ring the bell for the start of the day's play. A huge honour, I explained. He rang the bell with relish.

He was also asked if he would appear on *Test Match Special* during the tea interval to answer questions from Jonathan Agnew. With the Speaker's lack of cricketing knowledge, I was a little concerned about him being let loose on *TMS*, but Agnew played it with a straight bat and concentrated on parliamentary issues rather than cricketing ones.

To finish off the interview, Agnew asked the Speaker how he thought the last session would go, meaning the parliamentary session. The Speaker thought he was wanting a cricketing contribution, but Jonathan Agnew put him straight and we did not deviate from the agreed line of keeping clear of cricketing issues.

Even before I left Manchester United, I was involved in greyhound racing, a wonderful and popular sport which at its core had remained essentially the same throughout its history. On New Year's Day 2009, I became chairman of a new organisation known as the Greyhound Board of Great Britain (GBGB).

The Labour politician and academic Bernard Donoughue had written a report into greyhound racing which concluded that it needed to modernise to compete in the wider leisure market. GBGB was the response.

Greyhound Racing had a close relationship with Manchester. In July 1926 the first greyhound race around an oval track took place at Belle Vue.

In the foreword to the 2009 Greyhound Annual Report, the first to be published in partnership with GBGB, I wrote:

> From a commercial perspective, my own experiences in dealing with sport governing bodies and their leading clubs, leagues and

sporting personalities suggest that greyhound racing's difficulties are neither unique nor insoluble. There is no instant solution to bringing people back through the turnstiles or raising the profile of our major events, but I am sure that by working together we can succeed in turning round the recent trends and generating the positive public exposure benefitting a sport which continues to attract well in excess of three million spectators each year. At the same time, we will ensure that the sport operates in an efficient and modern regulatory environment.

Being new to the sport I thought it would be a good idea if I demonstrated my interest at the level of an owner. So I purchased a greyhound, with the benefit of apparent expert advice, which I named 'Bursary Boy'. There was considerable interest in my acquisition when it won its first race and I thought I had acquired a future Greyhound Trophy winner. Unfortunately, it was not to be, and my greyhound started to develop bad habits including disrupting the running of its racing opponents. I was advised to withdraw him from racing before I incurred some hefty penalties. I gave him one more race at Belle Vue. That was a mistake; he was disqualified, and I was fined. Enough was enough, and I arranged for him to be rehomed through the Greyhound Trust, a wonderful, caring organisation which rehomes more than 4,500 greyhounds each year.

If my parting with Old Trafford was unexpected and sad, there is one memory that I shall always treasure. This was a letter from Alex Ferguson.

> 31st July 2012
> Dear Maurice,
> Now that we are back from our major pre-season tour, I wanted to put pen to paper on your decision to step down from the board

of Manchester United, after 28 years' service. I know it will have been a difficult decision to make, having been so instrumental in making the club such a global success.

Maurice, I always appreciated your loyalty to me since my appointment with the club and your sound and measured advice in our dealings both on and off the pitch. I have always considered you a friend and confidant, and I am so pleased that you will continue to act as an advisor for the club going forward, you know only too well my thoughts on continuity, so you will not be escaping from me!

I know that you have many other 'hats' and I am sure that all the other institutions that you help and guide will benefit from your integrity, honesty and loyalty, and on that note all that is left to say is thank you for your support, and friendship, and I wish you well with your endeavour.

Yours sincerely

Alex

The letter means much to me and summed up Alex, the man I knew. The public persona may have been a ferocious, must-win football manager, but in private he was always very thoughtful and considerate, and treated people with respect. I wish I could say the same of many others I have met in football or in the wider world of sport and law.

Epilogue

Gandalf II

Not much that happens in football surprises me. But I must say I was surprised when I heard on 19 April 2021 that twelve of Europe's 'leading clubs', to use the terminology that they used in their press release, had come together to form a midweek European Super League.

My first response was surprise that no consideration whatsoever appears to have been given to history or lessons learned over 'Project Gandalf'.

It was clear to me this was a case, in the main, of American capitalist owners, not for the first time, driving business interests without appreciation for what football means in the UK and being completely disengaged from its fans.

None of the six Premier League clubs involved – Arsenal, Chelsea, Liverpool, Manchester City, Manchester United and Tottenham – seemed to have fully considered the Premier League's Rule L.9. I can well understand that chairmen and chief executives may not be familiar with the details of the rule book, but these big clubs, as I know from my experience, have very qualified advisors; that they had not drawn attention to the rule astonished me.

I am very familiar with L.9, having drafted the rule book, but following the announcement I looked it up again – since so many who now run our game seem not to know it, I feel it is worth quoting:

Except with the prior written approval of the Board during the season a Club shall not enter or play its senior men's first team in any competition other than:

L.9.1 the UEFA Champions League;

L.9.2 the UEFA Europa League;

L.9.3 the FA Cup;

L.9.4 the FA Community Shield;

L.9.5 the Football League Cup; or

L.9.6 Competitions authorised by the County Association of which it is a member.*

I would love to see the legal advice which told them they could drive a coach and horses through such a clearly stated rule. In making its announcement, the six founding clubs from the Premier League showed an unbelievable arrogance in trying to wreck the football pyramid in breach of Premier League rules.

When we consider what had happened with Gandalf I, was this purely a case of ignorance of history, or did the participants just forget or ignore what had happened before? It is very surprising that JP Morgan, who were financing the project, appear to have suffered from serious corporate amnesia, failing to recall that they were the financiers for the aborted ESL in 1998.

What they also underestimated was the reaction their plan would provoke from fans, other clubs and organisations, and also the politicians. By 10:45pm on 20 April all six Premier League clubs had withdrawn from the new competition in a humiliating climbdown.

* Since the time of writing the Premier League rules have been updated to expand the list of approved competitions to include the UEFA Europa Conference League, UEFA Super Cup and the FIFA World Club Cup. The substantive point of Rule L.9 remains the same but the wording has been expanded to make clear that it is a breach for clubs (or their officials/directors) to engage in the creation of, or be involved with, any competition formats outside the existing list of approved competitions.

Pep Guardiola, the Manchester City manager, attacked the plans. Chelsea's great former keeper, Petr Cech, addressed fans protesting outside Stamford Bridge. Shortly afterwards, the club announced their withdrawal and fans celebrated. Manchester City were quick to follow Chelsea in announcing their exit, and the other four clubs came in line in short order.

What are likely to be the consequences and effect of the collapse of the ESL?

There is likelihood of future breakaways being blocked by political/legal means and revisions of the Premier League handbook to ensure that this can never happen again, including an Owners' Charter, breaches of which will lead to significant sanctions understood to include potential bans from the League.

UEFA fined the breakaway clubs, and the Premier League, having considered whether the English clubs should have points deducted, also imposed a fine. It is very possible that these English clubs, who were the leaders of the game in this country, will suffer a loss of influence and lose their prominent positions on the Premier League, UEFA and FIFA working groups.

A more serious consequence is the effect on all of football. This is of power being ceded from the Premier League and the FA to politicians, with the Department for Culture, Media and Sport wanting to play a part in running football.

The review being conducted by former sports minister Tracey Crouch could lead to the imposition of a football regulator. This has often been talked about, but in the backlash of the failed ESL project it could become a reality.

There could also be changes to football clubs' corporate structure. Could this lead to a 50+1 Rule as in the Bundesliga? This is a clause in the regulations of the German Football League that in order to obtain a licence, a club must hold a majority of its voting rights. An exception to the rule is when a company or person has substantially funded a club for a continuous period of twenty years, it is possible for that person or company to own a controlling stake. An example is Bayer Leverkusen, which has been owned by the pharma company, Bayer, since its inception, which predated the Bundesliga.

In addition, television broadcasters could demand clauses in Premier League sell-off agreements to handcuff 'rebels' to England's top tier.

The ESL project failed as a result of a very significant fan action, and this could have long-reaching effects. The behaviour and actions of some Manchester United supporters resulted in the Manchester United v Liverpool match, due to be played on 2 May, being postponed as a result of spectators breaking into Old Trafford. A number of United fans joined the #NotAPennyMore movement, which urged protestors to boycott Manchester United's club sponsors, of which there are more than fifty.

There will be action from sponsors who will not be attracted to invest in clubs and their owners who have such disregard for their sport and customer supporters. The Hut Group, a Manchester-based company, pulled out of negotiations with Manchester United over a multi-million-pound training-ground sponsorship deal. Liverpool's sponsor, Tribus Watches, said they were withdrawing from their agreement with the club in protest.

Clubs could also find their powers to run their own businesses have been weakened. Representatives from supporters' trusts could be seconded to club boards for a minimum term.

While the European Super League is history, those who run English football will be well advised to take into account the various contributory factors that led to its collapse. This includes social media and immediate access to news online which meant information and views were shared much more quickly. Social media enabled fan movements to take off very rapidly.

The announcement, coming as it did in the wake of a pandemic and record economic inequality, was portrayed as a desperate move by cash-grabbing owners. The lack of engagement with players, managers and staff was very apparent and it became clear that many had not even been consulted.

Players started putting out their own statements on social media opposing the ESL. It is significant that during Gandalf I, or at other moments when there had been dramatic changes in the structure of the game, including the formation of the Premier League, there was no social media and such player response would not have been possible even if the players were inclined to take a stand.

Social media also provided a platform for influential sports pundits, including several prominent ex-players, to be vocal on this issue and this clearly fuelled the backlash from the fans.

It is an old cliché in football that goals change matches. It can be said that the failed ESL project has also changed football. The only question is how dramatic these changes might be and whether they will lead to a better-run football world. I must say, having seen how some of the biggest clubs in this country and Europe have behaved, I have my doubts.

Endnotes

1 Tommy Docherty, *The Doc: My Story – Hallowed Be Thy Game* (Headline, 2006)
2 See *Manchester Evening News* – https://www.manchestereveningnews.co.uk/sport/football/football-news/red-legend-is-cup-crazy-973088 – and *The Sportsman* – https://www.thesportsman.com/articles/man-united-legend-mcilroy-blames-ron-atkinson-for-sad-old-trafford-exit for further accounts of this story
3 See also the *Guardian*, 16 Dec 1999: https://www.theguardian.com/football/1999/dec/16/newsstory.sport
4 https://www.manutd.com/en/news/detail/utd-podcast-mark-hughes-on-transfer-from-man-utd-to-barcelona-12-april-2021
5 Alex Ferguson, *Managing My Life* (Hodder & Stoughton, 2000)
6 Alex Ferguson, *A Light in the North* (Mainstream Publishing, 1985)
7 See *Manchester Evening News*, 15 October 2023: https://www.manchestereveningnews.co.uk/sport/football/football-news/manchester-united-takeover-owners-news-20860903
8 Jon Smith, *The Deal* (Constable, 2016)
9 Alex Ferguson, *Managing My Life* (Hodder & Stoughton, 2000)
10 Martin Edwards, *Red Glory* (Michael O'Mara, 2017)
11 See the *Irish Times*, 20 July 2018: https://www.irishtimes.com/sport/soccer/english-soccer/how-manchester-united-stole-roy-keane-from-kenny-dalglish-1.3571214
12 'Book Review / How Irving Scholar won and lost his Spurs: "Behind Closed Doors"', *Independent*, 22 December 1992: https://www.independent.co.uk/voices/book-review-how-irving-scholar-won-and-lost-his-spurs-behind-closed-doors-irving-scholar-mihir-bose-andre-deutsch-14-99-pounds-1565025.html
13 Andrei Kanchelskis with George Scanlan, *Kanchelskis: The Autobiography* (Virgin Books, 1995)
14 Alex Ferguson, *Managing My Life* (Hodder & Stoughton, 2000)
15 From *Opus*, originally featured in *United*: https://www.thisisopus.com/opus-world/eric-cantona-by-royal-appointment/
16 Graham Kelly, *Sweet FA* (Willow, 1999)
17 Graham Kelly, *Sweet FA* (Willow, 1999)

18 Peter Schmeichel, *Schmeichel: The Autobiography* (Virgin, 1999)
19 Graham Kelly, *Sweet FA* (Willow, 1999)
20 See also https://www.fourfourtwo.com/features/rupert-murdochs-manchester-united-how-bskyb-nearly-bought-red-devils
21 Mihir Bose, *Manchester Unlimited* (Orion Business, 1999)
22 Gordon Taylor, *BBC News*, 12 November 2001: http://news.bbc.co.uk/sport1/hi/football/1651343.stm
23 An Irish solicitor who asked to remain anonymous, as quoted to the *Observer*, 1 Feb 2004: https://www.theguardian.com/football/2004/feb/01/newsstory.sport5

Acknowledgements

I would like to thank the following individuals:

My partner Elaine, for her support in my writing of this book, particularly on days when it felt like a real struggle, she was always there with words of encouragement and cups of tea!

My stepdaughter Emma, for her proofing of the book and her promise to me to ensure that she will take charge of making sure it gets published if I am no longer around to do so.

My son Andrew, for his work in compiling information from over the years of work which I have been involved with, which has been of useful assistance whilst writing this book.

Maurice Watkins

Before Maurice passed away, he asked me to ensure that this book, which he had spent two years writing, was published. I reached out to Sir Alex Ferguson, who was full of praise and offered to write a foreword. Alex contacted Roddy Bloomfield, his publisher at Hodder & Stoughton, and the book came into being.

I would like to thank Tim Rich, who did a wonderful job editing the book. I would also like to thank our publisher Roddy Bloomfield; Phil Shaw, whose eagle eye caught numerous important points; and Christian Duck, Managing Editor at Hodder & Stoughton, for their continuous support throughout the publishing of *Legally Red*.

Emma Shaw, Maurice Watkins' stepdaughter

A Note from the Author's Estate

The Manchester Grammar School (MGS) is the largest independent day school for boys in the United Kingdom. It was founded in 1515 by Hugh Oldham, the Bishop of Exeter (1505–1519), whose intention was to educate the boys of Manchester showing sufficient academic ability, regardless of background, in 'godliness and good learning', without any charge.

Maurice felt very strongly that his successes came about because of his access to good education. The free place at the MGS, where he was a Foundation Scholar, set him up for life. Following the government's abolishment of the Direct Grant System in 1976 and the Assisted Places Scheme in 1997, the door for academic boys like Maurice to enter such schools seemed to be closing. MGS endeavoured to raise money to ensure that this would not be the end of free education at the school, and Maurice spearheaded the fundraising campaign for over twenty years as a governor and later Chair of Governors of his former school. With an initial target of £10 million, the fund now stands at over £30 million and nearly the same amount has been spent in the intervening years. This has meant that more than 750 pupils from modest backgrounds, like Maurice, have been able to attend the school.

Maurice, a son of Manchester, helped ensure that Hugh Oldham's mission was not lost some 500 years later.

The royalties received from the sale of this book will go towards supporting the provision of bursaries at The Manchester Grammar School.

Photo Acknowledgements

Section 1
Page 1, top left and top right: © The Manchester Grammar School
Page 2 top: © Andy Hooper/Daily Mail
Page 2 bottom: © Manchester United Football Club Limited
Page 3 top: © Mirrorpix/Getty Images
Page 3 bottom and page 4 top: © Bob Thomas Sports Photography via Getty Images
Page 4 bottom: © David Cannon/Getty Images
Page 6 bottom: © Manchester United Football Club Limited
Page 7 bottom: © David Davies/Mark Leech Sports Photography/Getty Images
Page 8 top: © Reuters Pictures
Page 8 bottom: © PA Images/Alamy Stock Photo

Section 2
Page 1: © PA Images/Alamy Stock Photo
Page 2 bottom: © Colorsport/Shutterstock
Page 4 top and bottom: © Manchester United Football Club Limited
Page 5 bottom: © Charles Green
Page 6 top: © Emma Shaw
Page 6 bottom and page 7 top: © Elaine Shaw
Page 7 bottom: © Vatican Media
Page 8 top: © Emma Shaw
Page 8 bottom: © James Watkins

All other images are from the author's collection.

Index

A Light in the North (Ferguson) 66
Aberdeen xi, 34–5, 36–7, 38, 39–40, 56, 59, 66, 68, 168
AC Milan 35–6, 40–2, 188, 189, 190
Agnew, Jonathan 274
Aigner, Gerhard 191, 194, 195–6, 197, 198
Ajax 189
Albiston, Arthur 47
Alexander, Robert 51, 52
Amaral 186
Anderson, Chris 39–40
Anderton, Darren 124
Archibald, Steve 56, 59
Arsenal xii, 26–7, 64, 71, 90, 104, 107, 108, 113, 170, 189, 191, 192, 193, 196, 199, 200, 245, 277
Ashton, Joe 216–17
Aston Villa 108
Atkinson, Ron 25, 28, 34, 48, 56, 58, 59, 61, 64, 66, 67, 86–7
Azevedo, Joao Vale e 182–4, 185–6

Bailey, Gary 24
Baines, Alan xii–xiii
Banks, Tony 245, 248–9, 250
Barcelona 55, 56, 57, 58–62, 96, 100, 103, 168, 189, 190, 234
Barling, Gerald 52
Barnsley FC 270–1
Bateman, Jane 251
Bates, Ken 215, 255
Batson, Brendan 89–90, 173, 258, 259
Bayer Leverkusen 280
Bayern Munich xvi, 181, 189
Bean, Graham 133–4
Beane, Billy 271

Beckham, David xvii
Behind the Glory (Scudamore) 252, 257
Bell, Alasdair 237, 241
Benfica 182–3, 184, 189
Benn, Nigel 81
Bercow, John 273–4
Berlusconi, Silvio 41–2, 188, 195
Bertrand, Jean-Jacques 146, 148
Best, George 3, 6
Beswitherick, David 204
Bjerregaard, Per 166, 167
Blackburn Rovers 87–8, 89
Blair, Tony 232, 245, 250
Blatter, Sepp 237, 238, 239, 240, 244
Blueprint for the Future of Football 105–6, 108
Bobroff, Paul 92
Boli, Basile 142, 152
Boli, Claude 152
Bond, John 12
Booth, Mark 202, 203, 205, 206, 207, 208, 211–12, 213, 216, 217–18
Borussia Dortmund 181, 189
Borussia Mönchengladbach 7
Bose, Mihir 94, 96, 245–6, 252
Bosman Ruling 168–9, 235
Bournemouth 12–15
Bowyer, Lee 141
Boycott, Geoff 51
Bragin, Alexander 125, 127, 131–2
Brandman, Henri 81, 82
Bridgeman, John 189, 212
Brightman, Lord Justice 14
Brighton and Hove Albion 35, 227
British Basketball Federation 271, 273
British Swimming 268–9
Bromley, John 105

Bronckers, Marco 240–1
Brøndby 166–7
Brookes, David 216
Brooks, Derek 129
Brown, Laurie 7–8
Brown, Mary 7–8, 9–10
Brown, Mick 67
Brown, Terry 233
Bruce, Steve 80, 151
BSkyB 113–14, 202–13, 214–24
Burnley FC 243
Burns, David 258, 259
Burrows, Nigel 93–4, 96, 97, 98, 101
Bursary Boy 275
Busby, Sir Matt xi, xvi, 5, 6, 7, 8–9, 17–18, 20, 21, 22, 43
Butcher, Terry 56
Butler, Robin 49

Caldecott, Andrew 20
Calderbank, Liz 163–4
Campbell, Alastair 250
Cantona, Eric 88, 123, 135–65
Cantona, Isabelle 140, 141, 142, 143, 144, 159
Cantona, Raphael 142
Capello, Fabio xvi
Carlisle United 77
Carman, George 10, 14, 15
Carter, Philip 105
Cech, Petr 279
Chance, David 220
Charles, Gary 186
Charlton, Bobby 3, 6, 43–5, 65, 96, 97
Charlton Athletic 208
Chaytow, Barry 69
Chelsea 49, 108, 264, 277, 279
Chernenko, Konstantin 31
Chisholm, Sam 220
Clark, Frank 89
Clarke, Christopher 52, 53
Clement, Andrew 172
Clough, Brian 84–6, 89, 90
Cohen, Stanley 73
Cole, Andy 136
Cole, Peter 70
Coleman, Chris 136
Collins, David 228
Conn, David 216
Conway, Paul 271
Cooper, Glenn 95–6, 97–8, 102
Coppell, Steve 24, 86

Coventry City 33, 108, 175
Coward, Nic 191, 219, 246
Craig, Ernie 78
Crerand, Paddy 7, 11, 13
Crewe Alexandra 234
Crick, Michael 209, 216
Crickmer, Walter 6, 21
Croker, Ted 54–5
Crompton, Jack 23, 24, 25
Crozier, Adam xviii, xix, xxiii, 257, 258, 259, 260
Cruyff, Johan 57, 103
Cruyff, Jordi 181
Cryne, Patrick 270–1
Crystal Palace 85, 86, 108, 121, 135–6
Cubic Expression 265, 266
Cunnah, Michael 246, 247
Cusack, Nick 259
Cyril the Swan 225–30

Daily Express 34, 208–9
Daily Mail 173
Daily Mirror 29–30, 31, 250
Daily Record 38
Daily Star 87
Daily Telegraph 220, 245–6
Dalgarno, Les xxi, xxii, xxiii
Dalglish, Kenny 87, 88, 89
Dalglish, Marina 88
Davies, David 150, 172, 174, 175, 176, 247, 249
Davies, Ian 158, 160
Davis, Paul 147
Day, Peter 226, 227, 229
Deal, The (Smith) 79
Deane, Brian 185
Dein, David xvii, 105, 174, 176, 191, 196, 255
Denning, Lord 14, 15
Derby County 7
Docherty, Agnes 8
Docherty, Tommy 6–12, 13
Donald, Dick 67, 68
Donaldson, Lord Justice 14, 15
Double, Steve 172, 175
Draper, Rob 222–3
Du Cann, Edward 11
Du Cann, Richard 11
Dumbarton FC 168
Dundee United 56
Dunn, Steve 225, 228
Dunnett, Jack 51–2

INDEX

Duxbury, Mike 24
Duxbury, Scott 226
Dyke, Greg 204, 206, 209, 210

Edelson, Michael 43, 65–6, 69, 71, 96, 97, 101
Edey, Roy 152
Edwards, Louis 5–6, 8, 9, 10, 13, 16, 17–18, 20, 21–2, 43
Edwards, Martin
  Alex Ferguson considers retirement xii, xvi–xvii, xxi
  and Andrei Kanchelskis 119, 123–4, 125, 126, 127, 133
  appointment of Alex Ferguson as manager 64–5, 66, 67, 68
  and BSkyB bid 202, 203–4, 206, 207, 208, 213, 216, 220, 221, 222
  and Caribbean tour (1985) 48
  death of Louis Edwards 21
  doubts about Alex Ferguson 86
  and Eric Cantona 140
  and European Super League 193, 197, 198–9
  flotation of club on stock exchange 92, 93–7, 99, 101, 102
  and Gary Pallister 80
  and Gordon Strachan 33, 34, 35–6, 38–9
  and Heysel disaster 48
  and Joao Vale e Azevedo 183
  and Mark Hughes 60, 61
  Maurice Watkins joins club board 43
  and Oxford United 29
  and Premier League creation 105, 113
  and Ray Wilkins 35, 41
  removal of Jack Crompton 25
  removal of Tommy Docherty 7, 8
  rights issue in Manchester United 18, 20
  and Robert Maxwell 29, 30, 31, 32
  and Roy Keane 89–90
  shares in club 45
  takeover bid by Michael Knighton 69, 70–1, 74–6, 77
  and World Cup bid (2006) 246, 247, 248, 249
Edwards, Roger 29, 30, 31, 44, 45
Edwards, Sandy 20
Ekelund, Peter 188
El Khalej, Tahar 186
Eriksson, Sven-Göran xv, xvi–xix, xxii–xxiv

Essaoulenko, Grigory 121–2, 123, 124, 127, 133
European Commission 231–42
European Super League 187–200, 277–80
Evans, David 49
Evans, Roy 181
Evening Standard 173
Everton 35, 50, 52, 104, 107, 108, 113, 124–6, 129, 131, 133, 134
Exeter 226

Farina, Giuseppe 35, 36, 41
FC Cologne 36–40
Ferdinand, Rio 233, 267
Ferguson, Sir Alex
  at Aberdeen 56
  and Alan Shearer 88
  and Andrei Kanchelskis 119, 122–3, 133, 134
  appointed Manchester United manager 64–8
  and Archie Knox 102–3
  and Arsène Wenger 170
  awarded CBE 152
  considers retirement xi–xxiv
  doubts about 86
  and Eric Cantona 136–8, 140, 144, 146, 148, 150–1
  flotation of club on stock exchange 100
  and Gary Pallister 78, 81
  and Gordon Strachan 34, 36, 37, 39
  and Joao Vale e Azevedo 182
  and John Magnier and JP McManus 262–5
  and Karel Poborsky 179
  letter to Maurice Watkins 275–6
  and Neil Webb 84, 85
  and Peter Schmeichel 166, 172–3, 175, 176
  and Roy Keane 89
  tribute to Maurice Watkins ix–x
  and World Cup bid (2006) 249
Ferguson, Cathy xv, xx, 66
Ferguson, Jason xxi, xxii, xxiii, 264
Ferguson, Mark xxii
Figo, Luis 234
Financial Times 210
Finney, Nicholas 215
Fiszman, Danny 193, 196
Fletcher, John 18–19, 20
Flynn, Alex 106
Fox, Bill 105

Francis, Pope 269
Francis, Trevor 57
Friar, Ken 193, 194, 196
Fulham xviii

Galatasaray 189
Gallavotti, Mario 241
Gaspart, Joan 58–9, 62, 63
Gibson, Alan 8, 43
Gidman, John 47
Gill, David xix, 82–3, 192, 193, 204, 207, 208, 216, 220, 221, 222, 224, 264, 267
Glasgow Rangers 56, 102, 134
Glazer family 45, 224, 265–6
Goddard, Keith 14
Goldstein, Oscar 45, 93
Gordon, Alan 34, 36, 37, 65
Goss, Don 228–9
Graham, George 56
Grainger, Katherine 273
Grandstand 172–3
Greengrass, Paul 21
Greenwood, Jim 53
Greyhound Board of Great Britain (GBGB) 274–5
Griffiths, Emma 132
Grobbelaar, Bruce 175
Guardiola, Pep 279
Gulliver, James 18, 31, 44

Hansen, Alan 139
Haroun, Denzil 8, 44
Hateley, Mark 40–1
Hauge, Rune 119, 166
Hayward, Paul 216
Henderson, Colin 79–80
Hewison, John 221, 258, 259
Heysel disaster 48–55
Higton, Jonathan 105
Hill, Jimmy 138
Hill-Wood, Denis 27
Hill-Wood, Peter 196
Hillsborough disaster 69
Hirst, David 88
Hodgkinson, Alan 166
Hoey, Kate 250
Hollins, John 227
Horne, Barry 258, 259
Hughes, Mark 56–7, 58, 59–62
Hull, Rod 72–3
Humby, Nick 264

Humphrys, John 228
Hurst, Geoff 14

IMG 23–5
Ince, Claire 153
Ince, Paul 81–2, 140, 152, 153
Independent Manchester United Supporters' Association (IMUSA) 205, 211
Infantino, Gianni 237, 241
Insider Magazine 210
Inter Milan 40, 189
Irwin, Denis 208
ITV 104–5, 113–14

James, Eric 2
Jenkins, David 215
Johansson, Lennart 239, 240
Johnsen, Ronny 181
Johnson, Peter 125
Jones, Peter 35
Jones, Vinnie 235
Jordan, Joe 16
Judge, Igor 75
Juventus 34, 48–9, 189, 190

Kamara, Chris 147
Kanchelskis, Andrei 119–34
Kandaurov, Serhiy 184
Keane, Roy 89–90
Keegan, Kevin xvii, xix, 36
Kelly, Graham 51, 97, 139, 147, 148–9, 150, 173, 174, 176, 177, 178, 191, 219
Kelly, Ned 127, 128, 129, 132, 146, 153, 159
Kennedy, Michael 26–7, 35, 90
Kenyon, Peter
    Alex Ferguson considers retirement xv, xvi, xviii, xix, xx, xxi, xxii, xxiii
    and BSkyB bid 204, 206, 208, 214
    at Chelsea 264
    and European Super League 187, 188, 191, 197, 198, 199–200
Kidd, Brian xiii, xxi
Kingsley, Ben 2–3
Klein, Roland 120
Knighton, Michael 45, 69–77, 80, 94, 96, 97, 98
Knighton, Rosemary 72
Knox, Archie 66, 68, 102

INDEX

Lancashire County Cricket Club 273–4
Laska, Vladimir 180
Launders, Robin 98–9
Law, Denis 3, 6, 11
Law Society Gazette 210
Lawton, Matt 208
Leaver, Peter 52, 192, 193–4, 198, 199, 216, 220, 223
Lee, Chien 271
Lee, Mike 238
Leeds United 49, 108, 121, 233
Leighton, Jim 86
Lewis, Mike 227, 229
Lewis, Richard 269
Lineker, Gary 56, 96, 138–9
Linfield Football and Athletic club 129–30
Liverpool 6–7, 33, 48–50, 51, 55, 64, 104, 107, 108, 113, 189, 190, 192, 196–7, 200, 277, 280
Lloyd, Terry 143
Lo Verde, Rosario 41
Lorimer, Peter 21
Lucari, Rodolfo Hecht 187, 198
Luton Town 108–9
Lyall, John 81
Lynch, Marian 174, 185

Macari, Lou 11
MacDougall, Ted 12–15
Magnier, John xx, xxi, 262–6
Magnier, Sue 262–3
Machell, Raymond 14
Mail on Sunday 222–3
Malone, Mr 160
Managing My Life (Ferguson) 65, 133
Manchester City 108, 121, 277, 279
Manchester Evening News 29, 30, 60, 103
Manchester Grammar School 1–3
Manchester United
  in 2001/02 season xi–xxiv
  Alex Ferguson appointed manager 64–8
  Alex Ferguson considers retirement xi–xxiv
  and BSkyB bid 202–13, 214–24
  Caribbean tour (1985) 47–8
  and European Super League 187, 188–9, 190, 192, 193–6, 197, 198, 199, 200, 277, 280
  Far East tour (1981) 23–5
  flotation on stock exchange 45, 91–103
  Glazer family buy-out 265–6
  and Heysel disaster 50, 52
  Magnier and McManus shareholding in 262–6
  Maurice Watkins leaves 267–8
  and Premier League creation 104, 107, 108, 113
  removal of Tommy Docherty 6–10
  rights issues in 5–6, 16–20
  and Robert Maxwell 28–32
  takeover bid by Michael Knighton 69–77, 94
  and World Cup bid (2006) 243–51
Manchester United Basketball Club 271–2
Mandelson, Peter 212–13, 214, 216–17, 223
Mannings, John 154
Maradona, Diego 58–9, 79
Marsden, David 52
Maxwell, Kevin 103
Maxwell, Robert 28–32, 93, 96
Maynard, Russell 228
McCann, Geoffrey 151, 152, 154–5, 164
McClaren, Steve xxi
McClure, Neil 226–7, 228, 229, 230
McCormick, Peter 258, 259
McGhee, Mark 37
McGiven, Alex 245
McGrath, Paul 78
McGregor, Jim 81
McGuinness, Wilf xvi
McGuire, Mick 258, 259
McHugh, Francis 81
McIlroy, Sammy 24, 25
McKeag, Gordon 146, 149
McKenna, Arthur 5
McManus, JP xx, xxi, 262–6
McMenemy, Lawrie 65
McMullen, Arthur 50
McQueen, Gordon 16
Media Partners 187, 188, 189, 191, 193, 196, 197–201
Meek, David 31, 60
Mellor, David 215
Mendy, Ambrose 81, 82
Merrett, Ken 122, 163, 167, 173
Midani, Amer Al 70–1, 94–5, 96, 98, 101, 204, 207
Middlesborough 78, 79–80, 124
Middleton, Peter 218, 219
Millichip, Bert 50

Millwall 49, 225, 270
Minto, Scott 186
Mirdan, Boris 127, 128
Moncur, John 136
Monti, Mario 232, 238, 240
Moore, Bobby 14
Moran, Kevin 78
Morelli, Sandro 265
Morgan, Piers 250
Morgan, Willie 10–12
Morris, Dennis 214, 215
Morris, Derek 223
Mullery, Alan 139
Munson, Roger 215
Murphy, Colin 7

Nelson, John 20, 31, 74, 92
Neville, Gary 253
New Islington Free School 2
Newcastle United 246
News of the World 60, 62, 170, 227
Nicholl, Jimmy 24, 25
Noades, Ron 135, 136
Noble, Jonathan 82
Norwich City 51, 68, 108, 138
Nottingham Forest 57, 59–60, 64, 84–6, 89, 90, 108, 121
Notts County 108, 109, 168

O'Brien, Margaret 147
O'Farrell, Frank xvi, 12
Oldham, Hugh 1
Oldham Athletic 108, 234
O'Leary, David xvi, 90
Olive, Les 5, 6, 7–8, 10, 13, 20, 28, 44, 96
Olsen, Jesper 47
Olympique Marseille 189
Omdal, Per 238, 239
One Game, One Team, One Voice 106
O'Neill, Martin xvi
Owen, Gill 215
Oxford United 28–9, 68
Oyston, Owen 75

Packer, Kerry 51
Pallister, Gary 78–81, 108
Panathinaikos 189
Panting, Graham 143, 144, 145
Paris Saint-Germain 189
Parker, Paul 167
Parry, Rick 108, 109, 112, 113, 126, 130, 189–90, 192, 193, 196, 253

Paska, Pavel 179, 180, 181
Pearch, Jean 155, 157–8
Philips, Peter 270
Phythian-Adams, Mark 74
Poborsky, Karel 179–82, 184
Poole, David 141, 143, 144, 146, 151, 152, 153, 155–7, 158, 159, 160
Powell, Robert 2–3
Premier League
  and European Super League 187, 189–90, 192–4, 196, 197–200, 277, 278–9
  formation of 104–18
  negotiations with PFA 252–61
Professional Footballers' Association (PFA) xviii, xix, 51, 52, 53, 112–13, 129, 140, 173–4, 221, 235, 252–61
PSV Eindhoven 82, 83

Queens Park Rangers 10, 60, 108
Quinton, Sir John 112

Raba Gyor 45
Ramsden, Ken 134
Reacher, Fred 90
Real Madrid 101, 102, 189, 190, 195, 234, 242, 271
Richards, Dave 246, 247, 256
Rioch, Brice 79
Rivera, Gianni 35
Roach, Dennis 35, 40, 48, 57–8, 59, 61
Robertson, Simon 74
Robson, Bobby 65
Robson, Bryan 33–4, 57, 124
Rock of Gibraltar 262–3
Rodger, Jim 66
Romanosov, Yuri 127, 128
Rose, Mr Justice 111
Roworth, Maurice 84
Royle, Bill 5, 6
Rugby Football League (RFL) 269–70
Rummenigge, Karl-Heinz 40
Russell, Patrick 13, 14

Safiullin, Ravil 130, 132
Sanfrecce Hiroshima 168
Satinoff, Willie 5
Saunders, Ron 65
Scanlan, George 123–4, 144, 145, 146
Schäfer, Bernard 39–40
Schmeichel, Bente 174
Schmeichel, Peter 166–78, 181

INDEX

Scholar, Irving 54, 66, 92, 93, 96, 105
Schröder, Gerhard 232
Scudamore, Richard 220, 239, 252, 253–7, 258–60
Sexton, Dave 10, 23, 65
Shah, Eddy 75
Shakhtar Donetsk 119–20, 121, 124, 125–33
Shankly, Bill 66
Shareholders United Against Murdoch (SUAM) 211, 212
Shaw, Richard 136, 137
Shearer, Alan 87–9
Shearer, Lainya 88
Sheepshanks, David 215, 218, 219
Sheffield United 108, 185
Sheffield Wednesday 108
Shields, Tom 174
Silkin, Sam 31
Simmons, Matthew 137, 140, 145, 148, 152, 154–6, 164
Sinfield, Kevin 270
Sinstadt, Gerald 11
Slavia Prague 179–81
Smith, Herbert 192, 193
Smith, John 49–50
Smith, Jon 79
Smith, Sir Roland
  Alex Ferguson considers retirement xii–xv, xix, xx, xxi
  and Andrei Kanchelskis 127
    and BSkyB bid 202–3, 204, 206, 210–11, 214, 221, 222
  on club board 97–8
  and Eric Cantona 140
  and Joao Vale e Azevedo 183
  and Peter Schmeichel 172
  and Robert Maxwell 29, 30, 31
  and *World in Action* programme 21
  and World Cup bid (2006) 247
Solskjær, Ole Gunnar 181
Souness, Graeme 56
Southampton 6, 51, 52, 64, 108
Southgate, Gareth 137
Speedie, David 88
Stafford, Harry 44
Stapleton, Frank 25–7
Stein, Jock xix
Stein, Mel 88
Stelling, Jeff 214
Stewart, Martin 203
Stott, Ian 146, 148, 149

Strachan, Gordon xi, 33–40, 47
Strachan, Lesley 36, 37
Studer, Markus 185, 196
Suchauek, Jiri 180
Sugar, Alan 96, 113, 124
Sun, The 82, 133–4, 226
Sunday People 59
Sunday Telegraph 210, 211
Swansea City 225–30
Sweet FA (Kelly) 148–9, 178

Talbot, Mr Justice 13, 14, 126
Talbot, Patrick 189, 193
Taveggia, Paolo 135
Taylor, Ann 248
Taylor, Gordon 51, 129, 140, 146–7, 150, 173, 174, 195, 215, 221, 222, 237, 252–61
Teeman, Ronnie 41
Thatcher, Margaret 49, 55
Thielen, Karl-Heinz 36, 37
Thomas, Mickey 24, 25
Thompson, Geoff 146, 148, 149
Thornton, Robert 72, 73
Thorpe, Jeremy 10
Times, The 40
Tottenham Hotspur 51, 52, 53–4, 64, 66, 91–2, 96, 104, 107, 108, 113, 243, 277
Trafford Park Estates 101–2

van der Gouw, Raimond 181
van Miert, Karel 199, 200
van Nistelrooy, Ruud 82–3
Venables, Terry 56, 58, 62–3, 96, 152
Videoton 46
Vinelott, John 54
Vöge, Wolfgang 119–20

Wakeling, Vic 216
Wale, Sidney 92
Walker, Jack 89
Walker, Lee 104–5
Walker, Rupert Faure 205, 206
Walsh, Andy 208
Washbrook, Cyril 2
Watford 47
Watkins, Geoffrey 3–4
Watkins, Christopher 22–3
Watkins, Peter 159
Waugh, Michael 193
Webb, Neil 84–5

Wenger, Arsène xii, xvi, 170
West Ham United 49, 60, 81, 82, 108, 227, 233
Westbrook, Neil 101
White, Noel 105
Wilkie, Alan 136, 137–8
Wilkins, Ray 24, 35–6, 40–2
Will, David 243
Wilpshire, John 11
Wimbledon FC 108
Wise, Dennis 152
Wiseman, Keith 215, 219–20
Wolverhampton Wanderers 243
Wood, Mar 250
Woodcock, Tony 36
Woodford, Alen 51
Woodgate, Jonathan 141–2
World in Action 21–2
World Cup bid (2006) 243–51
Worrall, Garry 24
Wright, Ian 170–2, 174–8

Yarrow, George 222
Young, Bill 8, 43

Zahavi, Pini xvii, xviii, xxii–xxiii, 179, 182
Zen-Ruffinen, Michel 238